HEAD & HEART MANAGEMENT

DATE DUE

6 2008

Also by Adrian Furnham

Management and Myths
The People Business
Management Mumbo-Jumbo
The Dark Side of Behaviour at Work (with John Taylor)
Learning at Work (with John Taylor)

HEAD & HEART MANAGEMENT

*Managing attitudes, beliefs,
behaviors and emotions at work*

Adrian Furnham

palgrave
macmillan

First published 2008 by
PALGRAVE MACMILLAN
Houndmills, Basingstoke, Hampshire RG21 6XS and
175 Fifth Avenue, New York, N.Y. 10010
Companies and representatives throughout the world

PALGRAVE MACMILLAN is the global academic imprint of the Palgrave Macmillan division of St. Martin's Press, LLC and of Palgrave Macmillan Ltd. Macmillan® is a registered trademark in the United States, United Kingdom and other countries. Palgrave is a registered trademark in the European Union and other countries.

ISBN-13: 978–0–230–55512–9
ISBN-10: 0–230–55512–8

This book is printed on paper suitable for recycling and made from fully managed and sustained forest sources. Logging, pulping and manufacturing processes are expected to conform to the environmental regulations of the country of origin.

A catalogue record for this book is available from the British Library.

A catalog record for this book is available from the Library of Congress.

10   9   8   7   6   5   4   3   2   1
17   16   15   14   13   12   11   10   09   08

Printed and bound in China

To the memsahib whose strict editing improved a lot herein, and the dauphin who tried his best to distract me, usually with success, from scribbling any more

Contents

Introduction

Most of us like to think ourselves as cool, rational, objective people. We rejoice in data-based, analytical logic. We hope that we make wise, well-thought-through decisions throughout life. Strategy, planning, analysis are serious "competencies" at work. We are, we hope, *people of the head.*

We are warned not to let our heart rule our head. We are encouraged in making big decisions to "sleep on it". We know at some deep level that we should not pay attention to certain superficial cues (such as physical beauty) when making certain decisions, but we do. We are, of course, also *people of the heart.*

Head and heart; logical and emotion; cognition and affect. Inextricably linked or separate systems? At work, at any rate, we don't talk much about emotions, although the *Emotional Intelligence* movement has to some extent changed all that. But even that is discussed in a rather analytical way, particularly by men.

The idea of "two sides" to our behavior is very appealing. We have, after all, two eyes, two hands, two legs. We have two ears and two arms, and half of us have either two breasts or two testicles. And two of our most important organs seem to have two separate and separable halves. As a consequence it is a popular idea to talk of left versus right brain structure and functioning. The real brain scientists know that much of this left–right brain stuff is little more than *metaphor.* People are not left or right brained – but they do know that certain parts of the brain, sometimes located in the left hemisphere and sometimes in the right, do control different functions. The verbal area, for example, is in the left hemisphere.

Perhaps human beings are, as a species, somehow trained to look for opposites. We do a lot of this: good and bad, black and white, fair and foul weather. Some like to think that the clash of opposites may yield special benefits. It's the essence of the thesis, antithesis, synthesis idea so beloved of the media. If somebody is *pro-* something, it is essential to find some individual who is *anti-* the same thing, because out of their discussion/argument we shall find the truth. A magical emergence of sane, *via media,* moderation from the clash of the opposite forces. Try listening or watching to see if it works.

Left versus right brain

The consultants, trainers and educators who espouse the "two-brain" theory often talk of the split-brain experiment where the channel – the corpus callosum – between the hemispheres was severed. They also document studies where faces are "reassembled" from two right or two left images. But they make a quick and (rather right-brained) imaginative and evidence-free jump from this to two-brain theory.

The idea is essentially this: the left brain is the logical brain. It is the hemisphere that does facts, knowledge, order and patterns. It is the bit that does maths and science. It is the centre of detail-oriented, abstract thinking and processing. The words that pop up in the column are logical, sequential, rational, analytic, objective and parts-oriented.

Left-brained people are, it seems, lucky. Most educational and business organizations have been set up by left-brained people to do left-brained things in a left-brained way. Just as the world is dominated by right-handers (dexters), controlled, of course, by the left brain, so there is a quirky minority of people (around 10 percent) who, being sinisters, are left-handed because they are controlled by the right brain.

The right brain is all a bit fuzzy, it seems. It is the seat of emotions, symbols and images. It's where philosophy and religion are processed. It's big-picture territory; the zone of fantasy and possibilities. Right-brain words are random, intuitive, holistic, synthesizing and subjective.

Right-brained students like the big picture: outline before details. They are, however, not too concerned with sequential planning or proof-reading or spelling or ... other trivial details. They don't like symbols, but they shine at intuition. They like coherence and meaning, but are fantasy-based not reality-based.

You could forgive a left-brained teacher for believing all this pleading for a right-brained approach to be a series of quasi-scientific excuses for dim, incompetent students. An assignment handed in late, littered with typos and devoid of analysis is simply the approach of a right-brained genius? Oh, yeah! Left-brained education inhibits, deviates or blocks creativity? Umm ... well! The evidence?

Certainly people have strong preferences. These arise out of ability and personality differences as well as training. Some people are deeply troubled by a lack of order in their office. Others have no problems with apparent chaos. The trouble is, we impose our preferences on others, believing they represent a better, more efficient, way to behave.

But the left–right brained metaphor does begin to bring to the surface the rational–emotional divide. Most of our education strives to appeal to, and reward, logic, analysis and knowledge accumulation. Most education, particular in the sciences, is all about cognitive processes: people are reduced to no more than firing neurons.

In the arts, emotion creeps into art and poetry. Also into history, but less so to philosophy. But even children are taught to analyze emotion; to examine how a poet's brilliant use of few words can encapsulate a powerful emotion.

The problem with work is that it is treated like a classroom. Most organizations don't do affect. Perhaps this was part of the reason for the whole faddish embrace of *emotional intelligence*. Many people reiterate the evidence-free, and no doubt wrong, point that emotional intelligence is a better predictor of how well one works than conventional academic intelligence.

The emotionally intelligent, possibly right-brained, individual not only recognizes the importance of emotions at work, but is also able to read them carefully and manage them well, both in themselves and in others.

It is self-evident that people experience powerful emotions at work. They often feel angry about the appraisal process, but they can and do experience a whole range of other emotions such as guilt and shame and remorse. The angry customer; the abusive and competitive peer; the uninterested and distant boss can all cause chronic problems. People have "nervous breakdowns" because of acute and chronic stress at work.

It happens to us all, whether we are left- or right-brained, emotionally or academically intelligent, senior or junior. But it seems that we don't have the concepts, the language or the will to talk about them. "Emotion talk" is, sort of, not appropriate in business. In fact, it can be banned. Thus falling in love with a colleague may be deeply frowned upon, provoking an instant posting to a dim part of the organizational territory. Ever yearned for the Health and Safety Officer's job in Bulgaria?

If emotions are confronted they are almost always positive ones. It's OK to feel pride in the brand; it's OK to express joy in one's work; it's fine to say one has deep contentment at work. But all the others are a no-no – envy and jealousy and contempt and the rest. You are not supposed to have them, so they are ignored or rationalized, and we remain stubbornly people of the head.

Conscious versus unconscious processes

There is another distinction one should note for those at work. It's usually illustrated by the famous iceberg picture, making the fundamental Freudian point that much is below the surface. And they mean by this, below consciousness. The iceberg above the surface is considerably smaller than it is beneath, and below the water it seems more jagged, more menacing, more ominous and more unknowable.

Most business executives and consultants use the iceberg to make the point about corporate culture or values. That is, what you see in terms of interpersonal behavior, of customer service, of team-working and the like is in fact driven by things you do not see, such as the value systems of the organization.

They are probably right, but it remains interesting that talk of the unconscious is avoided. Business people, particularly in marketing, had a reasonably short affair with psychoanalysis in the 1950s. They were called the "depth boys", whose task was to understand things like the symbolism of logos, product names and product shapes. They did things like Jungian archetypal analysis. But they went out of fashion.

Business people seem to have caught the academic backlash against psychoanalysis. If you introduce yourself as a psychologist it's best to say you are a behavioral psychologist, to distinguish oneself from the Freudians. To the middle-aged, middle-brow, middle-manager, Freud was all about sex: the master of murky, dark forces; of mental illness, and even depravity.

So for most people at work, we tend not to talk about emotions or the unconscious. Work is all about left-brained, above-the-surface stuff. We treat each other like sane, logical analytic beings, and we assume that customers and shareholders are too. We prefer not to have to deal with emotional outbursts, wherever and whyever they occur. And we certainly take a pretty simplistic view of motivation. People are motivated primarily by money and status, right?

All sorts of people have been hammering at the solid oak door of the rationalists. Economic psychologists and behavioral economists have shown how people are consistently irrational when dealing with money. And economists have recently had to see that all-important axiom for their science – that wealth is directly, positively related to happiness – is unsupported by much longitudinal data.

The head and the heart; the wallet and the purse

Most people are far from rational with respect to money. Passions, parents and promotions influence their decision-making more than logical calculations.

People can be, and are all too frequently, *irrational and a-rational* about their money. This is because money is deeply imbued with symbolic meaning. Our attitudes to money have psychological meanings that are understandable, indeed predictable, often from early childhood experiences. However, they rarely follow economic or rational logic. Economists are often simply wrong because they describe how people *should* behave rather than how they *do*. Clever, educated, supposedly rational people simply do not behave as economic models say they should. People do not make sensible, well-calculated, logical decisions about their own money, let alone the money of others.

Our attitudes to beliefs about our spending and saving of money have much to do with our childhood and early education. A significant number of "money-troubled" people can trace problems to explicit and implicit messages they received in early life. Irrational savers, profligate spenders and anti-social misers often say they know they are not being reasonable but don't know how to change their illogical and "addictive" behavior. Their money habits can and do wreck relationships, and cause serious problems at work. These problems can be treated, but they first need to be recognized.

Money is a very important issue in marriage and divorce. Often, because people do not discuss money with their partner, they discover they have very different money beliefs and habits. This can cause friction and divorce, which inevitably leads to more money misery. There are two reasons why couples may not explore their money attitudes sufficiently; the first is that it remains a taboo subject; and the second is that many of the emotions associated with money are negative. Thus, in order to reduce both embarrassment and distress, the issue is quietly pushed under the carpet, often leading to much greater disagreement than if the issue had been confronted in the first place.

At work, money is a powerful demotivator, rather than a powerful motivator. There is quite simply a very weak relationship between pay and productivity, and pay and satisfaction, in the long term. But there is a very strong relationship between money and morale.

People who are happy about their money (income, wages, investments) are happy about other aspects of their life. This is not because money leads to happiness, but there tend to be happy people and unhappy people, and life satisfaction, job satisfaction and pay satisfaction are closely linked. There is therefore no major impact on happiness by adding or subtracting money. You can't decide to become happy or purchase happiness, despite the powerful underlying messages of many advertised products.

Pay is *one* of the rewards of work; there are others, both tangible and intangible, but it is difficult to separate these, as many are inextricably linked. People think about their total package. They make trade-offs: quality versus quantity. They may "downgrade" deliberately or even turn their back on materialism, but these are often a minority. There is a powerful distinction between those who value "to have" and those who value "to be". Money is a motivator in how people choose jobs, and how they work in them.

Money can decrease motivation, or at least change it. It can shift attention from quality to quantity; from intrinsic to extrinsic; from "we" to "me". If people *feel* unfairly rewarded (pay being part of the reward package) with respect to others inside *and* outside the work organization, they can easily and quickly become angry, disloyal, and demotivated. And they are able to adapt quickly to increases in pay, which makes money a very expensive and addictive way to attempt to boost morale. Further, satisfaction with pay is more a function of the perception of comparative fairness than the actual amount received. People are often quite happy to trade off money for job titles.

The emotional power of money is manifest at "bonus" time, when the predominant response of people awarded high sums of money is anger, because they feel as if they have been dealt with unfairly and negatively.

Money and well-being are only related tangentially: money cannot buy happiness. It certainly can in some instances prevent types of unhappiness, but it cannot, per se, be looked upon as an easy solution to life's problems. Most of us know that in our heads, but alas not our hearts. Witness the aggressive, health-costly pursuit of wealth and consequent "affluenza". By understanding what factors do lead to happiness and satisfaction in life and at work, we can better understand why money and happiness are poorly linked. It also explains why money is not as important as many other factors relating to work, motivation and productivity.

Money is a motivator in how people choose jobs and how they work in them. But its power is particularly limited if (i) people consider themselves amply or satisfactorily paid; (ii) they are not very materialistic; or (iii) they feel they are paid fairly compared both to others and to their own experience. In these cases, it remains relatively stable. By contrast, money works as a motivator where people can perform for it; they believe they need it; it is truly related to performance; and they find the work highly pleasurable and intrinsically rewarding.

The power of money to demotivate is higher than its power to motivate, however. It is more a source of anxiety and envy than one of pleasure. People see money as a demotivator if they feel they are not being paid fairly compared with others. Money is an easy, powerful, social comparator. It is a way of measuring or comparing people.

People do not behave as logical, rational individuals as economists assume. Even without money pathology, they make well-known and systematic "errors" in how they use money. Its symbolic power prevents them from being rational. Such odd money-related decisions are well known and well documented. Money is *love* and *power* and *freedom* and *security*. Its symbolic value confuses and confounds many people, resulting in them consistently making very bad money decisions. Again, it's the heart over the head. Knowing about such bad decisions helps us make better decisions. Attitudes and beliefs about the use of money are closely tied up with other beliefs, because of both its symbolic and its actual value. Formal and informal money education begins early. It has been claimed that the signs of early entrepreneurship can be seen in the school playground. Millionaires are born, it seems, not made. We can and should teach young people to be better managers of their own money, to make them more sensible about its use. Money education is, or should be, the concern of *every* parent and teacher.

Money attitudes are tied to other political, religious and economic beliefs. In this sense, money is an ideological issue: the distributions and correlations of wealth are at the heart of politics, and the uses and abuses of money are at the heart of religion. Thus all aspects of money usage, from charity giving to tax evasion, are linked. So many of our fundamental values are related to and emotionally focused on money.

There are a surprising number of "money-troubled" people – people whose beliefs about money lead them to behave in ways that cause and perpetuate unhappiness. Because of the symbolic value of money as a source of security, love, power and freedom, people can hurt themselves and others by their irrational psychological, rather than logical, behavior. They know they are being irrational, but are apparently unable to do anything about it. Some feel they are victims of the past or helpless in the face of money.

As society changes, so do our attitudes to money. People think about money quite differently in poor and rich countries, in high and low-tax countries, and in countries with high or low inflation. Governments can and do punish and reward certain money behaviors (especially saving), with mixed success. They certainly have the ability to raise passions about it.

The motives to acquire money, possessions and status have complex origins. Motivation is certainly about both head and heart and is very difficult to investigate. One problem is that people *cannot* rather than *will not*, tell you about what really motivates them. Regardless of the extent to which they believe in the power of the murky unconscious, what is clear is that people often do not understand what motivates them to do such strange things with their money. Therapists spend a lot of time helping people to become aware of the deep springs of their motivation. And this does not just apply to seriously disturbed patients – understanding and articulating our own motives often seems harder than understanding the motives of others.

Opposites

There are many "opposites" at work. Perhaps it is wiser to talk of different perspectives: management versus labor, or blue versus white collar, though both of these terms now seem hopelessly outdated. There is the amateur versus the expert; co-operative versus competitive; generalist versus specialist; and task oriented versus socio-emotional.

There is also hard versus soft training. There are cost centres and profit centres. Those in tall and those in flat organizations. Those that try to sell what others have produced. Those in "civvies" and those in uniforms. Those that dress down and those that dress up. And those who have a light rather than a heavy, carbon footprint.

What all this amounts to is a difference in perspectives, preferences and values. However, intelligent, empathic and non-egocentric we are, we are all products of our own personality, temperament and socialization. Most of us are not prisoners of our past, but certainly have been shaped by it.

Those blessed with a multitude of talents, and the opportunity to find and exploit them, may be in an organizational sense ambidextrous, bi- or tri-lingual and equally at home with words and numbers. But such individuals are, alas, rare. Great talents can be very limiting, as many biographies of famous people – both artists and scientists – attest. They find it really difficult seeing and doing in a different way. Their thinking, coping and interacting styles makes them predictable but not always productive.

Thus those who are attracted to the cool, analytical, deductive world of maths and physics, IT and engineering, eschew and even condemn the hot, passionate world of poetry, art and drama, and therefore perhaps also the world of human resources (HR), public relations (PR), and even marketing. The other world seems so alien, so problematical, so easy to condemn and then to stereotype. And that is not a good start in business ever, anywhere at all.

The psychology of coaching the head and the heart

Business coaching is now very popular. To be without one's trophy coach in certain companies is like being without one's famous psychoanalysts in New York. Getting help is good. Rather than be ashamed, we should rejoice in the wisdom of money and time well invested in one's sanity, morale and ultimate productivity.

It's all very understandable: it's tough at the top. There is a lot of stress, and demands from numerous stakeholders let alone the prurient press, neglected family and friends, and hostile competitors. It's lonely at the top; it's not easy to find a good sounding board; an outsider's perspective, time to muse, to doubt, even to brainstorm.

The complicated nature of the coaching relationship means that it can change a great deal. The coach or consultant may easily slip into being predominantly a confessor, simply a confidant or perhaps a counsellor. He or she is often a curious mix between teacher, therapist and trainer.

How to find, choose and assess such people? It's partly explicable in terms of their training and experience, and partly a matter of style and chemistry to ensure that the giver and receiver are compatible in terms of things such as energy, politics and even humour. There are issues of how the coach is supervised; what is their level of self-awareness as well as their theoretical orientation. And there is always the issue of how they personally measure success.

There is a thin line between counseling, consulting and coaching. There are many common factors in all three processes: all are attempting to improve focus, increase awareness and maximize opportunities. A lot of tears, ink, time and money have been spent in attempting to discover the best treatment, be it therapy or coaching or training. Is there one method or approach that works best? Or is it a case of what works best for whom? Does it depend on the nature of the problem/opportunity; and the personalities of the client and coach as well as the time spent working on the problem?

The answer is in part yes, but there is a surprising finding that suggests that all therapies and coaching philosophies have equal success.

This book of short essays is, alas, not a coherent exposition of the above. But it does have some roots in these ideas. As an applied and business psychologist, I am struck constantly by the fact that managers are ignorant of, and not even very interested in, human behavior. They seem often to rejoice in a very naïve view of their fellow humans, understanding very little of what makes them tick. The worst offenders are often the "techies", who have turned to the logic of technology because they can't understand or tolerate the capricious whimsicality of humankind.

All good managers are like good parents and good teachers. They understand the human condition, human needs and human foibles. They understand the complexity of human motivation, and that quite frequently the heart can rule the head.

This book is, I hope, something of a counter-blast to all those daft gimmicks, magic-bullet consultants, politically correct censors and dressed-up old wives' tales one finds on business book stands. The essays are meant to amuse, challenge and provoke. They are a smorgasbord, not a well-planned feast – designed for dipping into when the spirit moves. The essays are about marketing and management, sales and selection, and security and insecurity at work. Enjoy.

A day in the office

Teachers, it seems, have discovered a new ruse. Children of various ages are sent to work, on a normal school day, with their parents. "Take your child to work days" are ostensibly to learn about the world of work. Is this "edutainment" a dose of reality, or yet another daft scheme devised by trendy educationalists? A educational experience, or teachers simply organizing a day off? A good way to learn about the reality of graft in the post-modern, post-industrial world, or a wasted and distressing day for both parent and child?

Certainly, the idea of teaching a young person about work, as well as preparing him or her for work, is at the heart of the mission to educate. By doing so, society hopes young people will make wise vocational choices and become, in time, active, responsible and happy workers in the national economy.

For most of our grandparents and before, you learnt about work early, not by exchanging the classroom for your parent's office for a day, but by doing the actual work. Long summer holidays are the historical residue of children being needed to help with the harvest. Children were mandated to help after, or even before, school at many tasks in both agricultural and industrial society.

The paper round, the Saturday-morning job, the helping out in busy periods are all extremely useful educational experiences. And note that they are *experiential* and *sustained over time*, not just observational and one-off. People learn more by doing than by observing.

Nowadays many people work in Dilbert cubicles, sitting in front of computer terminals. The work is often complex, and the output pretty intangible. It looks neither interesting nor important, though it may be both.

The higher up the corporate ladder you climb, the more you attend meetings, the more perplexing it is to the outsider what you actually do. The paradox is perhaps this: lowly paid and unskilled jobs are much easier to understand from a child's perspective. They also look more meaningful and often more fun. Children fully understand what bus-drivers, shop assistants and nurses do. It's fun shadowing a policeman or a landscape gardener for a day, but imagine a fourteen-year-old observing a blue chip company chairperson or an actuary? Or even a secretary or, worse still, a security guard?

The idea that children should understand more of what their parents do to bring home the bacon and their day-to-day working schedule is a good one. But whose choice should this be? Some parents have little say over whether they can take their children to work.

Some single parents find the long summer holidays a terrible burden and attempt to go some way towards solving the problem by taking their children with them to work. Others simply can't do this: the job is too dirty, dangerous, secretive or complex for anyone to observe, let alone a child.

Further consider the role of the parent as a possibly unwilling and unprepared "teacher for the day". Many of us have witnessed bored and bewildered children tearing around cramped office space while harassed parents try to mind, let alone educate, them and perform at least some of the daily activities for which they are paid.

What should parents show or tell their children? Should it be a bright-eyed, Disney version of the working day, or should they confess to the ennui, the tedium or the insecurity of the job? Is the aim to encourage children to understand the nature of work, or the burdens of their parents? Is the objective to make them grateful, or to give them realistic insights? Is it to make them look forward to, or to prefer to postpone, ever going to work in the real world?

And what about a return match, when parents go to school for the day? The child could explain what goes on, and why; the politics of the playground; the monotony of the menus; the tetchiness of certain teachers. School memories are often highly selective and distorted. Some are rose-tinted, golden memories of innocence, but others are precisely the opposite: of being forced to do pointless activities by professional bullies.

Freud said, and this time he was right, that the most important things in life contributing to our overall happiness and contentment are our work and our loving relationships. You can detect passion at work and you certainly detect its opposite. The bored, angry, resentful worker is enough to encourage a child to wish to avoid the world of work completely.

Is this no more than the old-fashioned idea of shadowing a person to learn what they do? Probably. Gone out of fashion now, though. If it is thought through, well prepared and with some follow-up activity it might be a good idea. Otherwise it is of little merit. But wouldn't it be fun to go to school for a day again, all supported and sponsored by your boss?

Advertising archetypes

It was Plato, rather than Jung, who first talked about archetypes. The Jungians have, however, cornered the market in these, which are thought to be part of the collective unconscious. In this sense they are supposedly universal, limited in number and recognizable everywhere. All stories, myths and legends celebrate one or other of these powerful prototypic models or specimens. For Jungians, archetypes are universal thought forms and emotions resulting from the "deposits of the constantly repeated experiences of humanity" and which predispose an individual to apprehend the world in particular ways. Everyone inherits a tendency to fear things that our ancestors found to be potentially dangerous (such as darkness), but an individual who grows up enjoying only pleasant encounters with the dark will develop mental images and behaviors that are quite different from the inherent archetype. Similarly, the child's perception of its mother is influenced partly by her true characteristics and partly by the unconscious projection of such archetypal maternal qualities as solicitude, nurturance, fertility and secrecy. All a bit murky.

Jungian psychology incorporates the widely accepted viewpoint that humans are inherently bisexual, but differs from other theories in attributing this phenomenon to archetypes. A man's unconscious feminine disposition is connected to the archetype known as the *anima*, while the male archetype in women is the *animus*. The anima and animus supposedly develop from generations of exposure to the opposite sex, and imbue each sex with an innate understanding of the other. The anima's influence must not be ignored, as a relationship with a woman markedly different from this ideal is all too likely to prove disappointing. But if a man projects his own anima on to a woman who corresponds to its general characteristics, and the man becomes so infatuated with her that he ignores her true personality, he may find to his dismay that he has married his own worst weakness. Or the anima and shadow (an archetype incorporating the dark, evil side of human nature) may fuse, resulting in dreams or projections of a she-devil.

It gets more interesting: the inner femininity of the anima compensates for the outward masculine persona of power and effectiveness. Trying to deny this aspect of personality will result in a one-sided and conflicted individual, as when a man who prides himself on an overly virile persona is beset by inner feelings of weakness and moodiness. The masculine animus, on the other hand, produces unshakable and arbitrary convictions. The woman who suppresses her animus in a misguided attempt to appear extremely feminine will be troubled by spells of stubbornness and blind conviction, and these characteristics are likely to be projected on to males who seem godlike or heroic. The well-adjusted personality integrates the male and female attributes by means of the transcendent function (a higher-order process), allowing both to find satisfactory expression.

Other archetypes include the wise old man, the mother, the father, the child, the parents, the wife, the husband, God, the hero, various animals, energy, the self (the ultimate goal of personality development), the trickster, rebirth or reincarnation, the spirit, the prophet, the disciple, and an indefinite number of archetypes representative of situations.

But the Jungians argue that we never become aware of the archetypes themselves, which always remain within the inaccessible collective unconscious. The collective unconscious is like the base of a volcano that extends to the core of personality and occasionally erupts, shooting archetypal images, motifs or symbols up to the surface. Unlike such common signs as words and pictures, which merely denote the objects to which they are attached, archetypal symbols imply something vague or hidden from us. Since they are produced entirely by the unconscious psyche, not by personal experience or intellectual thought, they have a powerfully numinous or fascinating effect that clearly identifies them as something out of the ordinary.

So can they be found in that myth-building, legend-creating, wacky world of advertising? It seems they can. No Jungian would be surprised, but might quibble only with the language.

And there seem to be slightly different versions of the archetypes for men and women. Those who have studied men in magazine, radio or television advertisements say that eight archetypes are clearly apparent.

- First, of course, the *hero* – brave, idealistic and righteous. Heroes are not materialists but rather dreamers seeking a better world for everyone.
- Second, the *winner* is a bit different: competitive, venturesome and ambitious, his aim is power, money and career success.
- Third, there is the *macho man*: tough, instinctive and austere. Macho men can be impulsive and passionate, and unafraid of risk.
- Fourth – the *prince*: usually young, elegant, faultless, with juxtaposed features such as being both strong and delicate; both tender and tough at the same time.

- Next there is the *patron*, which is perhaps not the best word. He protects, supports and develops others. He takes responsibility and sets a fine example to others.
- Then there is the *creator* – quirky, adventurous and gifted. The creator is independent-minded, innovative and eager to understand things.
- Seventh, there is the friend, the *buddy* – cheerful, frank and supportive. They nurture relationships, are good at listening and understanding, and are always tolerant.
- Of course, there is always the *anti-hero* – eager to be who he really is. Sometimes childlike, always candid, the anti-hero is self-critical, wry and independent.

The female archetypes are sometimes almost identical to their male equivalents prince/princess, patron/patroness, creator/creator, friend/friend, but there are differences. A female hero is likely to be a *star* – adorable, inaccessible, unattainable, wishing to be, and are, admired and adored.

The female equivalent of the macho-man is probably the *seductress*: alluring, charming and enticing. She may be delicate, fragile or sensitive, but equally could be hard-hearted, manipulative and tough. And she is different from the *vamp*, who is the demon, mercenary, lustful anti-hero.

But studying commercials reveals that advertising people are far less imaginative, particularly in less developed countries. Here you have four female and three male types. Your choice is the middle-aged, domestic and demure *traditional housewife*; or the modern housewife who keeps up with technology, ecological issues and economic realities.

We still have the *sex symbol* – need one say more – as well as the *successful woman* – neat, enterprising, educated and resourceful.

And men: there is also the *professional* – independent and successful; a self-confident connoisseur of many things. And our *macho friend* still pops up. As does the *father figure*.

It is only the adventurous, it seems, who explore new images such as *metrosexual man*, which researchers have divided into three subtypes, namely androgynous; nancy; and new man. We can now have man as object, delicate man and sensitive man.

A fun project for a media studies student, perhaps: the question is, does finding the right archetype for the right product improve advertising effectiveness?

Attitude surveys

Are attitude surveys ever worth the money and effort? It's a pretty big industry, so there will be a lot of people eager to sell their multiple benefits. They provide, we are told, a snapshot of company morale at a period in time. They show, apparently, the things management needs to concentrate on. They can tell if a change programme or a merger and acquisition (M&A) is working.

Those who support doing surveys put forward all sorts of arguments in their favor. They believe surveys serve to:

- Separate fact from fiction.
- Obtain unbiased information.
- Help discover whether the organization is meeting its objectives.
- Identify opportunities for growth, change and improvement.
- Improve the morale and motivation of respondents
- Assess staff needs.
- Assess the status and capability of equipment and buildings.
- Provide an insight into recruitment and selection.
- Measure the culture of the organization.
- Provide an insight into employees' needs.
- Show potential fit and misfit in mergers, acquisitions and partnerships.

But there are three important objections to doing attitude surveys. *First*, they all yield practically the same results. *Second*, attitude surveys rarely offer any straightforward and realistic solutions to problems: it is far from clear what to do with the results. *Third*, attitudes do not predict behavior (the obverse is true).

Call them climate surveys, engagement trackers or morale monitors – an attitude survey is nearly always a set of statements about various aspects of life in the organization. Questions usually tap into issues such as attitudes to customers and supervision, innovation and communication. The output is usually a glossy, multicoloured report with bar graphs or pie charts. And often the results are broken down not by the old favourites of age, sex and class but by such things as level, specialty and region.

The first problem is that it is possible to predict the results long before putting the survey on the intranet. There is always a "communication" problem. People complain that they do not get told what they need to know: this despite avalanches of cc-ed emails, internal communication posters, magazines and newspapers, weekly meetings and the like.

Surveys always show people claim that they don't get enough information. They don't say *what* they want to know, *who* should give it to them, or *how* they are best informed. There seems to be a generalized belief that senior staff have a library of important secrets that they are not willing to share with their staff. A conspiracy of silence? Paranoia – perhaps?

The second predictable feature is pay disenchantment. Ask people about their compensation and benefits and they appear to be unhappy. Are they fairly and equitably paid? Are they paid well according to market rates? No, they are all under-benefited; they are badly paid. This result is so predictable and infuriating that those who commission the research often choose not to ask such questions. They usually know about market rates and can demonstrate that staff opinion is wrong.

Third, if you ask about morale you always get the same result. People believe three things about morale across the organization: they think it is clearly in a remorseless decline, and has been for some time. They also believe that things are OK in their small area; in their section. Their morale has held up, but it is bad elsewhere. They also experience stress, poor work–life balance and demands to do more work in less time to higher standards.

Attitudinal results rarely make fascinating reading. Ask the client to predict the results before the survey and many are so accurate you wonder why they commission the (expensive) study in the first place. But worse than that the results rarely even hint at what actions might be taken to change those attitudes. They do not explain how to improve communications and how to improve morale.

Attitude surveys describe attitudes. But they do not indicate what causes them, or more importantly, causes them to change. But should one worry? Aren't attitudes almost epiphenomenal? There has been a debate in psychology since the First World War on whether, how, when and why attitudes predict behavior. If the causal path is from attitudes to behavior, then changing attitudes leads to changing behavior. But if the causal nexus is the opposite, it makes attitudes far less interesting and important – change behavior and you change attitudes.

The data is back: we know the answer – and it is the latter. Remember seat belts and clunk-click and all that? Many people, despite all the advertisements and experts' advice and all that palaver, ignored the advertisement.

Then they changed the law, which changed behavior and consequently has changed attitudes.

One recent study looked at the attitudes/behavior debate in terms of the job satisfaction productivity link. Are happy people productive, or does productivity bring happiness? It was both of course, but more the latter.

This is not an argument for ignoring attitudes at work. But unless you know why you are investing in an attitude survey with and all the expectations that it might lead to, it is probably best to focus on specific behavior. Praise and reward what you like. Help people do better at what they are less successful at: that is harder, of course, than doing an attitude survey but considerably better value for money in the long run.

Base rate blunders

Everyone has worked for an incompetent manager. Not just abusive, cranky, sullen or obsessional, but dysfunctionally incompetent. Some believe they have worked for no others.

But what is the incidence of incompetence among the senior management population: 3–5 percent? Perhaps 8–10 percent of executives and chief executive officers (CEOs) turn out to be too dangerous, deranged or derailed? Others, looking at corporate blunders, firings or sudden resignations, think that it may be 30–50 percent. The data, such as it is, support the latter: around 40 percent of CEOs are incompetent.

Certainly, business news stories seem to imply that incompetence is widespread. So how do these people get to where they are?

It's partly through making all those classic selection decision mistakes: choosing in one's own image, or that of the previous incumbent; believing the story in the CV or the referees' comments; not being clear about what the job involves; leaving junior, inexperienced or untrained staff to do the hiring.

So you get incompetence. Attractive, articulate, super-confident, just-out-of-business school types with no real-world experience. Those eager to make their pile and duck out for a quiet life. Conventional meritocrats who don't understand the politics of influence. Confrontation-averse peace-keepers unwilling to ruffle feathers. Attention-seeking rebels who are consistently and unwisely always anti-conformist. Pointy-headed techies who can't sell the (often wise) decisions they make. Those with an impostor syndrome, who suddenly feel they do not deserve the success they have achieved.

They all share certain characteristics: a lack of self-awareness; an exaggerated sense of self-worth and concomitant entitlement; insensitivity or indifference to the needs of those around them; an ever-hungry and seemingly unfulfillable need for approbation and approval; and sometimes a heavily disguised and hidden insecurity.

Failed leaders can be perfectly articulate, dedicated and intelligent, but they cannot (sometimes will not) do what has to be done. This can be because they have chosen the wrong team, because they can't make timely decisions, or because they can't delegate authority and accountability. Some lose the plot: they drift, unfocused and unhappy. Worse, they take their eye off market realities.

Studies of failed, derailed, incompetent senior managers have yielded rich checklists:

- They cannot administer using the simple process of prioritization, delegation and record-keeping – so over- or under-manage.
- Being reactive, not proactive for major events.
- Poor judgement because of lack of intelligence, being too emotionally involved, too late or too unclear.
- Socially unaware, insensitive, egotistical: unable to build teams, persuade, charm or influence. Lack of adaptability and flexibility to change when the situation requires it.
- Not being sufficiently well-adjusted to "take the heat": emotionally unstable, unpredictable, fragile.
- Lacking in integrity, loyalty: dishonest, betrayer of trust.
- Personally over-ambitious.

So how to fix incompetence? First, what aspects of incompetent people can or cannot be changed? Some things – skills or competencies, for example – can be taught: intrapersonal skills (patience, courage, the work ethic), interpersonal skills (communication, compassion), technical skills (decision-making, process management), and leadership (delegating, directing, hiring). However, personality factors play a part in executive learning. These include *self-discipline* and *self-control*, which are linked to conscientiousness. Then there is *self-confidence*, which has a double-edged benefit: it may be related to resistance to coaching and difficulty in acknowledging mistakes but positively related to the ability to withstand criticism. This is related to stability and neuroticism. Next, there is the issue of insightfulness: perceptiveness, insight and social sensitivity. No doubt this is partly related to agreeableness and extraversion. Finally, there is the ever-present issue of rationality: the ability to evaluate data and make good decisions on the basis of it.

CEO derailment is costly to the organization, in both human and financial terms. An improved selection and appointments process, or succession planning, could reduce its incidence. And perhaps to consider serious, sensitive coaching all the way through the rocky ride that is now called "my watch".

Beware salespeople bearing gifts

Most of us love prezzies: the excitement and unexpectedness of it all; the idea of being liked and valued; the getting something for free. We talk of gifted children and "gift" our donations. But there is a darker side, not exclusively to do with Hellenic mischief.

Many people look forward to giving and receiving gifts from their relatives and loved ones. Ritualized gift-giving is, always and everywhere, a way of consolidating important (and not-so-important) relationships: a gift is a symbol of commitment – accepting a gift symbolically indicates a willingness and obligation to continue a relationship with the gift-giver. More significant gifts defined by cost or rarity symbolize great commitment by both giver and recipient.

We are obliged to give gifts to relations: it cements the social fabric; ties us together and symbolizes our bonds. Not receiving an expected present from a mother or son, for example, immediately sets off a train of questions about love, commitment, ungratefulness. All the insecurities and passions of close relationships are triggered by *not* giving presents, or giving those that are obviously inappropriate. We don't have to spend much time or money, but we do have to get the sentiment right.

Yet behind this seemingly innocent exchange of gifts is a complex set of rules and behaviors. Aside from the obvious matters of kindness, thoughtfulness and taste are the more subtle dynamics of reciprocity and obligation, psychological and economic debts, and understanding and obeying rules and conventions.

Broadly, gifts fall into six categories:

1. *Gifts with a personal history*

Gifts that are nostalgic or are a memento of a special time are very special. It may be an heirloom, or have been owned by a famous person. Heirlooms are likely to acquire a sort of sacred status if carefully restored. They can provide a great sense of family continuity, which extends beyond death. But they may equally signify a past occasion shared by the giver and recipient. They may represent a place, an occasion or an event shared by the two that has special meaning. Paintings, photographs, objects which capture and freeze an event are good examples.

2. *Gifts that have taken time and effort*
Some gifts, such as hand-crafted items, take considerable time and effort to produce. The hand-carved, sewn, embroidered or painted item may be of limited monetary value, but of enormous personal value to the recipient. This is emphasized by the personal nature of the gift, or the fact that it is personalized, perhaps by the initials, name, or likeness of the giver and receiver. They take time, but also reflect the ability of the individual.

3. *Surprise gifts*
The unexpected gift is special and valued precisely because it was not anticipated. The surprise might relate to when the gift is given, how it is given, or by whom. Of course, one can be surprised by disgust as well as joy. Beware the person who says "surprise me". They may not really mean it.

4. *Exotic gifts*
More and more people are buying gifts from abroad. The item from abroad is of indeterminate price (usually) because it cannot be compared in the home country, although it may represent a "bargain" for the giver. These gifts can make the recipient feel as if they were being thought of in the absence of the giver, and are particularly important for families/girlfriends/boyfriends left behind for business trips, as they strengthen ties in separation. These gifts are difficult to obtain, and have a rarity value and foreign cachet at home, which increases the "special factor" of the gift. This shows a significant "effort" in the purchase and transportation, negotiating a foreign language and currency, carrying it home. It can, of course, be seen as a show-off token of those who travel to those who don't.

5. *Gifts with a message*
Some gifts are chosen because they deliver an explicit message to the recipient. Many are passed of as "joke" presents: hot, spicy chewing gum (for the loud-mouthed), exploding cigarettes and cigars (for sexual harassers), gift-wrapped boxes of imitation faeces (for those who talk rubbish). Joke gifts may reflect a rather insecure relationship as well as a hint. But gifts may be an expression of guilt about a year's (or longer) neglect, or an attempt to compensate for some other deficit (such as woeful inattentiveness). Gifts make excellent items to use in the atonement of sins but they can easily be rejected as not being sufficiently compensatory.

6. *Monetary gifts*

Nearly all gifts of money are given by parents/grandparents to children/ grandchildren, and this appears to be one of the few acceptable situations in which to give money. In fact, research indicates that it accounts for 50 percent of all gifts received from grandparents. Further, cash gifts are common from employers to employees. And small money gifts are given to dustmen, newspaper boys, milkmen, postmen in appreciation of their services throughout the year.

Apart from in the situations listed above, money is generally unacceptable as a gift, for two reasons. *First*, it is impersonal. It says nothing about the relationship of the donor and recipient, and gives no clues about the personality or tastes of the giver, the recipient or their relationship. The giver has made little or no investment of time, thought or effort: even a gift voucher says more about the giver. *Second*, it might cause offence: the giver assuming he can "buy" the recipient (particularly in male–female relationships), or that the recipient needs the money.

In the working world there are business-to-business, as well as business-to-customer gifts. These can be tangible (in the form of goods), or experiential. They can be targeted or not.

What is the psychology of business gift giving? What are the motives of the giver? What is the marketing strategy behind the whole thing?

There are various possible aspects worth measuring for the management researcher in this area: how people evaluate the gift; their attitude to the giver; their feeling that they should (and later will) reciprocate; how this influences later choices; and their skeptical or cynical perception of the manipulative intent of the giver.

What are the key elements in the whole enterprise? First, the gift itself. There are at least three factors involved in this issue that seem important. The first, of course, is value, though that is not so easy to measure. Sometimes gifts are so "cheap" they are an insult – a bit like giving too small a tip. On the other hand, they might maybe too big to accept. What are the boundaries? Under £5? Between £5 and £20? Over £20? Over £100? It does make a difference ... or does it?

Related to the gift's value is the type of item offered. Various dimensions are relevant here. Is the gift essentially of a hedonistic or a utilitarian nature? Is it standard or personalized? Is it something the receiver likes, or wants, or not? Clearly, perfume is different from a pen; a bottle of wine with the recipient's picture/name on the label different from one with a fake chateau; a plastic watch with the gift-givers logo is different from one with a recognized (and respected) brand.

And then there is the implicit or explicit reason or request associated with the gift. Is it an opportunity for the recipient to try the "new and improved formula?" Is it a "little thank-you" for continued custom? Does it arrive once the recipient has spent some (semi-outrageous) amount on a product? What, in short, is the motive of the giver?

Also who exactly is the gift-giver? Is the gift from an individual with some authority and discretion, or is it simply a routine mailing from an anonymous organization? What is the reputation of the organization? There is a big difference between a time-share and a charity.

Most organizations that "do" (serious or semi-serious) gifts want the recipient to like and value the gift. They want to influence the recipient's perceptions and behavior, and reciprocate, perhaps in purchasing but also in word-of-mouth marketing. But they do not want to be seen as manipulative and cynical.

Research in this area has shown some interesting facts. First, perhaps surprisingly, the value of the gift is not that important in its evaluation or reciprocity. Two factors *are* significant, however. The first is the strength/nature of the relationship between giver and receiver. To receive a gift from a person/organization you know and where you are known is much more powerful. Indeed, it is seen as an index of that relationship: cement, blood-tie, bond and so on.

The second factor is the nature of the request or the explanation for the gift. How explicit or manipulative is the gift-giver seen to be? A giver who appears too pushy may experience a serious reaction that can backfire.

Do charities do themselves a disservice by enclosing a very cheap pen in the mass-marketed appeal letters? They have probably done their homework – it is cost-effective. Do stores that have loyalty shopper evenings or after-hours, party-bag-giving events get their money back? Does the free gift attached to the magazine help sales?

The literature says this: business gifts work best between two parties who know each other and do not make too much of any implicit strings attached. After all that's what a real gift is, isn't it?

Blindness, pretence and denial

Karl Marx called it false consciousness. Jean-Paul Sartre called it double-mindedness. Freud called it repression.

What did the Freudians mean by repression? Through repression, inner conflict at the unconscious level is not permitted to reach the level of consciousness. The unconscious life of each individual is made up of troublesome urges, strivings and impulses that are constantly seeking to be expressed. Psychologists assume the presence of some kind of critical, selective process that allows some urges to be expressed while others are held in check. At any given moment an individual does not express all the urges he or she possesses, but only a few. The rest are controlled by the powerful forces of repression.

Although repression takes place automatically and unconsciously, there are conscious forces supporting the process. The conscious part of this controlling mechanism is the conscience. When the conscience bothers a person, he or she has become aware of the struggle between his or her unconscious impulses and the code of ethics and morals adopted.

The purpose of psychological treatment is to explore the unconscious and to reach the deeper levels of the personality by releasing guilt-laden, pent-up experiences. Such treatment attempts to get below the surface, to find out what the critical experiences have been, to free them, and to help the patient understand how they have been responsible for the conscious conflict.

Suppression, which is sometimes confused with repression, is a defensive maneuver by means of which the individual consciously attempts to push disturbing thoughts and feelings out of the mind. It is not unusual for people to seek to forget their troubles and the unpleasantness of life by losing themselves in work, by being involved in needless activities, or by false love. This has also been called self-deception, misrecognition, or data blindness – a refusal to accept that certain facts related to important personal beliefs are wrong.

There is first the avoidance of evidence pointing towards these facts, and then pretending not to notice the avoidance of evidence. Comfortable illusions are maintained by ignoring the obvious, empirical truth about what is going on.

There are fascinating psychiatric cases recorded of hysterical blindness, where people faced with some personal catastrophe literally go blind.

Opticians, eye surgeons and the like can find no tissue or brain damage, but the person cannot see, but their sight may return as quickly as it disappeared. Psychological trauma seems to lead to this dramatic, if primitive, defense mechanism.

Take boardroom feuds. Most of the time, the grown-ups who run the show are involved in constant, vicious power struggles that use up most of their energy. They are continually out to create fiefdoms, immobilize contenders, build spheres of interest, inherit (and keep) the crown. They do this at the expense of their health, and the wealth and welfare of all stakeholders in the organization. They create dysfunctional boards … and everyone pretends this is not happening.

There are many fascinating stories of how families cope, albeit rather bizarrely, with difficulty. The author John Mortimer noted how his father simply ignored his blindness. Others do likewise with a variety of mental and physical handicaps. The response is part healthy, part not. It's good to believe that physical handicaps are not mental handicaps. It's good to try to triumph over adversity. But it's bad to not face reality, and not make others try to do so too.

And what of organizational pretence and denial? Does it occur? If so, why? When? How? What are its functions? Should we try to prevent it?

What evidence is there of this phenomenon – call it denial or hypocrisy, spin or PR? Look at a company's mission statement, job advertisements or recruitment campaigns – pure fantasy: no correlation with reality: talk to senior people about work "on the floor", or visit and observe a boardroom meeting.

Part of the problem arises because information flows downhill more easily than uphill. Those at the top are heard more clearly than those at the bottom. It's nicer at the top. And once there, it's easier to believe that it's the same throughout the organization.

People who have made it up through the ranks tend to have a selective memory. Perhaps they are promoted partly on their ability to see the glass half full; to be relentlessly optimistic.

Holocaust and global warming deniers are vilified for their wicked dissimulation, but those who deny organizational gloom and reality are rewarded, not punished.

People at the top receive filtered information. And some do not realize that those around them are not being exactly honest. Weak jokes are laughed at; third-rate ideas applauded; incompetence brushed over by sycophantic, self-effacing, Uriah Heap-alikes. You see this with fashion designers who bar bad press and who are bodyguarded by ever-adoring luvvies. The feedback is false. It feeds narcissism.

Groups are prone to "group think". It has certain characteristics, such as collective rationalization, illusions of invulnerability and self-censorship of dissenting ideas. Mindguards ensure that the party line prevails.

We are all prone to the primitive defence of denial. When things are too difficult to bear, a very simple and temporarily effective reaction is to pretend nothing is happening. It is associated more with pain than pleasure, but can occur when organizations or individuals have to explain why they are so successful.

To outsiders, consultants or later historians, it seems almost inconceivable how groups behave under pressure; and why there have not been more plays about boardroom feuds remains a mystery. There is often more interesting psychiatric pathology in a boardroom in the City than a wing of a secure psychiatric unit.

Brand discrimination

All marketing people want to, or should want to, fundamentally understand their customers, their peccadilloes, peculiarities and predilections. They are captivated by the idea of customer brand loyalty. Why, when purchasing cars, or computers, or cameras – or even whisky, washing powder or window cleaner, do some consumers carefully search out brand names? Are they naïve, discriminating or savvy? Manufacturers want to get inside the heads and hearts of their customers and those who, seemingly unwisely and irrationally, buy other brands, to see what makes them tick.

Marketing people have to "live the brand". They try to get "into the mind and under the skin" of consumers, to try to understand how they make their decisions. They need to understand how demographic forces, and changes in values and aspirations, influence groups of individuals to have very specific preferences. Their aim is to understand brand discrimination from the customers' viewpoint.

For at least fifty years, market researchers have tried to understand brand loyalty by borrowing psychological concepts to differentiate and segment the market. Early attempts were heavily influenced by *psychoanalysis*, with its emphasis on unconscious motives, crypto-sexual symbolism and deep-seated fears and hopes. Hence the appeal of certain chocolate confectionery based on the phallic shape – and the range of staple food products apparently enjoyed by happy nuclear families.

Freudians were the deep-motivational boys. But then the *sociologists* and *psychologists* got a look in. Some tried to categorize social motives and social needs: needs for acceptance and achievement, dominance and power. So brands fulfilled needs. A certain brand of whisky signaled that you had "arrived", were part of the "in group", or had high social status. Equally, some cars fulfilled the dream of ever-frustrated "boy racers" of beating all other cars off the traffic lights (starting block).

About this time the *self-theorists* entered the field. They believed it was self-concept or self-image that were the keys to understanding brand loyalty. People bought products whose images were like themselves. See yourself as a steady, practical, sensible sort of chap and you buy products that rejoice in those qualities. On the other hand if you see yourself as a bit of a rebel, a bit funky or "arty", then you choose brands to complement that image.

The *social psychologists* also had a go: they were interested in attitude systems and how they were related to brand purchase. So authoritarians with conservative, dogmatic, anti-change attitudes were attracted to quite different brands from open-minded, flexible, individuals tolerant of ambiguity, who rather like variety and change.

Naturally the *personality theorists* waded into the fray. But one celebrated study at the end of the 1950s failed very convincingly to show any meaningful personality differences between Ford and Chevrolet owners. Other attempts met with a little more success, and the application of standard personality inventories to those who owned, chose or preferred different brands showed very modest effects.

A natural outcome of this research was to develop concepts and measures of consumer-based personality traits. So a list of these were constructed like the novelty-seeking personality, or the high self-monitor.

But none of these delivered what they promised. They did, however, lead to the psychographics industry. Thus you can segment markets demographically (results broken down by age, sex and class concept) or geographical segmentation (by television region or by political boundaries). Psychographics is about the values or life-styles of customers. Values are divided up into a person's preferred activities, interests and opinions, and are thought to be formed by institutions (primarily families, schools and religious organizations) and early childhood experiences.

Various psychographic systems or models have been developed based on lifestyle and values. People are classified into groups such as "achievers", "belongers", or "emulators". These classifications are used to segment markets for everything from booze to breakfast cereal, as well as media preferences and purchases.

But does it work? It depends on your hopes and expectations. Does it help marketers to understand brand preference? Probably. How accurately can you predict the purchasing behavior of different groups? Moderately. Can you differentiate between those who seek out a Bentley versus a Roller? A Datsun versus a Nissan? Probably not. But a promising start.

Brand is everything

For marketing people, the concept of *brand* is everything. It is like the Almighty: omnipotent, omnipresent and omniscient.

Technically the brand is a set of characteristics associated with a product or service that give added value, beyond its tangible benefit. To an outsider it seems that marketing people are so obsessed by the concept that they have well over two dozen concepts/definitions with "brand" as a prefix, and a similar number with this word as a suffice.

Some are highly pretentious. How about *brand custodial blue print* defined by Iain Ellwood (2002) as "A sequential process for new brand creation that starts by defining the brand DNA in a media neutral frame of reference". Or there is *brand narrative,* which is "the biography of a brand that develops over time, matching a developing relationship with the customer".

We have *brand length* (the stretchability of the brand across products or services) as well as economic terms such as *brand equity* (the financial value of a brand) or *brand personality* (the chosen character or temperament for a brand). One can have *brand displeasure*, a *branded customer journey,* a *niche brand*, a *sub-brand, entry brands* and *diffusion brand*.

The marketer is after brand breadth, extension, identity, leadership, length, power, spread and weight. A lot to ask, you might well say. People buy brands, not products. Brand names have entered everyday vocabulary: hence we Hoover the carpet and Sellotape the parcel.

And some have stood the test of time. Everything from Avon cosmetics to Wedgwood pottery. Coca-Cola and Quaker Oats have been going well over a hundred years. People have spent their entire lives in the service of Heinz baked beans or McVitie's biscuits. They live the brand and are eager for us to do so as well. They are in charge of the aura: that semi-mystical, all-important "stuff" that surrounds the brand; that differentiates it; that brings it to life.

Skeptical observers are always amused by the shopper who is a life-long advocate purchaser, and indeed enthusiast, for a particular brand over others but who on blind usage cannot distinguish one brand from another. Popular consumer television programmes as well as magazines show that the vast majority of the public often cannot tell the difference between types of products (brandy versus whisky; China tea versus Indian), let alone specific brands. Further, there is no relationship between price and disinterested expert evaluation of quality.

All this means that the brand boys have won; they have persuaded people through persistent but consistent marketing that enters the popular imagination. This has not occurred by accident. Fine minds have been at work on the brand, theme, name and identity; they have sought to understand the image of the brand, its "emotional benefits" and personality.

They have labored on the *brand proposition*: in short, the promise of the marketing. They have worried about the name, particularly if they have tried to develop a new one. Ever wondered why cars in particular have such odd names? The brand-name Johnnies have, you see, to fulfil various criteria: the name must be simple so that everyone can spell and pronounce it correctly; it should be universal, and not have special (odd, negative) associations in some places; and it must give people a feel-good experience when hearing or seeing the name. Cars go in for conceptual names; perfumes for proper names.

And you need to think through brand logos and trade marks, colours and typefaces, strap lines and supposed attributes.

Buying a brand can be a political statement. It may be patriotic or political. You express your "greenness", your ecological mind, through brands. Brands bring psychological pleasure: they confirm your identity as a "person of taste", and discrimination, and money and exclusivity. They even have sociological benefits: they can show group identity and belonging. And they can even have religious and ideological functions.

And you thought you were just buying washing powder when you chose Persil; you naïvely believed you chose Kellogg's randomly when buying cornflakes; and that Colgate was just another toothpaste....

Marketing people know that we are not entirely rational shoppers. We are people of the head and people of the heart: emotional and rational. And they knew we are social animals with complex needs, whose decision-making to purchase one brand over another can be understood and managed.

Reference

Ellwood, Iain (2002) *The Essential Brand Book: Over 100 Techniques to Increase Brand Value*, 2nd edn. London: Kogan Page.

Brand sickness

Everything and everyone is, if you are to believe the ad men, a brand. Brands have a life story, a history. They also have a personality. Advertising executives live their brand and try to get us to do so as well.

You have brand relationships, brand identity, brand recognition, brand extension, even brand DNA. But, perhaps, you can also have brand illness, brand sickness, brand senility. As well as physical illness, there is, of course, mental illness. While psychologists talk of personality traits, the psychiatrists talk of personality disorders.

Personality disorders are serious, difficult, if not impossible, to treat and pervasive in their effects. Some people believe such disorders are really just manifestations of extreme personalities. In this sense, they are pretty inflexible. So can a brand have a personality disorder? Consider the following hypotheses:

Borderline brands

These are moody, fickle, unstable brands that have intense, short-lived and passionate relationships with their owners. They are mercurial, fickle and prone to unpredictable swings of idealization and devilishness. They are impulsive and often not quite sure who they are. They create "scenes" and are often high-maintenance.

Paranoid brands

These are cynical, distrustful and suspicious brands that doubt others' true intentions. They believe that others are inherently malevolent, and they are super-vigilant. If they believe they are being treated unfairly, they retaliate. They don't compromise and can be self-centred.

Avoidant brands

These are (unusually) coy, socially sensitive brands. They are super-sensitive to criticism and react terribly badly to any form of rejection. This brand is easily embarrassed, easily shamed and socially reticent. All too often they look cautious, indecisive or dithering.

Schizoid brands

Aloof, detached and cold, they are solitary brands, seemingly equally indifferent to criticism or praise. They appear to lack any interest in, or indeed any awareness of, the feelings of others. They are solitary, detached and self-absorbed, with unflappable sangfroid.

Passive-aggressive brands

They take the line of least resistance. They are leisurely, lazy and independent. They resist doing what is expected of them, but become argumentative and irritated when asked to do something they don't want to do. Sulky procrastinators, protesting laggards, sniping critics: very unappealing brands.

Narcissistic brands

Bold, unusually self-confident, haughty. These brands do grandiosity, self-importance and a real sense of entitlement. Their conceit and confidence can look like charisma, but they are too vain, pompous and overbearing to be really attractive. But they energetically and effectively sell themselves in the search for the red carpet of life.

Antisocial brands

These are the adventurous, mischievous brands which tests the limits. They take risks, love excitement and pleasure (now). But they are cunning, deceitful and manipulative. They are not only rule breakers but also law breakers. They like outwitting the system; being rolling stones who gather no moss; and react badly to routine, processes and procedures.

Histrionic brands

These are the drama queens, theatrical, attention-seeking brands. They are animated, expressive and want to be noticed. They do serious exaggeration and excessive emotionality ... darling! They are often seductive, provocative, easily influenced, spontaneous and applause-seeking.

Schizotypical brands

Oddballs, idiosyncratic, eccentric and peculiar brands. Somewhere between creative and disturbed, they certainly portray themselves in unusual ways. They seek rapture and nirvana, and often seem pretty peculiar.

Obsessive-compulsive brands

These are the diligent, conscientious, perfectionistic brands. They rejoice in rules, orderliness, following procedures. They are inflexible, precise and controlling. They can be seen as miserly, stubborn and over-scrupulous. They like to do the right thing, the right way, at the right time. Always.

Dependent brands

Dutiful, devoted, dependent brands are dreadfully eager to please. They need advice, reassurance, guidance and support. They desperately need approval and would never dream of independent action or going against the crowd. They really need TLC, companionship and nurture, always seeking harmony and togetherness.

It's not too difficult to see which products might be branded with certain personality-disordered characteristics: home alarms with a touch of paranoia; cosmetics with narcissism; 'boy racer' cars and bikes for the anti-social; frocks for the histrionic. Even obsessive-compulsive traits might suit some products, such as personal organizers or household cleaners. Not quite as clear for the avoidant and the passive aggressive characters.

The story of the personality disorders is that having some of the characteristics might even be beneficial. But too much of a good thing and you are in deep doo-doo.

Bullying at work

Is bullying really on the increase at work? Is this simply over-reporting by incompetent, lazy, vengeful staff eager to punish their bosses and sue their organizations? Or does the stress and complexity of modern business life lead to stressed managers who then bully, harass and victimize innocent and vulnerable workers? Workplace bullying supposedly takes many forms. It includes assaults and threats, verbal as well as physical attacks, ridiculing, nit-picking and even patronizing someone.

Lots of interesting questions arise related to workplace bullying. What is the typical gender of the bully, and that of the victim? At what level in an organization are people most likely to be bullied? What events typically coincide with the onset of bullying? What is the typical duration of bullying? And then there is what do, or what should people typically do? Is it best to confront the bully and/or seek help from colleagues? Should you see the known representation, or HR or your GP? While some people seek help, others simply try avoidance, humour or stoicism. Some even feel pressured to resign from the organization.

Bullying is usually defined in terms of duration, frequency and intentionality by people in positions of power, to unduly accuse, criticize or humiliate others. For most adults, bullying is a psychological rather than a physical process, though of course it can be both. In essence, at work it is the abuse of power, though victims can also be bullied by peers and subordinates.

One central question for those interested in the whole issue is whether bullying can or should be explained by organizational, personality or social factors; that is, does the organization condone or even promote bullying as a management technique? Or is there something about the make-up (personality, intelligence, social skills) of both bullies *and* their victims that leads them to seek out each other for their bizarre and beastly rituals? Or is it social factors at work that lead to, or indeed prevent, bullying?

Certainly bullying is more likely to occur in some environments than others: where there is role conflict or ambiguity; where there is acute or chronic work overload; where workers have little autonomy; or where there is an atmosphere of fear of redundancy, sacking or whole organization collapse. In these circumstances, bullying is more likely to happen. Whenever there is win–lose rather than win–win as a philosophy, there is conflict and, often, in the shadows, lurks bullying.

Further, some organizations have a history of autocratic leaders, whose style becomes not only acceptable but required. None of that consultative, democratic nonsense with the authoritarian leader who admires strength.

Authoritarians demand rigid adherence to rules, an uncritical acceptance of authority and a strong, open, aggressive condemnation of the weak, outsiders or those who do not obey the rules. Many project their inner emotions and impulses on to others and have a sort of free-floating, generalized feeling of anger and hostility. Authoritarian leaders admire power and toughness. They have a preoccupation with dominance over others.

But what of the personality make-up of both bullies and their victims. Various groups do not want this discussed or researched because it might do two things they do not want. First, it might indicate that the bullied, as well as the bully, are to blame for the situation. Second, it might imply that very little can be done to remedy bullying, because personality is difficult to change.

There has been a lot of research both in schools and in the workplace, on the vulnerable personality who is likely to be bullied, and the provocative personality who is likely to end up being the bully. And there are no surprises. Bullied people tend to be less stable – more anxious and depressed. They also tend to have low emotional intelligence and few social skills, which means they find it harder to make and keep friends. They tend always to avoid conflict, and to be submissive and passive. And they have poor coping skills, so they are both super-sensitive to bullying and unable to cope adequately when bullied.

And, yes, bullies are in the playground, shop-floor and boardroom: aggressive, competitive and impulsive. They too aren't too good at being assertive. Bullies are aggressive, the bullied are passive; neither seems very assertive.

But is all this research flawed? Does not the bullying experience change the individual? Is not the neurosis of the bullied a consequence rather than a cause of bullying? Does this personality research not amount to victim-blaming and perpetrator-condoning?

While it is true that the victims of bullying do appear to share various personality traits, there are differences between them. And we have little evidence from the bullied being tracked over time to sort out the cause and effect direction.

Everyone agrees with three issues. *First*, bullying is a serious problem that blights people's lives and affects workplace efficiency. *Second*, there are things we can do to prevent it, though some just mask it, others might increase it, and some genuinely help. *Third*, it has multiple causes: bullying is likely to arise from various factors happening at the same time.

It is therefore just as unwise to ignore the individual difference correlates of bullying as it is to insist that they are the predominant cause.

Burnt out but opulent

It's over a quarter of a century since the burnout at work concept was formulated. Initially it was thought that certain professionals were particularly prone to it: health care professionals, teachers and the police – those in remorseless, demanding, people-oriented service jobs.

The early work focused on doctors who were thought to be particularly prone because of the pressure of too many patients, having to make critical decisions based on ambiguous information, and having to face the consequences of those decisions. Also interaction with patients and their families and friends is often fraught because it is charged with anxiety, embarrassment and, more unpleasantly, tension. So this leads from acute to chronic stress, and thence to burnout.

Burnout is associated with physical exhaustion and illness, with increasing use of legal and illegal drugs, and with marital and family conflict in addition to the usual suspects associated with neuroses: anxiety, depression, hypochondria and low self-esteem. This leads to the feeling that someone has nothing left to give, that he or she has essentially achieved nothing and that in some way it is the clients (patients/students/customers) who are the cause of the problems.

There are physical, behavioral and work-performance indicators of burnout. Burnout victims suffer from headaches, sleep disturbance, colds and flu, skin and stomach problems. They may lose or gain weight, depending on their personality. They certainly appear moody, grumpy and suspicious. They make bad decisions, and are easily frustrated. Many pop "uppers and downers" to help with the tiredness. And they become dulled, dampened and diminished in the workplace. They seem to work hard but not smartly; to waste energy and bite everyone's head off.

Those interested in burnout have usually suggested that there are three distinguishable but related factors that make up the syndrome. The first is *exhaustion*. Burnt-out individuals report being physically and emotionally drained, about feeling "all used up", and with little more to give. They feel under constant strain and always tired. We all know these feelings, but for the burnt-out they are both acute and chronic.

The second symptom is *cynicism*. The burnt-out doubt whether they really make any contribution and are hence less interested, enthusiastic and committed to their job. They are more than alienated, with a sense of anomie. They cannot be bothered. At work they are automata. They are cynical about management and peers, customers and subordinates; in fact, about anybody and everybody with whom they come into contact.

The third symptom is a total lack of *personal efficacy*. Effective employees can feel confident, competent and considerate at work. They feel they accomplish worthwhile things, and make a real contribution to the lives of their employers, clients, friends and family. They can report exhilaration at work and are really happy to be there. The burnt-out never experience any of this. Indeed, their reaction is the precise opposite.

So what are the antecedents of burnout? The usual suspects are implicated: long working hours with a heavy "psychological workload". Work culture and a lack of decision authority are also factors.

It seems that there are various reactions to burnout. Some people may feign burnout for ulterior motives, while others try to hide it. Equally some organizations deny that it exists among their employees, while others appear to be happy to try to help those who are burnt out.

Easy enough to describe and diagnose, but what to do about it? Some jobs are not easy to change in order to reduce burnout, but things can be done to help individuals at risk.

Some organizations, aware of the pressure put on employees, try to screen out the more vulnerable. Hardiness, not hard-heartedness, is a major prophylactic to burnout. People need to be resilient, to be able to keep their self-esteem when faced with personal criticism. Everyone has their tipping point, but some are more easily tipped than others. When people say "the wheel is still turning but the hamster is dead" they are indicating a sort of cognitive burnout. They have lost all their energy, burnt up all their fuel and as a result burnt out their engine. They may also have burnt their psychological contract with the organization. The real puzzle, however, is why they don't leave earlier. Are they enslaved and handcuffed to their generous pay and conditions, and therefore happy to pay the price?

So, the answer is: select resilient people; put in place support mechanisms that are effective and acceptable; help staff to work smarter rather than harder; understand the benefits of play and relaxation … and neither sweep burnout under the carpet nor expect it to be commonplace in the organization.

Career planning

Jobs for life are, we are told, dead. We are all now, like it or not, *portfolio people*. The safe, old-style, jobs-for-life story where you climbed the greasy pole from tea boy to CEO is no more.

Career progression and development are now, and for always, in your own hands. With regards to your career, you are now captain of your ship and master of your own fate. You, and you alone, are responsible. Not your boss. Not your organization – YOU. So you had better think about how to do it.

And this is no longer something you do only after leaving school or university. Indeed, career planning is something you do, or need to do, more so as you get older. It is those big "0 years" (30, 40, 50, 60 years) that offer a perhaps sobering, if not frightening, time to reflect, re-evaluate and plan.

But how to do it? Do you need an expensive business coach? How about comprehensive 360° evaluation with personal feedback? A fishing or golfing trip with a few old friends who will give you brutally honest feedback? Perhaps. But as a starter for seven why not consider the following simple questions, in this order.

1. Describe your dreams

OK, goals will do. Where would you ideally like to be? Given your experience and values, knowledge and ability, what sort of job provides you with that ideal combination of satisfaction and reward? Think outside the box. Be radical. But be prepared to justify your choice with some data. Ponder, dream, but end up with a highly specific short-list of jobs, goals or dreams. Do you really know what they will entail? Have you thought about all the implications?

2. Describe your real values and lifestyle preference

No flimflam now. No political correctness. What really is important? You are allowed to say money, fame and power ... if you really mean it. You don't have to say family, giving something back to the community and all that stuff you do at interviews.

But do some serious introspection. What is important to you? For what are you prepared to die? Or at least make major sacrifices? Have you experienced for any period of time, the lifestyle you say you want? The grass often looks greener where you superficially inspect others lifestyles. Be clear about your energy, involvement, and activities that *really* bring satisfaction.

3. Do you believe you have the ability to achieve the goals?

There is all the difference in the world between desire, motivation and talent. The journey and the destination requires more than determination, though that should never be underestimated.

The older we get, the more opportunities we have to "try out" various activities, jobs and tasks, and hope we get feedback on whether we can really do them or not. It is as dangerous to under- as to over-estimate abilities. Some people do excessive (and often false) modesty, while others do very unattractive arrogant hubris.

Find your strengths; your real talents. Don't underestimate them, but don't brag about them. Some require constant practice. But if some things come to you more easily than others and you enjoy exercising those abilities, then build your career around them. Think of them as special gifts, for that is what they are.

4. Do you think you can develop new talents/abilities?

Sure, there is natural talent, high ability, giftedness. But it often needs to be nurtured, strengthened and practiced. More important, perhaps, is both the exploration of other (perhaps hidden) talents and the development of new skills and new insights.

As one gets greyer, wider and more wrinkled, more rigid and often more threatened by the energy and enthusiasm of youth, it is comfortable to retreat into a quiet, calm world that tries to resist change. Development is a threatening word. Take that attitude and you are somebody with a fine career *behind you.*

Do an audit of your abilities. Work on those you have neglected. It's pointless wasting great amounts of effort on things you don't do well. But practice, improve, update.

5. Have you planned milestones and options along the route?

There may be more than one way to get from A to B. Some leave their organizations quite deliberately so that they can return later. Some favor an educational sabbatical. Some like the idea of a coach.

The question is: what experiences may be gained fruitfully or opportunistically by different moves? The Japanese model used to be to move people around the whole organization systematically (from HR to Finance to Planning) so that they could gain not only a full understanding of the organization itself, but also of the skills, values and preferences of people in different parts of it.

Different paths have different hurdles. Some have pretty impermeable blockages; others seem the long route.

The journey has lessons, and it provides opportunities. It may have reverses. But there are different routes. You need a "sat-nav". Yet it is important to remember that though there may be a preferred route, all should be considered.

6.   Are you willing to let go of personal baggage?

Most of us carry backpacks of stuff. Call them hang-ups or memories, self-limiting beliefs or complexes: it's all the same. It's often the job of counselors and therapists to help us reframe our views in a healthy way.

Cognitive behavior therapy is all the rage at present. The idea is an old one and is simple. The way we think about ourselves, others and the world has an impact on how we behave: and if we have distorted, dysfunctional or daft cognitions we under-perform. The past is another country: they do things differently there. But these things are difficult to let go. It's easy to talk about disposing of personal baggage, but it is essential.

Many things can hold us back. Things that happened a long time ago. Things that have a negative influence on our whole career development. The dark shadows, the murmuring voices, the near-phobic reactions. These need to be confronted head on. The invisible backpack can get heavier and heavier. A millstone and then a tombstone. Let them go.

7.   Identify those who can help on the journey

We all need encouragement and support. We constantly need emotional, intellectual, moral and social support. We might even benefit from technical and financial support.

Many people help us on the journey: bosses who give one a chance; spouses who take the burden at crucial times; friends who listen.

There are also professional people who can make all the difference. They might be a cost but are best seen as an investment. One needs to enlist experts and support staff for the journey. This is a practical, not a cynical exercise.

People help in different ways and at different times. Think about who and what you need. No man is an island … and all that.

No one gets to the top without ability, planning, determination and support. Yes, maybe luck does play a small part, but as all successful people know, you make your luck. It's never too late to take down, dust off and reconsider your career plan.

Character strengths and competencies

Most people are deeply bored by the competency industry now reaching its senility phase. For over twenty years, HR people have sought to design competency frameworks and architecture that supposedly form a bridge between silos and the organizational DNA, and are the uniting force behind everything, from selection to training.

Often, to the outsider, this pompous talk is really little more than a list of human characteristics that the organization says it wants (nay requires) in its employees. There are four clearly observable facts about organizational competencies.

First, they are almost identical for every organization. They all make a song and dance about theirs being unique to the organization and its mission, history, brand (blah, blah), but they are nearly always identical.

Second, they nearly always have some HR gobbledegook from a past age. So crucial competencies include "helicopter view", and "think outside-the-box" – never strategic perspective or divergent thinking.

Third, it is assumed that these competencies can be observed relatively easily for selection. This must be the case, because it is these competencies that seamlessly knit together recruitment, selection and training and … well, everything. But some of these concepts seem very difficult to define behaviorally and therefore to observe.

Fourth, with a charming, evidence-free naïvety, it is assumed that each and every one of these competencies is happily trainable. So you can send someone on an innovations or teamwork or customer responsiveness course and they will return willing, able and fired-up to fulfill their competency.

Competency thinking persists because nothing has yet really replaced it. But look no further than the blossoming field of positive psychology. The positive psychologists, whose mission is to understand the essence of well-being, meaning at work and the like, have attempted a taxonomy of what they call character strengths and virtues.

You will recall that we have strengths and …? "Developmental opportunities", of course. The W-word has been airbrushed out of the lexicon. One fundamental message of the positive psychology movement is that you get more value out of HR by exploring and exploiting your strengths rather than your weaknesses. Weaknesses are more difficult to correct or eradicate than strengths are to use.

So why not make the virtues the new competencies? There are six, which are further subdivided into twenty-four character strengths. So is this a runner? Consider the virtues:

1. *Wisdom and knowledge*: very desirable, but what is it? Curiosity, open-mindedness and a love of learning. It is to do with having and enjoying the acquisition of skills, ideas, insights. It's also got to do with having perspective, putting things in context and the proven ability to give wise counsel to others.

2. *Courage*: the strength to pursue worthwhile goals in the face of (continuous and strong) opposition. It's about bravery and persistence. Energy and zest. It's also about this now rather overused word 'authenticity', which is being who you are really are and speaking the (plain) truth as you really see it.

3. *Humanity*: empathy and kindness and warmth. It's about awareness of the needs of others, the skills to help and befriend, and to manage social relationships. You may call it emotional intelligence but it is clearly broader than that.

4. *Justice*: "Civic strengths that underlie healthy community life". It's about fairness. But it is where leadership and teamwork come in. It is about co-ordinating social and task activities equitably, fairly and efficiently.

5. *Temperance*: the anti-excess virtue. Excess does not lead to success, so a very important character strength is self-regulation; of beliefs and behaviors, of passions and possible addictions. It is about prudence and modesty, not hubris and aggrandisement.

6. *Transcendence*: this is about meaning and beauty and hope and gratitude. It is about seeing the meaning and purpose of the whole endeavor.

Will it fly? Will the hard-bitten accountant stomach nineteenth-century religious talk of temperance and transcendence? Will they believe you have just missed the last train to Sanityville? Possibly.

You can, if you try hard, find interesting, contemporary, work-language synonyms. It is an alternative to the competency framework that is perhaps past its sell-by date and has the benefits of being supported by modern psychological research.

There is nothing wrong with accentuating the positive. And nothing wrong with celebrating and reinforcing strengths than spending massive effort trying to correct weaknesses flippantly called "developmental opportunities".

Charismatic speakers

What is the difference between a charismatic and motivational speaker? Do great orators have to be charismatic? Is it in the script or in the delivery? Do you really have to believe in what you are saying, or can actors fake charisma?

Perhaps our hunger for motivational speakers is a function of the decline of religion and the really good sermon. In fact, motivational speakers share many similarities with good preachers, in both style and content.

Never forget "pitch, pace and pause". Hit the right notes; vary the speed; pause for effect. Learn rhetorical devices, such as the power of repetition, the magic number three, the influence of body language to punctuate and emphasize.

And the content? Tales, narratives, sagas? We are designed, it seems, to take in information via stories. And good stories have structure: beginning, middle and end. They can contain puzzles and dilemmas. But they need resolution: ideally, a victory for the truth, the right and the virtuous. The story itself is a journey and they often tell of travels and pilgrimages.

Nearly all stories have happy endings. Nearly all business books are upbeat, positive, moral tales. They are full of homilies, heart-warming stories of "little people" whose simplicity, essential goodness and wisdom won the day.

Motivational speakers learn fast. They have a relatively simple Darwinian feedback mechanism: it's called re-hire. If you are good you get more work: if you aren't you don't and it's thanks, but no thanks. Don't call us. Stand-up comics know this. They know the viciousness of the Glasgow Empire or the northern club. If the audience doesn't like you, you soon know it. The feedback is loud, immediate and unprintable. So you learn what works ... and what doesn't. Survival of the motivational.

There are various others whose job is speaking: barristers, teachers, lecturers. The latter are now being regularly, rigorously and remorselessly assessed. Their job might be to educate and develop; to instill insight and enthusiasm. To ensure skills development. To provoke and satisfy curiosity, and, of course, to get their students through exams.

But teachers and lecturers are, more and more, being evaluated by the students. Just as trainers hand out the "happy sheets" after courses, lecturers may be obliged to collect student evaluation forms. But even this is changing. First, the lecturers are not trusted to give full, fair and frank details of what the students wrote. Far too easy to "edit out" a few (or indeed many) maverick, negative, bitchy comments or ratings. So disinterested and dispassionate outsiders (consultants) are hired to do the job.

More and more, this is web-based and driven by the blogger generation. So the hapless, helpless, hopeless lecturers have their "score-card" up on the web for all to see. One is fully exposed to the petty demands of the dimmest, most demanding students who have been taught all the tricks of external attribution ... the stuff of litigation.

But what dictates good ratings? There are various theories. First, it is believed, some subjects are just more intrinsically interesting than others. For a psychologist, it might be better to teach "The Origin and Treatment of Sexual Perversion" rather than "Advanced Multivariate Statistics". Equally, those studying English may find "Turning Novels into Movie Scripts" easier than "Irony in Restoration Comedies".

Others believe that all courses can be made equally appealing. It's what one might call modular attributes: that is, what is taught and how (the methods), and how it is examined. Videos, visiting celebrities and visits all help. Using many didactic methods to bring the material alive is the stuff of education. Note how people on television have made archaeology, geology and (even) cookery exciting and popular.

The other factor is, of course, the lecturer's ability and personality. Enthusiasm, energy and commitment go a long way. Complex issues need to be illustrated with examples. Giving clear explanations, being open to suggestion and examples, all count.

The lecturer needs to be stimulating, inspirational and influential: in short charismatic. But charisma cannot compensate for not being organized, knowledgeable or up-to-date.

Cynics believe the modern, passive, demanding student wants PowerPoint slides and spoon-feeding, and is helpless against the plagiaristic opportunities of the web. Maybe! But all of us respond to charisma: that is what a memorable teacher is all about.

Charisma is a function of three things: ability, motivation and personality. It is probably identifiable in childhood or early adolescence. Many aspire to charisma but few have what it takes. It helps to be good-looking, and fit and young. It helps to be up-to-date and passionate as well as compassionate. None of this, alas, can be acquired through training. Have you ever seen a "Training in Charisma" course? Certainly, it's not all or nothing, but it is the greatest asset in all forums, be they cabaret clubs, conference halls or classrooms.

Competitiveness

Competitiveness: a dangerous drive that must be repressed in schools and the workplace, or the essential motivator of success, even survival?

All that 1960s drivel about competitiveness being morally evil and interpersonally dysfunctional has returned. We were told that competition led to winners and losers, and that this was all so unfair on the latter because they lost self-esteem and self-respect and descended into a vicious cycle of failure. Because all must have (equal) prizes, it was wrong to show that some people had greater ability than others.

Competition was a capitalist conspiracy that set people against one another in a crypto-Darwinian survival-of-the-fittest scenario that cause nothing but misery. Competition, we were told, led to wars and conflict. It was forgotten that competition led to cheaper prices, to innovation and to constant improvements.

The business world always seeks that magic bullet – sustainable competitive advantage. Theorists argue that competition both lowers prices and improves products.

But there are those who believe that competition may bring out the best in products but the worst in people. And it is particularly harmful if competition is encouraged *within* as opposed to *between* companies.

The pendulum swings back and forth among educational experts as much as with business gurus. At one time, all competition was frowned upon because of its supposed long- and short-term negative effects on the losers. They labeled themselves as failures and this produced a sort of self-fulfilling prophecy. Once a loser, always a loser. So *all* had to have prizes or no competitions were allowed.

No one ever thought of the benefits to the winners, or to those talented people who, through lack of feedback, never got a sense of their gifts and hence never exploited or developed them.

So what is competitiveness, and where does it come from? Can there be good versus bad competitiveness, or hypo- and hyper-competitiveness?

The very first experiment in social psychology – in the year of Queen Victoria's Diamond Jubilee – involved competitiveness. A researcher showed that racing cyclists rode faster when they were up against another (competitive) racer than when simply riding against the clock.

And just before the Second World War a neo-psychoanalyst worried about the evils of hyper-competitiveness, described as "an indiscriminate need to compete and win (and avoid losing) at any cost as a means to maintain or enhance self-worth". The idea of the poor competitive soul was that they had poorer self-concepts and more negative interpersonal relationships than had co-operative individuals.

Those interested in measuring individual competitiveness have made the distinction between good, healthy competitiveness and its opposite. Good competitiveness is the drive to accomplish a goal, to bring out the best in individuals; indeed, to help them understand themselves. Bad competitiveness is winning at any cost: it sneers at the outmodish negativity of the old aphorism "It's not whether you win or lose, but how you play the game". Losing is for wimps, failures, *Untermensch*. It is the self-aggrandizing, other-denigrating factor associated with competition that is bad, but the self-improvement is good.

It has also been suggested that competitiveness is domain specific. Thus one may be highly competitive on the sports field, but not in the family: in the classroom, but not at work.

And consider sports. Nearly all are competitive, but some are team-based and some individualistic. Some are contact sports, others not. The long-distance runner and the boxer certainly appear to have rather different motivations, though both might seek to win.

Competitive individuals tend to be ambitious, achievement-oriented and dominant. But like everything else, moderation is a good thing. The hyper-competitive individual might be masking all kinds of inadequacies. But so might the hyper-cooperative individual who is unable to make a decision, go it alone, or challenge the group.

Hyper-competitiveness has its downside. It is associated with poor interpersonal relations and incidence of road rage and accidents. On the other hand, competitiveness can bring out the best in people. It can make them go that extra mile to put in a special effort that can bring about results.

The dilemma for the manager is to encourage *optimal* competition. We live in an individualistic Western culture, the very opposite of the collectivistic Eastern culture of most parts of Asia. So from an early age we are placed in teams or in houses at school to encourage both inter-group cooperativeness and extra-group competitiveness. The idea is that the one enhances the other.

But those who are competitive cannot be sure of a real desire to win on the part of all team members, so adopts the attitude of "Love many, trust few, always paddle your own canoe".

Sales people thrive on competition; IT people do not. But both need encouragement and stroking. Both need rewarding for productivity. Both need to understand how and when and why in-group cooperation and out-group competition help the organization to thrive. And there is probably no room for the narcissistic, hypercompetitive, self-doubting pugilist ... except perhaps in the ring.

Concentrating on blunders

Do you learn more from failure than success, or the other way around? Do you learn more from others' "war stories", blunders, disasters and errors, or from their wins, triumphs and victories?

Many business people, and certainly all business book writers, appear to believe that one learns best from stories of success: stories of humanity, perseverance and good common sense that lead to great rewards. The stories may contain setbacks but definitely not blunders, because we need to know how to overcome obstacles.

But does this lead to bias? In his book *On the Psychology of Military Incompetence* (1981), Norman F. Dixon studied some of the great military defeats and disasters of the nineteenth and twentieth centuries. He shows how hubris, bloody-mindedness, or simple dim-wittedness cause defeat. The sheer recklessness of military managers beggars belief. The moral is that there are lessons that should inform selection and training, processes and procedures as well as strategy and tactics.

We appear to have developed a North-American, crypto-evangelical taste for inspirational speakers. Many are sports people who proudly fondle and display their gongs. They often show "Chariots of Fire" clips of their greatest moments.

The good ones try to tug at the heart strings. They tell of their journey to success; the quest; the handicaps overcome on the way. Self-belief, practice and more practice lead inevitably, justly and naturally to success. And you too can become successful if you only....

Another form of the success story is business autobiography. This is often a rattling tale of adventure, of courage and of just desserts. These books appear more like novels than history, but they sell well enough.

Most case studies used in business schools are about success stories too. They are sort of modern-day parables: complex, ambiguous and moralistic.

But there are case studies of failure; of moral and strategic error; of corruption and stupidity; and of simple incompetence.

We like happy endings. We like success stories. We need to believe that the world is a just place. But what is better for learning and training? We certainly know one thing. Doing is better than telling. We always learn best by practice. The question is, should we build in or allow for errors, blunders and failure as aids to learning, or try to minimize them?

Researchers have explored this issue. *Error management training*, as it is popularly called, has been shown to be rather effective. This may involve learning through committing/experiencing errors or watching others do so. It is argued that errorless learning promotes happy, quick and seemingly effortless skill acquisition. But error exposure training teaches people better how to react in unexpected situations. And people remember error exposure training better.

There are various arguments in favor of focusing on mistakes. First, it helps *understanding*. Errors illustrate underlying principles clearly. Second, errors are seriously *memorable*: students tend not to repeat them. Third, errors underline the message of thinking before acting, of *being attentive*, being "all there". It helps to concentrate the mind, identify problems and generate sensible solutions.

Error training delays the *automatization of skills* and makes the pupil think more deeply. Curiously, this improves motivation. But does it lower self-confidence, self-esteem and self-efficacy? It might reduce cockiness, but does it increase anxiety?

And what of war stories? This is the telling of true-ish stories of actual events by people in them. Old soldiers talking of lost battles, accident and emergency people relating serious mistakes. Does the story of the *Herald of Free Enterprise* ferry that capsized help seafarers? Does the Hillsborough soccer disaster story improve police crowd control? Should one rake over the coals of these tragic events as an educational experience?

Researchers have genuinely tried to answer these questions. A study recently published in the *Journal of Applied Psychology* (2006, vol. 91) examined the training of fire-fighters. Some learnt with case studies that described errors and their consequences, while others had errorless versions. They also varied the complexity of the scenarios, from simple to complex. The different groups were later measured by the number of appropriate alternative actions they could generate when given a unique and novel scenario. They were also evaluated on the problems they could identify in realistic scenarios.

Results showed that the group learning with case studies that described errors did the best. Stories of others' mistakes, particularly when addressing complex problems, clearly helped people to learn lessons.

Stores of failures, near-misses and poor judgments are often suppressed by organizations dedicated to sexing-up and spin. They might be doing themselves a disservice if this policy is training, especially safety training.

Reference

Dixon, Norman F. (1981) *On the Psychology of Military Incompetence.* London: Jonathan Cape.

Conference neuroses

They cost a lot of money but they are a good day out if, of course, you are not a speaker. The conference business is a big one, but it's fickle. Some things catch the potential audience's attention and others cause cancellations.

Conference satisfaction seems as much to do with the quality of the luncheon, the party-bag and networking opportunities as any to do with the speaker's fame or content. But they can provide serious PR opportunities for senior executives to produce a nicely sanitized and very positive version of "latest developments".

Organizations can run their own in-house conferences, which really are a lot of work. Last minute hiccups, difficult speakers, petulant technicians doing the lighting all make it far from simple. For the chairperson, the speaker, the set-designer, the marketing staff and the catering officer, conferences can be a real challenge. Hence the emergence of a new and hitherto neglected psychiatric family of neurotic disorders and conferences neuroses.

Research, however, has shown that this is not just a single syndrome but made up of various important but distinguishable disorders, fetishes and complaints. The following are now under serious investigation:

- *Dysfunctional conference committee disturbance*: a problem caused by egocentric types trying to impose their daft and impractical ideas about the conference on other members of the committee equally committed to wasting time and money.
- *Adolescent exhibitor/sponsor malady*: a problem when sponsors find out what they really get for their money, leading to many tears before bedtime.
- *Substance-induced gala dinner reaction*: often the result of being seduced by the catering manager to test wines for the big event. This may be similar to wedding-reception planning disorder.
- *Acute keynote speaker exhibitionism*: a problem especially for over-paid, vacuous, motivational speakers who want to be loved, treated like royalty and never follow any guidelines, particularly about invoicing.
- *Mixed plenary session malady*: a post-breakout group neurosis, where dull attention-seekers try incoherently to describe the tedious drivel and uninspiring process that resulted from being locked in a small room for nearly an hour.

- *Unconscious parallel session fixation:* that terrible worry that one made the wrong choice and that the other sessions are having more fun. This is akin to the well-known "the other queue always moves faster" neurosis.
- *Chronic PowerPoint technology fetish:* the phobia induced by having seen some gormless, hapless presenter struck dumb when their computer technology failed. Another version of the fetish is to believe slide design somehow compensates for content.
- *Psychosexual poster tendencies:* the powerful feeling of what it must be like to be a past-their-sell-by-date hooker when standing in front of a poster as people avoiding eye contact pass by.
- *Delusional presidential address complex:* a delusion on the part of both the committee and the CEO that people look forward to their shop-front PR speech written by somebody else and containing little in the way of humor, insight or truth.
- *Bipolar program order disturbance:* a vacillation between believing it is best to be first (primary effect) or last (recency effect) on the program. Related to this is "filling the post-luncheon dip slot" with an energetic and amusing speaker.
- *Periodic spouse itinerary reaction formation:* only for small, board-level conferences in nice resorts, where two programs have to be considered: one for the board and another for their spouses. Clever organizers find out over time that the latter's satisfaction is more important than the former.
- *Borderline workshop deficit:* this is the persistent misunderstanding about the whole business. Is one at a conference to listen or to share? To receive or to give? Workshop deficit is a complaint that occurs because people come to a conference to talk rather than listen.

Anyone who has tried to run a conference knows the stress attached to the whole enterprise, particularly if the conference has to make a profit. There are whole rafts of difficult people one has to charm, negotiate with or placate to ensure the thing goes smoothly. These include prima donna speakers with petty, egocentric demands. It includes uncharmable IT people as well as vicious uncooperative security staff. There are members of the audience who want diabetic, kosher or vegetarian food for lunch. There are those won't leave the lecture and those who won't have a lecture. There are those who want to rehearse and those that won't. There are those who like to show off their up-to-date, state-of-the-art IT knowledge and skill, and those who freeze at the sight of any equipment.

It is said that public speaking is the most widespread and probably the most debilitating of all phobias. It shows at conferences.

It takes considerable effort, skill and patience to plan and run any conference. It's not an activity for the faint-hearted. But it does allow the psychologically minded to observe many of the above-mentioned quite specific neuroses.

Delicate delegation

The word "delegate" can be a noun or a verb. A conference delegate is an emissary or representative. To delegate means to assign, appoint or entrust authority, duty or responsibility to another. Its etymology is to send or give or bequeath legal status.

Sounds rather grand, but delegation is at the heart of management. All leaders have to decide who should do what, when and why. They have to delegate certain tasks or processes to other people in a team to ensure they can use their own time effectively and efficiently.

Many managers struggle with delegation. It can cause massive problems, even ultimate derailment.

There are four types of delegators: refuseniks, abrogators, vacillators and deliberators. *Refuseniks* don't really do delegation. There are essentially four reasons for this common, near obsessive, problem. The first is the fear that the subordinate will fail at the assignment and this incompetence or subsequent failure will reflect very badly on the delegator. So best not done … ever. Second, is the belief that the *Refusenik* can do it better, faster and to their exact standards more easily than anyone else. This may be based on delusion or fact. But it certainly traps the individual into continuing and never passing the baton to anyone else.

The third reason is that the delegator may be seen (probably unfairly) as simply unloading their work on to someone else. In this sense they may be thought of as lazy by both superiors and subordinates, and therefore be resented. The fourth reason is they fear losing power, uniqueness or mystique. If you delegate a task that others master (possibly better than you), how long will it be before they threaten your whole position?

Then there are the *Abrogators*, who are only too happy to withdraw to the inner office, the golf course or for a quiet snooze while hardworking, well-informed and conscientious staffers keep the whole show on the road. Ronald Reagan was famous for this. If, and only if, you have a well-trained, trustworthy and responsible staff it's not a bad policy … in moderation, of course.

The third type, the *Vacillators*, are essentially ditherers famous for their inconsistency. They seem to delegate some things but not others, with no rhyme or reason. They delegate to some people and not others. And even that seems a function of caprice, of whim. They are, as a result, unpredictable, which is not good for anybody.

And then there are the *Deliberators*. They understand the purpose, indeed the necessity, of delegation. They also understand the process fully. They understand that to achieve a particular set of actions, optimal delegation is required.

The first step is *analysis* – deciding which tasks to assign to whom. This means thinking about your skill set and theirs; the present and the future.

Good delegators think carefully and gather data. They usually start with self-contained, clearly-defined tasks that are stretching but achievable, reasonably easy to measure and whose successful completion gives the individual a sense of achievement.

So, the steps are first analysis, then *appointment*. A few potential questions for the delegatee: Can they do it? How will they react to this added responsibility? Will they relish it and see it as a developmental opportunity? And does this really mean the delegate has too much work to do, and needs to delegate something to free up time for the extra tasks? It's a potential chain, you see, so needs a bit of thought and proper process.

Next, the all important, clear, sufficiently detailed *briefing* to include explicit statements of the how, when and what questions. The clever delegator also sets up meetings and control mechanisms to encourage, monitor and observe so that helpful corrective action can be taken if necessary. And, most importantly, there should be a detailed and clear evaluation process to review and if necessary revise for further action. It's logical, it does not have to be bureaucratic, and it's difficult to imagine how delegation can really happen without these steps.

So why does delegation often go wrong? Again, four reasons. First, some managers only delegate those tasks they can't do, don't like doing or find tedious. That is, to put it mildly, a non-optimum approach. Your staff soon detect this and it can undermine both respect and authority. Second, you delegate the wrong tasks: perhaps those you want to absolve yourself of responsibility for because you believe they really should not be part of your job. Third, you tend to delegate to the wrong people, making your judgments more on liking and personal attraction than the confidence or indeed the competence of the individual. Fourth, you don't make things clear enough, or keep interfering; or both. This results from poor process: establishing a contract with the individual stipulating rights, responsibilities, outcomes, etc.

To some, delegation feels like letting go and losing authority. To others, it's a blessed relief to have others to carry the can. Delegation is a business process as well as a training activity. All managers have to understand the necessity and requirements of delegation. They also need to see it as an excellent developmental and training opportunity, both for themselves and for their staff.

Does God approve of venture capitalists?

Religious traditions have a powerful impact on how people view their money. Consider, for example, the Islamic rules on bank interest and usury. Consider the behavior of the Amish, or indeed many Christians who still give tithes. Faith is ultimately related to values about things in this world as much as things beyond it. It dictates how people see the rich and the poor, and how people desire to acquire and spend their money.

Within the Christian tradition it appears from numerous biblical passages that people are meant to work, to work honourably, well, and with passion *(Ecclesiastes 3:22)*. St Paul made it clear that if a person refused to work, that person had no right to eat *(Thessalonians 3:10)*.

The New Testament shows fairly unambiguously that people are meant to work – and to work honestly, cooperatively and conscientiously. All work, however humble or mundane, is for God's glory. There is no better test of a person than the way he or she works. It is how people work, rather than what they do, that is important. It is better to do ordinary things extraordinarily well than to do extraordinary things. It is the fidelity with which work is done that is the real test. Work is a contribution owed to the community at large. Things are due from, as well as to, people at work. The parable of the laborers in the vineyard *(Matthew 20: 1–16)* suggests that people have a right to work, to a living wage, and to reasonable working conditions.

The Christian view of pleasure is both proscriptive and prescriptive. No pleasure can be right if it is harmful to the person who indulges in it or to others, or if it becomes addictive. Any pleasure is wrong if in enjoying it the essentials of life have to take less than their proper place. Any pleasure that leads to regret is wrong. But Christianity does not deny or minimize leisure, or pleasure, or money. Leisure and pleasure relax the mind and refresh the body.

It is generally true that the Old Testament connects goodness with prosperity, whereas wealth is associated more with affliction. From the many references to money and wealth in the Old Testament it seems that wealth is seen as a gift from God, but it is not everything; it is essentially a secondary goal. Possession is much more a blessing than a sin, and can be a danger to character. Wealth is to be enjoyed but it is not worth making a dedicated pursuit of. Care for the poor is the duty of the rich. To help the poor is to help God.

The New Testament is certainly clear about the danger of riches. The danger of the love of money is well recorded and well known in the story of the rich young ruler (*Mark 10: 17–31*). Poverty is not a virtue because wealth is dangerous, however. Wealth is dangerous for many reasons, partly because it can lead to arrogance, haughtiness and snobbery (*1 Timothy 6:17*). The value of life cannot be measured by income or wealth, which are diminishing assets. The single-minded pursuit of wealth can blind people to more important things. The parable of the rich man and Lazarus (*Luke 16: 19–31*) suggests that wealth can blind people to the needs of others as well as to any sense of responsibility for their state.

The story of the cleansing of the temple by Jesus (*John 2: 13–17*) includes a major moral or teaching point that it is wrong to make money out of people's credulity, trustfulness, or simple need. Christian giving (of money) through the Church is important; it should be systematic, proportionate, and universal. The New Testament is replete with messages about the dangers of wealth. It can give a false sense of independence; it can cost too much, and it can be addictive.

There are various crucial principles that the Bible teaches will save a person from the dangers of wealth:

- Is money acquired in a way that has harmed/injured no one but in fact has helped and enriched the community?
- How do we regard money – as master, enemy, servant, or friend?
- Is money spent exclusively selfishly or in the service of both self and others?
- People are more important than things; people are more important than money.
- There are times when to give money is not enough. It is impersonal giving, whereas it may be that personal giving is what is required.

Every generation, it seems, has the need to translate the Bible or at least specific passages from it, into the language and imagery of its time. Like performing Shakespeare plays in modern dress, updating is thought to aid communication of the message.

So here is a new version of the Parable of the Talents (*Matthew 25: 14–20*). After attending an assessment centre and taking some test that had been well designed and psychometrically validated to measure "venture capitalist wealth-creating ability", three individuals were given scores. They had been sent by the head of a major international Wealth Creation Trust.

Based on their prospective earning ability, the CEO gave one chap two million pounds (five talents), another around three-quarters of a million and the third a paltry quarter of a million. It was a way of validating the centre.

Just as the Assessment Centre Ratings had predicted, the really talented chappie doubled his stake. Even the bloke who got much less did likewise, doubling his stake by careful trading in pork bellies, platinum and gas futures. But the third chappie lost his nerve waiting for a more opportune moment and left all the dosh in a safety deposit box, fearing who knows what.

At the end of the validating exercise the CEO inspected the results. He was delighted by them. He told the top performer he would now head up the New York Office and be in charge of the Americas. The second chappie was likewise complimented, sent to Sofia and made head of emerging East European markets.

But he was pretty angry about the serious under-performer. And, knowing him to be a person of the book, he read him part of verses 26 and 27 of Matthew: "You wicked and lazy servant … you ought to have deposited my money with the bankers, and at my coming I would receive back my own with interest". He took the meagre £250 K from the incompetent investor and gave it to the top Johnny. So the rich get richer and the poor get nothing.

And so the moral, the point, the bottom-line? Perhaps deposit accounts are the very bare minimum you can do with your and others' money. But you should try some wise, carefully evaluated risk investments. If you have the ability, use it.

You are rewarded according to your effort (labor) and ability. It's a performance management system. It's not about job title or years of service. It's all to do with performance. Diligence is rewarded, negligence is punished. Hey presto! The Protestant Work Ethic.

All financial wizards and even independent financial advisers will be accountable for the investments entrusted to them. And the better you do, the more people will choose you. It's a vicious and virtuous cycle.

So let's try a bit of non-PC heresy. We can learn from the Parable of the Talents:

1. People are not born equal – they differ considerably in ability, which they are expected to exploit.
2. Using your ability with hard work is, and deserves to be, equitably rewarded: to he who hath shall more be given.

3. Risk-averse, lazy people deserve the sack (outer darkness).
4. Performance management is just.
5. Taxation, perhaps, is unjust and stupid.

A complete misinterpretation of the received meaning of the parable? Or a useful and fair interpretation for our times? Well, that's the beauty of case studies: they are easily open to misinterpretation. Maybe this explains why there are so many Christian sects.

It's not hard to find pretty good biblical justification for wealth creation; for the idea that wealth is indeed a sign of God's grace; or that it is very easy to distinguish between the deserving and the undeserving poor.

Do leaders really matter?

There are various critical questions about the whole issue of leadership. What is leadership? Does leadership matter? How are leaders chosen? How should leaders be evaluated? Why do we choose so many flawed leaders? How to forecast leadership? Why do leaders fail? How do leaders build teams?

There are many different definitions of leadership, which include directing group activities; initiating/maintaining expectations and interaction; the influence, through communication, of goal achievement; providing a shared vision; creating opportunities and building confidence; inducing followers to act; creating social order; giving purpose to collective effort; a catalytic force that empowers others. But there are some pretty straightforward facts about business leadership.

The fundamental task of leadership is to build and maintain a high-performance team, a team that wins, that beats the competition. A person's performance as a leader should be evaluated in terms of the performance of his or her team, and not in terms of how much the boss likes him/her. Leadership is related directly to organizational effectiveness – an effective organization is composed of high-performance teams. Effective leaders are seen as honesty/trustworthy, decisive and able to make good decisions, competent at the business, and visionary – having a sense of direction and purpose. There are a large number of bad managers in every organization; their staff know who they are, even when the bosses apparently don't. The fewer the bad managers in an organization, the more effective it will be.

Researchers in the area have tended to look at six different but related topics:

Topic	Research focus	Research questions
Power that comes with the role	Influence tactics; use of power; role requirements	How does organizational history and structure affect leader's power?
The leaders themselves	Personality traits; cognitive ability	What most differentiates effective versus ineffective leaders?
Those who are led	Group dynamics	What types of subordinates desire what type of leadership?

(Continued)

Influence process	The range and type of influence attempts	When are leaders susceptible to influence?
The situation and setting of leadership	Situation effects on leader behavior; physical, social and political	How does the environment modify leader behavior?
How do leaders emerge?	Group dynamics and history	How do leaders become recognized and stay in position?

Judging by the money they are paid and the publicity they seek and receive, you would imagine the fate of great organizations lies squarely in the hands of their leaders. The inspirational vision, the motivational charm, the brilliant strategy that leaders bring – or don't bring – is the key factor to organizational success.

But, of course, there are contrarian voices. There are three alternative approaches. The first is *situational* or *contingent*. The argument is "it all depends on the situation". Winston Churchill was a war leader; Margaret Thatcher a turnaround leader; and Richard Branson an entrepreneurial leader. Cometh the hour, cometh the leader. Yes, but the theory maintains that there must be a close fit between the leader's make up and the particular organization that they lead. They are, in short, limited to specific situations and might well be disasters in others.

The second approach is *fatalistic*. Leadership, power and influence are really illusory. World events determine organizational outcomes. Socio-political and economic events shape company success much more than one person's charisma. A rise in the price of oil, a change in EU regulations, militant unions or sudden customer disaffection can seal a company's fate irrespective of what leaders do. In this sense, their power and influence are no more than a chimera.

With the third approach, it is argued that the *followers* make all the difference. It is their drive and determination that really turn the wheels, not the person at the top. A fine conductor can do very little with a weak orchestra.

Another view is that leaders do have real power and influence, but almost always make things worse. It's a sort of one-side-of-the-coin argument suggesting that bad leaders can cause chaos and mayhem but good leaders can't (on their own) transform organizations for the better.

But the data are not on the side of the situationalists, fatalists, follower fanatics and doom mongers. There are some excellent empirically verified case studies which show that new leaders can transform institutions very positively. Whether it's morale, productivity or profit, with all else kept constant, the leader (alone) does make a difference.

There are various ways to become a leader. You can inherit a position, or simply usurp it by force (even just by force of personality). You can self-nominate, or be (democratically) elected by others in a bottom-up way. Of course, you can also be appointed top down by those in some sense to whom you report.

Just as with school prefects, it really matters if leaders are elected or appointed. Prefects elected by the pupils are somewhat different from those appointed by the staff. Elected leaders tend to be more agreeable, friendly and extraverted than do appointed leaders. They tend to be more political. Their ability to make great speeches may be more important than their ability to do strategic planning. But one thing followers really do want is integrity. Call it morality, trust-worthiness or honesty, it is valued seriously. Leaders have power, authority and obligations.

Ask followers if they are prepared to trade-off moral integrity for technical competence and most (though they want both) choose the former. It is as if a technical skill can be taught, but not morality. Also, moral integrity seems to be in some way in shorter supply.

It's a bit like IQ and EQ. Ask people if they want a "bright but cold" versus "average but warm" boss and they seem to choose the latter. The soft stuff counts to the staff. But those that appoint go for intelligence and dominance, for sociability, resilience and the technical expertise stuff. They can overlook the power and importance of the moral dimension. And that is why the most common complaints everyone has about their leaders is that they are dishonest, two-faced spin doctors.

Leaders do make (a hell of) a difference. We know it's complicated and we know what factors seem to be important. The method by which they got to become leaders often dictates what sort of people they are. Leaders have moral as well as economic challenges. They need moral in addition to financial reasoning, whatever the particular situation they find themselves in.

Electrophrenology

The new sexy prefix to practically all activities is "neuro". It used to be "psycho", but that is all so twentieth-century. We now have learned Professors of Cognitive Neuroscience, and scientific journals of the same name.

It's all about brain scanning. Of course, we have had ways of measuring "brain waves" for ages. Indeed, the films are in black and white that show people (usually in white coats) attaching little electrodes to certain parts of the scalp, often with sticky gel. Those waves could be measured literally as the output is a continuous line that traces in real time how the brain responds. Where the line jumps we have the all important "spike".

It looks much the same as seismography or cardiography. And its not that different from the output of the famous "lie detector". In short, brain scanning shows how people respond to words, pictures, smells or whatever.

The difference today is in the quality of the toy the boffins have. Through such things as PET (Positron Emission Tomography) scanning and MRI (Magnetic Resonance Imaging), we can now peer into the working brain and see what lights up and when. It's all very exciting.

And, of course, the marketing boys are quick to see if the new toys can help them. So we have neuromarketing. It's the "science" of brain responses to marketing messages. It's about how we really (physiologically) respond to advertisements.

The great appeal of this approach is that marketing people believe that people *can't* or *won't* really tell you how they really respond to brand names, symbols, icons or products. It is believed they can't because the process operates below consciousness. This is what explained the long love affair marketing people had with the Freudian "depth" experts for over fifty years in the twentieth century. The idea was that all sorts of things – the half-open door, the train speeding into the tunnel, the white-haired avuncular actor – all had powerful symbolic influences. They triggered cultural archetypes that are universal and that profoundly, if subtly, influence behavior.

All this preconscious processing was seen at its starkest in the "hidden persuader" world of subliminal perceptions. Of course, this process does happen – people do see without awareness. But the claims of advertisers and their critics for the magic power of subliminal messages were described by scientists who investigated the problem in depth as absurd, laughable, ludicrous and preposterous.

The idea of having a flashed image or word leading to massive purchasing, odd behavior or the like was appealing but bunkum. However, the idea that marketing messages could stimulate the unconscious in some way has never gone way. And neuromarketing has revived that idea.

Certainly, traditional market research methods had drawbacks in identifying "true" customer responses. As a result of numerous social processes, what emerges from focus groups and even in-depth interviews is tainted, biased or distorted. Most of us have been interviewed by a clipboard-armed researcher outside a supermarket. And more and more we have been enticed by monetary rewards to attend social focus groups to discuss with bizarre earnestness the soft filling of biscuits or the color of crisp-packet wrappings.

And we have all said what we think will please our interviewers, or better still shuts them up so that we can get on with life. There are garrulous show-offs at focus groups, inarticulate interviewees in malls, undiscerning, lonely people eager to add their two-penn'orth. But their views are not worth one penny, because they are not being honest. Perhaps they are asked the wrong questions; perhaps the situation is not optimal.

So identifying real responses to marketing messages is tricky. And we know that brand recognition, recall and positive associations is the first, but all-important, step in the long walk to a purchase.

Enter neuromarketing – the exciting, new, expensive science of telling how people really respond. No more murky, Freudian, sex-obsessed unconscious; no more subliminal messages; and no more dreary focus groups. Wire them up, or scan them over, or preferably both, and all will be revealed.

Or is it? Is this merely electrophrenology? Will we soon have those beautiful nineteenth-century ceramic heads again, replacing those areas labeled (so charmingly) "domestic propensities", "selfish sentiments", "constructiveness" or "acquisitiveness" with "Big Mac" or "Porsche"?

But there are two good reasons to assume that neuromarketing will attract a reasonable chunk of the billion-pound budget that goes on advertising. The *first* is a result of our understanding that *where* the brain responds to messages is really important. If your ad lights up the reward centre of the brain, you really are on the road to something serious.

Second, the strength of the signal and the association between features of the message or picture and the signal no doubt contain highly significant information for advertisers.

We have known for a long time – since the Morris Minor, in fact – that round, baby-shaped cars elicit a warm, positive glow. Recent neuroimaging studies confirm that, when seen from the front, friendly, smiling cars lit up the face recognition area – the headlights being the eyes; the grille, the nose; and the fender, the mouth.

Did you really need neuroscience to tell you that? Cartoonists have known that for a hundred years. Neurostuff really does appear to offer seriously exciting possibilities, but at the moment it is more about mapping than anything else. But it may also be like all those other magical techniques that promised so much and delivered very little.

Elite performers

How do you get to the Royal Albert Hall? How do you represent your country at the Olympics? How do you really get to be good at your job? Practice, practice, practice.

Studies on this topic have shown, however, that not all experts really *are* experts. In some embarrassing revelations it was found that expert stockbrokers did little or no better in their choice of stocks than pigeons pecking randomly at the lists. Not all expert wine-tasters and masters of wine do terribly well at identifying wine without the label.

In some jobs, expertise is either not affected or (worse) negatively affected by experience. Thus the length of training of teachers and psychotherapists has little effect on performance. And years of doing the same job in the same way leads to lower productivity.

It's often easier to describe elite performers than to understand how they became so good. They seem to see patterns differently and read situations faster; they seem to have a bigger repertoire of options; and they seem to be more confident and in control.

Studies of elite performers have thrown up some really interesting findings. *First*, there is the ten-year rule. As a rule of thumb, it takes ten years of intensive, focused, "full-on" training to reach the top.

Second, elite performers seem to know how to maximize the efficacy of practice. Thus they may practice for as little as 4–5 hours a day, break this into sessions of no more than one hour long at a time, and they often have little naps in between. It's what creativity researchers call "incubation".

Third, these people challenge themselves. They make things difficult. They prefer not to automate responses. They try out new ways of doing things. As a result, during practice they often look less skilled and polished than less talented performers.

Thus a performance of thirty minutes to an hour by an elite athlete or musician has 20,000 hours of practice behind it.

For how long, and how, people practice skill and knowledge acquisition is crucial. They have to invest time and money for the sake of their art or sport or discipline. And this inevitably involves eschewing other, often very attractive, activities. In this sense, some, but by no means all, elite performers seem a little narrow ... a little naïve. When others went partying, on holiday or to leisure events, the aspirant elite practiced. They have to have iron discipline and a very real desire to "win" to make it to the top.

But is that all? What about talent, abilities and genes? It seems clear that sports demand certain physiological shapes. While you can certainly sculpt your body through training exercises, you see few basketball players who are under five foot ten; and no musicians who are tone-deaf or ham-fisted.

Training unlocks the genes; practice helps biology become destiny. Many a flower is indeed born to blush unseen and waste its fragrance on the desert air. Many people with prodigious talent seem to ignore it, downplay it or simply fail to exploit it.

The training required to be an elite performer in any field is exceptionally demanding. It looks very easy, but it is patently not. So they need ambition and motivation.

Consider the following 2 × 2 box: high versus low motivated individuals, success and failure at their tasks. One box is more difficult to explain than all the other three: the highly motivated individuals who don't succeed. Certainly they exist, but why? Are they naïve, untalented types whose lack of self-insight means that they have just too little latent talent to exploit? Do they practice inefficiently, or believe success is the result of other social factors more than their ability to improve? Are they simply victims of unfair systems that prevent them from being successful?

People receive feedback on their abilities and the effect of practice through their coaches, but also by observing their peers. Many give up, either believing they don't really have enough talent, or rather that to achieve the status they desire is just too much effort.

And there is one other factor: social background. Privileged children are more likely to become elite survivors. Why is this? Many explanations are possible but, clearly having access to education, equipment and specialists does help. As does having ambitious parents. These all develop self-confidence, which helps social success.

So elite performers need a good start in life in two ways: their genetics and their parents, which are obviously closely linked. But they also need ambition, motivation and the sheer drive to succeed. This drive is their investment in doing the training. It is practice that is key. It is how, for how long, and to what end performers practice that really unlocks the genetic endowment and background advantages.

And sadly there is no way of getting around this. The British admire those with some special natural talent. They empathize with the "Chariots of Fire" types who come home from work, eat a Marmite sandwich, put on their trainers and pop down to the track to win the Olympics. The idea is that any fool can win with practice; practice is slightly vulgar.

But this amateurism has no place in the desire to be an elite performer.

Everything intelligence

Even if we have never taken an intelligence test, most of us know intuitively what intelligence is. It's partly very impressive general knowledge exhibited by wunderkinds on "Mastermind" and "University Challenge". It's partly about speed of uptake: explain the issue once and it's understood. And it's partly about problem-solving.

Dictionary definitions of intelligence are succinct: the ability to learn, understand and apply knowledge or think in an abstract way in relation to new situations, or situations that cause anger. The act of comprehension, reasoning or understanding. Synonyms are: bright, brilliant, brainy, clever, quick-witted, smart.

From quite an early age most of us are acutely aware of peer differences in intelligence. Through long years of schooling we all notice that some students are quite simply brighter than others. The brightest one may even have been teacher's pet. In the old days, before all had prizes, a chosen few seemed to walk away with all the awards. This was made worse if they were sporty and handsome to boot!

Bright people have often been the target of envy, and hence of prejudice and ridicule. It all seems so unfair in our happy, egalitarian land that some people are brighter than others. And this might have led to the post-Second World War demise of the intelligence test and to the many attempts to undermine the very concept of intelligence. New terms such as capacity, cognitive ability or information processing have been reintroduced as substitutes to avoid using the word intelligence at all.

But all this changed in 1995 with the runaway best-seller, *Emotional Intelligence* by Daniel Goleman. The book clearly struck a nerve. It argued that emotional sensitivity and awareness (in oneself and others), as well as the ability to manage emotions, are not only very desirable characteristics but also a major predictor of success at work. In fact, it was argued, in a data-free sort of way, that emotional intelligence was a stronger predictor of work success than academic intelligence. Note at this point the discomfort of having to put a word in front of intelligence.

Thus the emotional intelligence industry was born, riding on the back of the multiple intelligences idea popularized by two American psychologists. Though they could not (indeed still cannot) agree on the number of or names for the multiple intelligences, they both agreed that we needed to broaden the term "intelligence". One (Howard Gardner) claimed there were seven (now eight), including the charmingly titled body-kinesthetic and naturalistic intelligence; while the other (Robert Sternberg) reckons there are three, including creative intelligence, and all of which fall under the general label of successful intelligence.

And soon the floodgates were open. The next to appear was spiritual intelligence. This movement to explore spirituality at work was confined to North America; always struggling with how to reconcile religion and materialism.

Consider the following list:

1. *Verbal* or linguistic intelligence (the ability to use words).
2. *Logical* or mathematical intelligence (the ability to reason logically; solve number problems).
3. *Spatial intelligence* (the ability to find your way round the environment and form mental images).
4. *Musical intelligence* (the ability to perceive and create pitch and rhythm).
5. *Body-kinetic intelligence* (the ability to carry out motor movement; for example, to be a surgeon or a dancer).
6. *Interpersonal intelligence* (the ability to understand other people).
7. *Intrapersonal intelligence* (the ability to understand yourself and develop a sense of your own identity).
8. *Existential intelligence* (the ability to understand the significance of life, the meaning of death and the experience of love).
9. *Spiritual intelligence* (the ability to engage in thinking about cosmetic issues, the achievement of the state of being (for example, achieving trance states), and the ability to have spiritual effects on others).
10. *Naturalistic intelligence* (the ability to identify and employ many distinctions in the natural world; for example, categorizing species membership).

And then we had a whole host of intelligence "discovered" by authors and researchers jumping on the bandwagon. So there is *network* intelligence and even *intuitive* intelligence. Perhaps the best is *sexual* intelligence, defined as the ability to seek out and maintain a fecund relationship with a partner. In short it's about wise mate choice.

Here is a list of a few more "intelligences".

Political	The ability to use formal and informal powers in a company to accomplish objectives. The ability to know how to use power in the organization prudently, judiciously and artfully.

Social/Cultural The extent to which one is adequately socialized in a society, an organization, or a subculture. Recognition and understanding of roles, norms, routines and taboos, in various settings.

Organizational Having a detailed and accurate understanding of how the organization operates, both functionally and the time that is needed to accomplish certain tasks within the company. The detailed knowledge of how "to get things done" in the company.

Networking The ability to get things done with multiple organizational units. Accomplishing the goals of the company successfully by effectively recognizing, understanding and managing inter-organizational relations.

Creative The ability to diverge/innovate in thinking and create novel ideas and solutions to problems. The ability to address problems/issues with insight and resourcefulness and to find unique solutions.

Intuitive The ability to gain quick insights into how to solve problems or to address situations without previous experience of the problem, and without formally processing information (for example, street-smart).

There are a raft of managerial intelligences, of course. It seems that all you have to do now is take a business concept, preferably what used to be called competencies, and put the word intelligence after it. So there is innovative intelligence, strategic planning intelligence, and customer service intelligence. A new concept, a new book, a new discovery.

The word/concept of "intelligence" is everywhere. We have intelligent design for a God-created universe. We have intelligent systems at work. We have now, publicly acknowledged intelligent agencies.

But we seem still to remain terribly wary of good old-fashioned timed intelligence tests. We allow selection into our schools based on metaphysical beliefs, but we dare not advocate an IQ cut-off point.

So, paradoxically, everything is an intelligence except real intelligence. You may happily take an emotional intelligence or practical intelligence or even a spiritual intelligence test. But try taking a MENSA-type test and suggesting the results might be predictive of success at work and life in general... So let's hear it for intelligent intelligence!

Reference

Goleman, Daniel (1995) *Emotional Intelligence*. New York: Bantam.

E-worries

While e-commerce continues to grow by leaps and bounds, it has not seen the phenomenal growth that was predicted by the wide-eyed futurologists at the end of the twentieth century.

Certainly, there are eBay addicts and those who swear by their web-purchasing, be it airline tickets, books or computers; but there are also those people who remain cautious, unconvinced and hesitant. These are not people cut off from modern life by computer phobia, ignorance or Luddism. Nor are they necessarily at the bottom end of the socio-economic scale. On the contrary, many are well-heeled, sophisticated shoppers who use the web a lot.

So what are their concerns, doubts and issues? How realistic are these? And will they go away eventually? There are at least ten major worries, and they do not appear to be diminishing over time; in fact, some are growing.

- *Safety*: Identity theft is the fastest-growing type of fraud, so giving your credit card number to all and sundry perhaps seems unwise. It is unclear often how you are "covered" if things go wrong, don't arrive and so on. People are rightly concerned about safety in other ways as well. What if the item arrives damaged? What if it leaks? But above all, the worry about how safe individuals are from increasingly sophisticated gangs of people who can clone your cards and empty your bank account before you've noticed.
- *Privacy*: While most of us do not worry about people knowing what brand of cornflakes we prefer and the destination of our last holiday, people can and do feel threatened by others recording their personal information, such as the trashy novels you read. What sums you spend on clothes. How much you drink. This may be more than taxman paranoia or a concern with keeping up appearances. We know that retailers keep records, sell lists, and target groups of high spenders. And many of us do not like it.
- *Product quality*: Buying from catalogs makes it eminently clear that what you see is not necessarily what you get. The camera, like the eye, can deceive. The blurb is one-sided. What the big print giveth, the small print taketh away. Many of us like to feel the quality and the width. It is quite simply a matter of "buying a pig in a poke".
- *Environmental impact*: It is not only your tree-huggers and good-lifers who worry that buying on the web rather than helping the environment

actually does it harm. Items have to be carefully packaged to avoid breakage. There are a lot of wasted raw materials in this process. And then there are the added transportation costs. Popping down to the local high street can sometimes seem altogether the more environmentally considerate option.

- *Shopping experience*: Shopaphobics and deeply dysfunctional shoppers excluded, purchasing goods is for many a pleasurable experience. Big shops, even malls, are the cathedrals of the twenty-first century. They are designed to enthral and entice. They can engulf the senses and even be an aesthetic experience. Going shopping can be a fun, sociable activity. It can appeal to both the hunter and the gatherer within us ... a far cry from tapping some keys in the spare bedroom.

- *Time spent*: How easy is it to book a holiday on the web? Or order the groceries? A no-brainer or a sore-brainer? Geographical remoteness may provide a simple answer but, paradoxically, given the demands of purchasing systems it can take ages. The problem is choice: stand in front of packed shelves of any product – instant coffee, soft cheese, jams and preserves, and there is an overwhelming choice. Some people are extremely brand loyal and consistently choose the same brand, seemingly uninterested in cost or innovation. But most like a modicum of experimentation. Often, therefore, it takes longer "filling your trolley" online than it does by walking the aisles.

- *Time to receive product*: The Achilles heel of the web is the delivery process. The near collapse of the Royal Mail, problems with urban transport systems and the unreliability of foreign suppliers mean that it may take an hour to purchase but a month before you receive your goods. You pay more for priority post, but that is sometimes little more than a bad joke. You could go to the nearest town and back and carry home your product in a tenth of the time it sometimes takes to arrive by post.

- *Convenience*: What could be more convenient than doing your shopping in your pyjamas, in the spare room on a Sunday morning? No traffic wardens, no crowds at the till, no lugging things around. But, wait – many shops these days are open 24/7. They understand the threat of the web. There are people to help (sometimes). There are food bars and the like. While the pyjama-clad shopper may cry "convenience" it is unclear what is traded off for this factor.

- *Cost*: Remember the "p & p" in the small print. Postage and packaging, delivery charges, premium rate or whatever, all have an impact on the cost. To buy cheap, shoddy goods and then pay for postage and packing means the line about savings is clearly more hype than reality. Those who do regular comparisons and take into account all the hidden costs soon realize that a cost–benefit analysis doesn't always support the web.

- *Delivery*: It might be convenient to order, but not necessarily to receive the goods. We have all waited in for non-appearing delivery people, received cards requiring us to travel across town to depots manned by surly customer-avoiding staff, or found the case of wine delivered to someone at No. 42, who at 82 years old was the only person at home in the street and has forgotten what she was supposed to do with the box in the hall.

Of course, fervent internet shoppers will have objections to each of the above, accusing those who put forward these arguments of being ignorant, out-of-touch fogies from another age who refuse to get a grip, keep in touch, or simply embrace the new world. But most of us have experienced numerous little but frequent frustrations from internet shopping which reveal the rhetoric and the reality still remain poles apart.

Failing in business

The statistics on business failure, especially with respect to small businesses, are depressing. In some sectors, such as restaurants, more fail than succeed. And success is defined merely as staying in business ... sort of solvent ... for a year or two.

Why do businesses fail? Can failure teach us about success? Probably, but under a number of specific circumstances. The most important is *not* to ask individual entrepreneurs why they failed (or indeed have succeeded). The reason is that they are nearly all victims of what psychologists call the *fundamental attribution error*. This means explaining away failure as being caused by bad luck, wicked politicians, demanding customers, unreliable staff and greedy banks.

However, success is attributed to personal motivation, talent and ability. "I succeed because of hard work, natural ability and flair: I fail because of bad luck and a host of people who let me down."

It is like that ubiquitous phenomenon called stress at work. Stress now comes exclusively from the environment or from others: bosses, shareholders, customers, the market all cause stress. Being neurotic, having poor coping skills or being a shirker does not. On the other hand, people are happy to explain their promotion or size of bonus in terms of how hard they work or how talented they are.

Consider frequent reasons given for business failure ... and the truth. The first (and rarest), is that old insurance favourite, *Act of God*: fire, flood and brimstone. This does happen, but very rarely. We don't have serious earthquakes or tornadoes in Britain. But there is global warming, and there are strange and unpredictable weather patterns and so on.

And that is the point of insurance. You can, and should, insure against these rare events. Paradoxically, some businesses have been saved by disaster. Hence the crimes associated with insurance fraud. It's usually cost effective; sometimes a legal requirement.

Second, there is *economic recession*. But recall that statistics from America show that even during the Great Depression, start-up business failure was less than 2 percent. In the early 1980s it was less than half of that. Well-run businesses can thrive in hard times. And Britain has been doing well for over a decade now.

Next is *fraud*: another pretty rare event. Less than 5 percent of companies go under because of a psychopathic partner: the addicted accountant; the bent bookkeeper; the devious and dishonest director who defrauds the business. But the puzzle is why and how they get away with it for as long as they do: fraud, theft and sabotage do happen but they are often a consequence of bad management.

Anyone who runs a business must understand the numbers. They show trends and patterns, and allow one to see the effectiveness of campaigns, offers and so on. The financially illiterate deserve to fail. This is not to say that hiring professional help is not a good thing. It is, however, important not to abdicate or abrogate power to them. Fraud and deceit are invited by ignorance of finances, unfair practices or poor monitoring.

A fourth reason is simple *neglect*: the absentee landlord; the manager with his eye off the ball; the distracted. There may be many reasons associated with this cause. The first is the haste of owners to open other branches or outlets before fully bedding down the business: too many balls in the air.

Or perhaps quite the opposite: the obsessional, possibly nervous, manager who cannot or will not delegate any power or responsibility. And then the paranoid tyrant falls ill and nobody knows what to do or how to do it. The manager has retained all the knowledge of procedures and policies because of fear of, or inability to handle, real delegation.

And managers have been known to lose the plot quite suddenly. The "menopausal" middle-aged manager may drop everything for a leggy blonde half his age. Drugs, drink and sudden obsessions, from collecting to gambling, can lead to the business owner to neglect the business, which then fails.

A fifth, certainly more common, cause is *lack of* sufficient business *experience*. This is often because of enthusiasm by what are essentially amateurs. More than cooking skills are needed to run a successful restaurant. Brilliant hairdressers need not necessarily have the skills to successfully start up and run a thriving salon. And authors probably make bad publishers. Businesses need to understand customers, suppliers, shareholders, accountants and tax specialists.

Indeed, there is a good argument to be made that managers need to understand the operation of business in general, rather than a specific business. Hence the rise of interim managers who can manage any business.

Another related reason that might account for over a quarter of business failures is unbalanced experience. This occurs when a well-trained enthusiast who knows a lot about a little, thinks they understand how the whole business works. The stories are legion about the optimistic salesman who did not understand cost control; the clever engineer who did not believe in marketing; the savvy accountants who thought people were motivated exactly like them. The *idiot savant* approach to management is alas doomed to failure, because business is just too complex.

Brilliance or extensive experience in one area is likely to bring about too much focus on that area and not enough on others: Enthusiasm, good intentions and a good grasp of one area of the business is just not enough.

But the most common reason for business failure? It is certainly unlikely to be admitted to by the fired, bankrupt or simply depressed business people. It is *managerial incompetence*. Management is about setting sensible and attainable goals; it's about using scarce resources wisely to support these goals; it's about understanding the various stakeholders in the business; and about motivating staff. Good managers can turn around failing businesses and bad ones can cause healthy organizations to stall and fail.

Being creative, bright, hard-working and driven helps, but it is not enough. You have to understand the business, the competitors and the market ... as well as having a grasp of the basic principles of accounting (even a little), law, psychology and engineering.

Management has, for too long, been thought as little more than applied common sense. Sadly, not that common, and alas not that often applied.

Flowing with the go

Lots of people have talked and written about "peak experiences" – that feeling of total absorption, completely focused attention, intense joy.

In 1990 a Transylvanian psychologist called Mihaly Csikszentmihalyi wrote a book called *Flow: The Psychology of Optimal Experience*. His research had involved watching and talking to people who were creative and successful in various fields from rock-climbing to rock music.

He also introduced a method called *experience sampling*. People carried a bleeper. Eight times a day this went off and carriers were required to write down immediately both what they were doing and how they were feeling.

People felt best, he found, when engrossed in some challenging activity. During "flow" they lost track of time, felt more capable, more sensitive and more self-confident, even though the activities might be work-based challenges. Flow occurs when challenges meet your skills. Combine high challenge with high skill, and you experience flow. But high challenge with low skill equals anxiety. Low challenge with low skills leads to apathy; and low challenge with high skills to boredom.

The activity was its own reward: intrinsically motivating. Flow banishes depression, distraction and creeping dispiritedness. So what are the preconditions of flow? There are five:

1. A clear goal in mind.
2. Reasonable expectations of completing the goal in mind satisfactorily.
3. The ability to concentrate.
4. Getting regular and specific feedback on their performance.
5. Having the appropriate skills to complete the task.

We all know the flow experience. Young people might find it in elaborate computer games, while their parents might experience it in the potting shed or workshop, making music, or in art or writing.

You see flow in those jobs where people experience the greatest work satisfaction. They include mainly artisans – potters and painters, writers and weavers, thatchers and designers. They exercise their talents, work at their own pace and are the opposite of "alienated from the products of their labours". Indeed, they *are* the products of their labour. They are what they produce. They are bound-up in the product. Their identity, their being, are in the product of their talents.

The question is this: if flow is such a deeply motivational experience and one that leads to great productivity, can jobs be designed so as to encourage flow? The answer is "possibly", but it requires serious attention to the business of selection, job design and management.

First, you need to select people with the skills for the task – people with sufficient talent for the task at hand and who enjoy exercising that talent. *Second*, you need to design the job so that people receive regular and specific feedback on how they are doing, so that that they understand precisely the consequences of their various actions. *Third*, you have to set, with them, clear, stretchable goals. Both the manager and the managed need to have appropriate expectations of what it is they should be attempting to achieve.

But some rather crucial things seem difficult to find and manage. Call it passion, or intrinsic motivation or captivation: it's the absorption that occurs when one is fully concentrating, fully caught up in the activity.

Is this a personality variable? Is it just that some people are lucky both to find and to exploit their talents? Indeed, actually to have talents? Is flow a gift or talent, or can one be trained? Can the ADHD adult ever experience flow? Or the impulsive, sensation-seeking boy-racer? Is flow an attribute of age and wisdom as well as ability and temperament?

We don't know, but what we do know is that job design and management style can certainly turn off the flow tap. Job design should match skills to the job; have enriched jobs; encourage people to use and rejoice in and extend their skills; have a way of giving them feedback; and reward them for their labour.

Flow might be a semi-trance-like state, but it is elicited by very clear and explicit conditions.

Seligman, founder of the positive psychology movement, offers a fourfold recommendation to increase flow at work:

- Identify your signature strengths.
- Choose work that lets you use them every day.
- Recraft your present work to use your signature strengths more.
- If you are the employer, choose employees whose signature strengths mesh with the work they will do. If you are a manager, make room to allow employees to recraft the work within the bounds of your goals.

Reference

Csikszentmihaly, Mihaly (1990) *Flow: The Psychology of Optimal Experience*. New York: Harper.

Heart-sinking staff

Doctors, lecturers and managers know of the heart-sinking patient, student or staff member. They are harbingers of doom and gloom; they seem perpetually pessimistic; they are carriers of the dark cloud of negativity.

The glass is always half-empty: the future the bleak; the hope none. Nothing can be done. Nothing will help. No-one cares. The system is biased and unfair and always has been.

Fortunately, there are those at the other end of the dimension, sometimes called "life-enhancers". They make all around them feel better, appreciated and therefore appreciative. They reduce blood pressure, encourage the flow of those feel-good endorphins and light up happiness centres in the brain.

So what causes someone to become a heart-sinker or a life enhancer? Is it the result of an unhappy childhood, persistent poverty or erratic parenting? Nature or nurture? Can their world view be changed? Can the "sinkers" be coaxed, coached or "therapied" into being an "enhancer"? And at what cost?

You certainly see them on training programs. I have noted six heart-sinking types on training courses: each, in his or her own little way, a "pain in the butt".

1. *The prisoner*: The scowl on the face, and arms folded across the chest, and in their pocket the letter from the boss or personnel manager demanding (requiring) that they attend the course, characterize this type. They have probably succeeded in avoiding this course, or ones like it, many times before, but eventually have been caught. They are prisoners: they don't want to be there and wish they were somewhere else. They are sour, negative, unhelpful and certainly uncooperative.

2. *The escapee*: This type is the course junkie who jumps at the opportunity to get out of the office. They may hate their work or simply enjoy education and training at the company's expense. The escapee is usually rather too experienced at course activities, games and questionnaires and may well have done them before. They are easy to deal with from the trainer's point of view but not good value for money from the perspective of their company.

3. *The old dog*: There are various reasons why some people believe they cannot be taught new tricks. Some delegates are on-the-job retirees, in

the departure lounge of the organization. They may in fact be quite a long way from retirement, but they are not interested in learning anything new. Others believe courses are too abstract, too theoretical, too vague and have nothing to add to their day-to-day working lives. These cynics have few critical facilities. This makes them too gullible and too unfocused, though certainly easy for the trainer.

4. *The intellectual*: Whereas the old dog may reject what he or she is told because it is too vague and theoretical, the intellectual wants to know the empirical and epistemological bases of the data being presented. Many are snobs who think they know more than the trainer (and sometimes do). These high flyers may believe either the content or the style is not appropriate for their level. They may enjoy humiliating the trainer if they can.

5. *The bastard*: These are arrogant know-it-alls. They usually believe that personnel departments should be closed, all consultants fired, and the money put into the company's pension fund. In a curious way, they enjoy courses in the same way that they enjoy meetings, because they have learnt to be maximally disruptive. They may be simple attention seekers, and in some organizations are intellectually seriously underpowered. They are a nightmare for trainers, because they are solely interested in scuppering or damaging the proceedings.

6. *The ingratiator*: Many people are anxious when attending courses because they fear being shown up in front of others. Those who fear being exposed as the product of the Peter Principle tend to be what Americans charmingly call "apple polishers". The ingratiator tries to do a deal with the trainer: "I will be a good boy/girl if you don't expose or humiliate me." And for trainers it is a good deal.

The question is really how to increase positivity, how to change heart sinkers into heart enhancers it in short, how to increase happiness. The happiness industry is growing. After all, there is a stress industry, so why not a happiness industry? When once there were a hundred academic papers and books on anxiety and depression for every one on happiness, joy or contentment, now the positive psychologists are asserting themselves in the face of the negative psychologists, who are now almost demonized for being the cause of the problem.

There are various strategies that the happiness-making Johnnies recommend we try out. These are not new, nor are they rocket science, but are long-forgotten practices known to our parents and grandparents. So try counting your blessings – each day, before you turn in, make a list, prefer-ably in writing, of five things you personally have to be seriously *grateful for every day*. It focuses on the half-full, not the half-empty. It gives you comparative data. Who was it who said, "I cried because I had no shoes until I met a man who had no feet"?

Next, *express thanks*. Most of us can nominate people, many from the distant past, to whom we feel both gratitude but also half guilt because we never fully thanked them for their kindness, thoughtfulness and help. They are often neighbours and teachers, relatives and professionals who may or may not have had any inkling of the effect of their actions. Thanks bring happiness to both to the bearer and the receiver of the news.

Third, is to give up the concept of "weakness", even of "developmen-tal opportunities". Rather than waste time, effort and money on trying to do things better that do not come naturally, *celebrate, indulge and glory in your strengths and gifts*. It is often debilitating and depressing to keep try-ing to do things better that do not come naturally, easily or happily!

But do these strategies/therapies work, or is happiness more hard-wired? Indeed, it is a paradox for the positive psychologists that the behavior geneticists have shown from studies on twins as well as longitudinal research, that as much as half of the cause of the sunny or cloudy personality lies in the genes.

But, cry the optimists, if genes cause 50 percent, then at least the other half can be changed. Possibly, but how and when? Is there a critical period (such as adolescence) which when passed means that little can be done?

The problem is this – life enhancers seek out situations that make them happy, while gloom carriers do the opposite. Enhancers seek to change what they do not like, while gloom-carriers endure fatalistically. Life enhancers seek to find the positive among the negative, while gloom carriers do the exact reverse. Looking back on an identical experience, it is noticeable how differently the two types recall what happened.

This is why it is so hard to change the one into the other. Why some survive misfortune so well and others do not. There is a "happiness gene" which works its way out through personality, coping strategies and world views. To him who hath shall more be given.

How advertising works

Is the question *how* advertising works, or *does* advertising work? It is not through want of research activity that the question remains unanswered.

In fact, there has been so much academic research since the 1920s that we now have a plethora of models and theories of how it all works. So we have the AIDCAS model, which stands for attention, interest, desire, conviction, action and satisfaction; and the DIPADA model, which means definition, identification, proof, acceptance, desire and action.

Most of the models – of which there are over a dozen – essentially claim a three-state sequence.

The first is *cognitive* and the jargon is attention, awareness, exposure, leading to knowledge. So the first task is to make people aware of, and knowledgeable, about a brand – a product, a service or an issue. Cognition is cold; it's the rational stuff; matters for the head.

The next stage is *affective*: matters of the heart. It's the hot bit. This is the state that involves liking for the brand; feeling warm towards it; having a preference. It's about desire and conviction.

And then, having engaged the heart and the head, it's time for the hand-in-the-wallet. The *volitional*, behavioral bit, where one acts – goes out and buys the product.

Alas, it is not as simple as this, though. There are other complicating factors. One is the attitude towards the advertisement itself, which affects both attitudes to, and judgments about, the brand. Another is involvement with the product. Thus, for less significant products, there is less of the head and heart stuff and more trial and error. In this sense, behavior – trying the product – leads to emotions and ideas. But if the product is important (expensive, ego-involving) the advertisements may be very carefully processed by the consumer.

In fact, these neat "hierarchy of effectiveness" models have fallen out of favor and been replaced by more sophisticated models or persuasion. One, called the ELM framework, suggests that four factors are important:

1. The source of the message – how attractive, credible, powerful, representative and trustworthy is the source of the bottom-line advertising message.
2. The message itself – complexity, quality and number of arguments.

3. The processing of the message – the viewer's ability and motivation to understand the ad.
4. Attitude change and buying behavior.

More important, there is a context for all advertising messages that is pretty important. Try the following: What is the goal of the advertiser? To introduce a product, remind someone of a brand, attack competitors? What is the product category? Ads for credit cards, cheese and cosmetics are different and probably work differently. What about the competition – how many competitors, how easy is it to differentiate the product? What is the product life cycle – long or short, on the way up or the way down? And who is the target market – adolescents or the aged? As, Ds or Es?

Just getting too complicated? That's the trouble with social science research. Too many variables. And worse: to study something may involve people being asked to take part in experiments where they do not react naturally. They may be wired up to sensitive physiological equipment or they may have to sit through ads of similar types. They will certainly be asked if they intend to buy, but that is quite different from actually buying.

No wonder there remains a lot of confusion and debate around how, if, when, or indeed whether, advertising works.

HR for dummies

One of the major academic growth areas is that of newly fashionable disciplines. Degrees in fashion and estate agency; in publishing and tourism; in photography and catering. This means that there are now departments of, and professors of, some really odd "disciplines".

Old-school veterans complain that a "discipline" by definition needs a coherent body of knowledge; a set of theories and products; and an ability to establish boundaries, not in the exclusionary sense but also in the area of focus sense. Thus economics can be differentiated from finance; sociology from psychology; geography from geology.

There has been a great fad for taking jobs – not even professions – and trying to give them an academic respectability by inventing university departments and even chairs to support them. Can you imagine three years of an estate agent degree? What on earth are they taught? Yes, they need some education on the law; something on economic drivers of market values; a few lectures on marketing; even a dabble in emotional intelligence. But a three-year honours degree?

Further, there is pressure to dress-up such degrees to make them look academically respectable. Thus one has the old-fashioned, quasi-pompous language in exams and seminars. But is this covering a serious problem of a gaping hole at the centre of the enterprise?

Even "disciplines" that have been sort-of partially accepted struggle for respectability. What about HR, or personnel (or staff dept) as it was known? This used to be part of a diploma in administration; then it was one of many MBA electives; now you can do a degree in the topic. Three years of it.

So what would the exams look like? Consider the paper below and see how you would do. Three hours; choose three questions. Be critical, creative but concise. If there are any, quote theories and empirical results. Justify your prejudices. And long, rambling personal examples are discouraged.

1. Distinguish between an annual performance appraisal interview and a cosy chat.
2. "HR is a girly world; powerless, poorly paid, pointless". Answer without being too cross.
3. You call it EQ; your colleague calls it interpersonal skills; your boss calls it maturity; your mum calls it charm; your dad calls it "bullshit". Who is right?

4. One of the following is true and critically important in selection and assessment decisions: Choose and justify your choice:
    - Men with beards are untrustworthy
    - Redheads are prone to temper tantrums
    - Oxbridge graduates tend to be spoilt, supercilious know-alls
    - iPod usage is a good index of computer literacy
    - Men who wear short-sleeved shirts will never make it
    - You can train any fool to be a good senior manager
    - Technical types just don't get it, do they?
5. Job Analysis is simply too boring to waste your time on. Illustrate your answer with poignant, witty examples.
6. Who said HR is an anagram of profligate waste, psychobabble and an unacceptable internal tax on the organization? Were they even partly right?
7. "HR directors rarely reach board level because they don't understand enough about business." After all, haven't you got to be an accountant, actuary or marketing specialist to make it to the top? Does that mean you've chosen the wrong degree?
8. A good HR professional is a cross between a psychiatrist, lawyer, hairdresser and gynaecologist. Discuss.
9. Is it true that training only really works if:
    - It is done in a nice country hotel
    - People play daft, non-threatening games during the day and get drunk at night
    - Every "dele" gets a really good party bag
    - You wheel-in a mega-guru to bless your proceedings
    - You don't measure anything.
10. What are the most useful data to acquire to make better selection decisions: astrological signs; graphology analysis; head, bust, waist and shoe size (if it's called anthropometrics – it is all PC); postal code; daddy's job; the type of car owned; number of visits to either an aromatherapist or spiritual healer; has the car got sat-nav?; knowledge of post-Freudian defence mechanisms.
11. A psychometric test is (tick all that are true):
    - Great fun
    - A way to make what you are doing look scientific
    - Damn expensive but indispensable
    - An essential tool to uncover the powerful unconscious drives of people

- A marvellous way of fooling people by telling them what they told you
- A way of looking professional without the training
- A tool to turn intuitions into numbers.

12. Compare and contrast the role and job of the business coach; the moral confessor; the essential confidant; and the psychopathic confidence trickster.

13. Freud said that all children were polymorphous perverts. How do you stop them getting to board level?

14. Performance management systems are a bourgeois attack on the solidarity of the neo-working class. Furthermore they advocate "ranking and spanking" where "sharing and caring" is required. Is this all old-fashioned Marxist tosh or a really good critique to prevent new change programs working?

15. Gender differences are a pernicious, positivist, pusillanimous attempt to create glass ceilings, glass lifts and glass trapdoors. Examine how some HR people (that is, who read that "Venus and Mars" book) are trying to attack the feminist revolution.

16. What people have in common is that they all are different. So how on earth can you devise policies and procedures to fit them all? Illustrate your answer with big words like nomothetic and idiographic.

17. How would you go about teaching creativity and emotional intelligence to someone from health and safety with a diploma in warehouse management?

18. Psychiatrists have observed that: narcissists do well in Marketing; paranoids in Security, schizoids in R & D, and psychopaths in senior management. Are they right? Illustrate your answer using any other sexy terms from the Personality Disorder nomenclature or just rave on about the mental instability of bosses that you have had.

19. Paradoxically, the verbal dexterity and casuistry, even sophistry, of Sir Humphrey in "Yes Minister" has a thing or two to teach an HR manager. If you disagree, find another sit-com character who does better.

20. Most business books could be boiled down to half a dozen bullet points, are badly written, and worse, are misleading. Draft a letter to Tom Peters, Raj Persaud or John Adair making this point.

Ideology at work

It's both a rather old-fashioned and semi-dangerous word, *ideology*. People who are ideologically driven seem easily categorizable into the good and the bad.

The Protestant work ethic is an ideology. It asserts the following:

1. People have a moral and religious obligation to fill their lives with heavy physical toil. For some, this means that hard work, effort and drudgery are to be valued for their own sake; physical pleasures and enjoyments are to be shunned; and an ascetic existence of methodical rigor is the only acceptable way to live.
2. Men and women are expected to spend long hours at work, with little or no time for personal recreation and leisure.
3. A worker should have a dependable attendance record, with low absenteeism and tardiness.
4. Workers should be highly productive and produce a large quantity of goods or service.
5. Workers should take pride in their work and do their jobs well.
6. Employees should have feelings of commitment and loyalty to their profession, their company and their work group.
7. Workers should be achievement-oriented and constantly strive for promotions and advancement. High-status jobs with prestige and the respect of others are important indicators of a "good" person.
8. People should acquire wealth through honest labor and retain it through thrift and wise investments. Frugality is desirable; extravagance and waste should be avoided.

And those who believe in this ethic are fiercely committed to self-improvement and personal responsibility. They don't approve of state hand-outs and welfare, particularly to those they see as the (many) undeserving poor. They believe that welfare payments:

- Reduce self-help – the idea that welfare payments make people less willing to look after themselves.
- Increase the tax burden – whether they are good or bad, it increases taxes intolerably.
- Reduce the work ethic – they sap the will to work, which presumably is extrinsic or intrinsic.

- Reduce the family ethic – making people less ready to look after their relatives and children.
- Increase stigma – making people who get welfare benefits and services feel like second-class citizens.
- Help the undeserving – providing people with a source of income who do not deserve it.
- Increase indiscriminate allocation – paradoxically they tend to help people who do not need help.

These various values were shown to be strong statistical predictors of attitudes to welfare payments. Interestingly, very few studies have sought to compare those on welfare with those not receiving benefits. But it is all terribly old-fashioned, never mind politically incorrect. Is ideology at work dead?

The selflessness and dedication of the empathic Third-World teacher or doctor is often dictated by a powerful belief system born out of experience. The Mother Teresa of Calcutta or Albert Schweitzer examples are typical. It was their faith that persuaded them, though there are examples of non-religious humanitarianism too.

In the other corner are suicide and other bombers, whose religious and socio-political beliefs lead them to identify a homogenous, evil enemy they are hell-bent on destroying at any cost. There was the "Unibomber" who hated modernity, the Timothy McVeigh case of bombing a government building, and those whose religious faith lead them to take pleasure in the killing of the "infidel".

A sad world – yes. But what has all this to do with the world of work? After all, office politics seem mild in comparison to all this mayhem and destruction. How does ideology play out in the modern workplace?

We are, in Europe at least, in a post-Christian world. Declining church attendance reflects a decline in religious beliefs. At best agnostic, at worst militant atheists, most but certainly not all people find their lives guided by metaphysical beliefs or religious practices.

Equally, after the end of the Cold War, we seem less politically committed. We choose to vote in fewer numbers, are deeply skeptical, if not cynical, about politicians, and find it harder to differentiate between the blue team and the red team as they bicker over the middle ground. We don't join political parties, and the great "isms" of the period between the First and Second World Wars are a distant memory.

So, if it is not politics and religion that give us an ideological world view, have we stopped believing in anything? Are we not guided in our daily lives by a coherent set of principles we might label as ideological?

Perhaps the paradox of the decline of religion and politics is that the workplace is *more* ideological than ever. What, after all, is political correctness; what are business ethics and ethics committees, and what is the deadening hand of "health and safety" but the manifestations of subtle, insidious and legally based ideologies?

Just as there are militant agnostics, so there can be militant work-based practice enforcers of various kinds. There are many powerful lobbies based on self-help groups with powerful beliefs about right and wrong, justice and injustice, the chosen and the damned.

They may support a special group which is, they feel, discriminated against. And they do so not only with the zeal of the inquisition, but also with all the tools of the modern electronic age. And, of course, they also use the law.

Ideologies of the past were grander and greater than they are today. Many were Utopian. Now they seem smaller and often dystopian. The great "isms" are now much reduced, though environmentalism remains the biggest and can itself clearly have an impact on the world of work.

Never underestimate or ignore the power of belief-systems to influence behavior at work. We may not be legally able to enquire, or comfortable about enquiring about these at selection interviews, but they can be the most powerful driver of productivity … or its opposite.

Image versus quality

In the pre-1980s world of advertising, researchers distinguished between ads that emphasized image and those that emphasized quality. Thus soft-sell ads don't focus on the nature or cost of the product, but rather on the image associated with using or possessing the product. Those ads suggest that we can be a particular kind of person (strong, handsome, sexy, above average, caring) if we own a particular product. They also suggest the specific kinds of reactions we are likely to get from others.

Image-based, soft-sell ads suggest a lifestyle that is associated with owning, using or just displaying the product. Quality-based, hard-sell ads, on the other hand, emphasize the utilitarian features of the product. These ads usually mention quality, durability and value for money.

While it is true that the product itself often dictates the sort of ad the gurus make, it is possible to conceive of making ads from *both* "perspectives". Cars are usually image-based and detergent usually quality-based, but experimental psychologists have devised ads that show an identical product from two quite different perspectives.

In a famous study, two American psychologists chose three products: whisky, cigarettes and coffee, and devised good-quality magazine-style advertisements for them. The difference between the two types of ad lay in the written message rather than the picture.

The whisky ad showed a well-known brand of Canadian whisky resting on a set of architectural drawings. The words beneath the picture were different: one (image-oriented) said "You're not just moving in, you're moving up", while the other (quality-oriented) said "When it comes to great taste, everyone draws the same conclusion".

The cigarette ad has a pretty predictable picture – handsome chap looks into a mirror at sexy female companion while lighting up. The woman's hand is resting (semi-suggestively) on his shoulder. The image message says "Brand ... you see the difference", while, quite subtly, the other reads "Brand ... you taste the difference".

The third ad was for mint-flavoured coffee. A couple, smiling at each other in a candle-lit room, drinking the coffee. The different accompanying messages read "Make a chilly night become a cosy evening with Brand ...." and "Brand...: A delicious blend of three flavours – coffee, chocolate and mint."

After the ads were shown, the viewers were asked questions such as which ads they liked better, and which were more persuasive. A second group was shown the same ads and asked how much they were prepared to pay for the product.

In a third study, people were asked to what extent they would be willing to try a shampoo that had just left clinical trials. Half were told it had average cleaning ability, but was the best in terms of how it left their hair looking; the others that it was average in how it left the hair looking but was best at cleaning.

All those studies were aimed at testing a theory of two types of individual: the high self-monitor, self-aware, socially flexible and responsive to their environment; and the low self-monitor, less concerned with fitting in but more loyal to beliefs and values. Predictably, the high self-monitors liked the image-based ads, while the low self-monitors preferred the quality-based ones.

There have been replications of these studies. The experimenters have used clothes, beer, chocolate, fizzy drinks, even cassette tapes, to test the theory.

But alas, as ever, it turned out to be a bit more complicated. Often the strength of the advertisement was more important. Equally, some products seemed pretty resistant to believable image ads. So it's pretty difficult to take utilitarian products such as aspirin or air conditioners and write believable image-based advertisements for them. Equally, some image-enhancing social-identity-based products, such as greetings cards, seem to resist quality-based ads. Others, such as sunglasses, swing both ways, so to speak. Luxury products are more prone to image type ads than necessity products, and vice versa.

And, of course, evaluating products depend on other features too, such as country of origin. Further, some products tend to be consumed or shown in public, while others are mainly used or worn in private. This can also make a difference.

But the studies have highlighted some important ideas: know your typical customer; aim your ads at customers' values and preferences; and experiment with both image-type and quality-type ads if your product allows it, of course.

Interview porkies

A common objection to the use of personality or motivational tests in selection is that people fake the results. They dissimulate, attempt impression management or provide empirically non-veridical, socially desirable responses. In short, they tell porkies. Maybe.

But what on earth leads one to believe the situation is any different – indeed possibly even worse – in the selection interview? Is the whole interview business not a smoke and mirrors charade, with both parties trying to outsmart one other? Hence the sale of books with useful killer-questions for interviewers and clever-clever answers for interviewees.

What do people mean by faking? It's the intentional distortion of ideas aimed at creating a favorable impression which, in turn, leads to an enhanced chance of being selected. But who fakes, and when and how? Interestingly, it seems that candidates distort their responses in a job- desirable, but not necessarily a socially-desirable, way. In this sense, they may perform what is called "role-faking": giving answers that seem to be desirable for a particular job. Clearly, there is a lot of "it all depends" stuff.

So what does it depend on, then? In a very thorough and sophistical review of all the research in the area, two American psychologists, writing in the latest issue of the *International Journal of Selection and Assessment* (vol.14, no. 4), found as many as nineteen factors that related to the faking of job interviews. Fortunately, and hopefully, they categorized these under three broad headings.

The first was *capacity* to fake. There are various features attached to this. You need to be skilful to fake convincingly. You also need to be articulate, socially perceptive and persuasive. As well as being socially skilled, expressive and emotionally intelligent, you need to be bright enough to know what the correct type of answer in fact is. You need to remember to whom different lies are told, and about what/whom. In short, you need sales skills and smarts to be convincing.

Equally important, you need to do your homework and know what to fake. Essentially, you need to know two things. The first is the sort of psychological constructs or organizational competencies that are being rated in the interview: basically, what are they looking for? Good team players, creativity and innovation, good with customers? Get the rating form and you are halfway there. But you also need to understand the job requirements as specified by the job analysis (if that was ever done) and the job advertisement. The latter have double-speak and spin but they should be interpretable.

If you know what they are looking for, the questions are more predictable and transparent. Crude stereotypes won't do. Know what they want … and give it to them.

The second big issue is not the capacity to fake but the *willingness* to do so. A number of factors seem to come into play here. The first is personality. What traits have been shown to be clearly related to faking? There is Machiavellianism: the rejoicing in the manipulation of others. Then there is the need for approval – this amounts to valuing others' acceptance and approval over the truth. Another is self-monitoring, or acute sensitivity to contextual rules of behavior, and adjusting one's "performance" to them. Extraverts enjoy the theatrical aspects of social interaction and should be better at the whole thing.

Third, the most important and obvious candidate is integrity. Those labelled as honest, reliable and trustworthy are (almost by definition) less likely to indulge in the dishonesty of faking at interview.

Another factor is the pretty obvious restraint of being caught out. The more someone believes they can get away with it, of not being caught out, challenged or made to provide proof, the more likely they are to partake of a spot of faking.

Don't underestimate or ignore a person's work and interview history. The more people have (or simply believe they have) been badly, unfairly or inequitably dealt with in previous interviews, the more willing they are to engage in interview faking. Those who believe they have been the victims of unfair discrimination may feel justified in a spot of restitutive faking.

And then there is the issue of job interview experience and coaching. Coaching is aimed at learning what are the best answers to questions, and how to give them. It increases capacity. Indeed it is precisely and explicitly what coaching is all about, though the issue of dishonesty rarely surfaces!

So we have the *capacity* and *willingness*, but we also need *opportunity* to fake. This lies more in the way the interview is conducted than in the nature of the individual. Unstructured, unplanned, essentially unprepared and idiosyncratic interviews provide many more opportunities to fake than those that are structured. But a lot depends on the nature of the questions. Some interviewers ask questions that are really easy to fake: the hypothetical (what if), subjective, unverifiable question. Situational interview questions really just ask for porkies. These are tests involving hypothetical but problem situations, with multiple choice answers.

The briefer the interview, the more the faking. Why? Well the interviewer does not have the time to address the same topic from different angles, to tease out the answers fully, and more important, to check the consistency or reliability of specific answers. Candidates slip up because they cannot "keep in role" for long periods, and long interviews show this up.

It's probably easier to bluff a single interviewer than a panel. Single interviewers can be too overloaded to notice all the little cues of the porkie-teller. Use of follow-up clarification questions can be very useful for the lie-detecting interviewer (CVs, test scores, and so on).

Worse for your typical interviewer; where interviewers' questions are trying to assess interests, personality, preferences or organizational fit, faking can easily occur, but where they attempt to measure intelligence, knowledge and skills (which are in fact better predictors of work), faking drops.

One final, pretty crucial point is the fundamental purpose of the interview itself. Is it recruiting, initial screening or final selection? Recruitment interviews are to increase the number of people in the applicant pool, while the selection interview is designed essentially to pick the best one.

Quite a list. It does help to unpack the process and reduce lying. But let's not assume the faking is all on the side of the interviewee. From the job ads to the interview there are those in the company itself who are very astute and active at self-presentation processes. Both sides in the interview are on their best behavior. Both are trying to impress, to seek the truth in others but conceal it in oneself. Perhaps this explains why some organizations pay little heed to the data that arises from interviews. It's just all too dodgy to be at all useful.

Investigative salespersons

Despite the glut, ever more books on How to Sell appear on the market. Most are short, all are upbeat, and universally they promise that secret, magic formula called "How to close the deal".

Most sales books are written by successful salespeople who have taken on guru and author status. Guest appearances at jolly conferences which offer the easy trousering of large fees confer a nice lifestyle. The conferences sell the books, and the books lead to conference invitations. The perfect win–win virtuous cycle.

While most authors of these books are reasonably frank, what they are trying to do is to explicate their particular strategy in a memorable model, phrase or metaphor. They tend to imply that selling has various phases, and that you need to apply certain techniques and strategies to move, encourage, or even shunt, the interaction along the lines you want. And, hey presto, the closed deal.

The problem with the books is not their naïveté, but the rather mechanical way in which the process is described. But worse than that, they really aren't based on research. It is possible, and it has been done, to describe and differentiate the processes and procedures of top salespeople. As in all other areas of endeavor, it can be shown that the top 10 percent or so have two to four times the productivity of the bottom 10 percent, and well over twice that of the average employee – and that's measured and well documented. It's true of teachers and executives, scientists and artists.

Studying the successful salesperson dates back to the 1920s. And all that the studies do show is that while there are phases and techniques, these are subtle. It's not particularly about eye contact, smart suits, cost–benefit analysis or "bogof" deals. It's actually about questioning. A good salesperson is more like a psychotherapist than a television presenter; more like a teacher than a manager. They know about high-yield questions. About making people think differently by reflecting on what is really important. By seeing the familiar as less so. Interestingly, answers to these questions can have a very long influence, partly because they are often rarely asked, and partly because it is the client who provides the answer.

The primary skill is diagnostic. And this is best done by getting the customer to do the talking. Psychiatrists at £150 per hour spend only 10–20 percent of the time talking to patients. It is their job to understand their clients. And they do so by using open, subtle questions. They need to pick up on cues: to listen, not to ask standard, mundane questions.

You can call them problems or frustrations or hopes or needs, but it is the job of the salesperson to understand where the customer is coming from, and quite naturally how the sales product or process will solve a problem or at least improve the situation.

Create a need and then fulfil it? Well not quite. Good salespeople, through attentive, open-ended, investigative questions let the customers describe their situations with reference particularly to how those situations could be improved. But then, rather than pull out the shiny catalogue full of special offers, they focus on the consequences of inactivity.

What will happen if the situation remains the same? In a sense, what is the prognosis for the complaint? But this is a controversial approach because it lowers the tone. Gloom and anger can replace simple frustration.

Traditionally, salespeople like positive, enthusiastic up-beat staff. They are selected for it and trained in it. They tend not to do negative emotions in others or themselves. But the "trick", in getting the customer to focus on the bleakness of inertia with respect to the future, is to introduce the ideal solution: namely, the product. The product solves the problem. It has a great pay-off. It becomes not only a useful but a necessary investment.

In this sense, customers sell themselves the product. Just as good therapists and change managers know that actions only come about if people "buy into" a solution, which they think *they* have found, so the salesperson lets the customer do the QED thing.

So what is different about successful salespeople? They ask more insightful questions of clients they have done their homework on. They steer the interaction to very common sources of frustration, ineffectiveness, poor productivity. They listen, they take their time. They then try to get the customer to look forward if the problem is not solved, and what that would involve. Then, and only then, does the good salesperson put forward the product as the best answer to the problem. As a sensible, rational, thing to do under the circumstances.

The skill is in the questioning more than in the presentation. And it's in the listening as much as in the pay-off blurb. Selling is a relationship business, but it is also about probing and counseling. And helping the client to persuade themselves to buy the product.

That is what good therapists, teachers and managers do. It's not through power but persuasion, and this comes of finding ways to make people really want to change to the product.

IT disorders

It's easy to make fun of IT geeks, nerds and eccentrics, but some have become super-rich. They also still have enormous control over our daily lives. They can, it seems, persuade big business and governments to pour millions of pounds into high-promise, low-yield schemes that supposedly save time, money and effort.

Remember the Millennium Bug? Poor countries did nothing, while the paranoid First World made the IT harbingers of doom very rich. Did aeroplanes fall out of the sky? Did military computers trigger off the firing of multiple nuclear warheads? Did your PC lose its entire memory? Not one Millennium Bug disaster has been documented.

And the "dot com" fantasy? The South Sea Bubble of the new millennium. Remember those super-cocky, ultra-confident masters of the web with their brave-new-worldspeak and contempt for the past? They got their just desserts.

But it's a hard life in this fast-changing, acronym-addicted world. The IT chappies have to keep up with frequent new inventions and please multiple constituencies. So they suffer stress and breakdown. Recently, psychiatric research has in fact identified some problems very specific to the industry:

1. Abnormal *acronym* fixation. This is the inability to speak or write a sentence without two or three acronyms rendering it utterly meaningless to the outsider. It's a way of confirming your identity, but renders one friendless and isolated after work.

2. Post-traumatic *backup* neurosis. This is the realization that mistakes are so common that everything has to have a recovery back-up system or program when the original system crashes and burns. The really paranoid have back-ups for back-ups, ad infinitum.

3. Episodic *customer-service* phobia. This is a morbid fear, coupled with a deep loathing, of people who use the system. Callers are addressed as *users*, not customers. Phobics will do anything to avoid contact with real human beings, preferring machines.

4. Delusional *helpdesk* malady. This is the idea that, in providing one helpdesk or helpline, customers will be both happy and channel all their anger, frustration and bewilderment on to the naïve, innocent person manning it.

5. Generalized *infrastructure* delusions. This is the idea, based on curious metaphors and jargon terms, that IT systems are in some way like the "information and communication architecture" of a company. It's a delusional state among those at the top.

6. Atypical *integration* dysfunction. This is the yawning gap between all that joined-up, interlinked matrix talk and the desire to have little to do with any other part of the business. It's a compensation for silo addiction.

7. Intermittent *password* disturbance. This is one manifestation of rampant paranoia that requires people to change their passwords frequently. Its aim is to humiliate senior people and make sure IT is respected and never overlooked.

8. Borderline *portable* psychosis. This is close to wireless syndrome and has two contradictory manifestations. It rejoices in the transportability and flexibility of all IT gadgets, but fears that people can literally walk off with everything valuable.

9. Psychosexual *technical support* fetish. This is related to, but different from, user support. These are purists who don't do people, only wiring, maps and gizmos. They can install and service them. Most fun is changing your system just when you have finally understood it and need it most.

10. Generalized *upgrade* compulsion. This is the use of the quite dishonest language of airlines to force random change on people who don't want "up", "re" or any other sort of grading, thank you.

11. Acute *virus detection*, *debugging* psychosis. This is part of the firewall paranoia that is a base requirement of the IT world. It is the belief that invisible, evil forces of doom, mayhem and destruction are everywhere and are trying to infect your system, leading to acute loss of memory or a painful death.

12. Habitual *web-enhanced* impulse. This essentially means trying to stop people communicating in any way except via computers.

It seems to be a young persons' game. Just as you master a new system, somebody changes it. No wonder the psychiatrists have had to spend time and effort describing the new ailments listed above.

Jocks, loners, druggies and nerds

Many Western governments appear to have awoken up at last to the fact that high numbers of their population are floating (pretty precariously) on a sea of debt. Many of us have very few, if any, savings, and worse – have credit card and other debts we do not seem able to pay off.

Whence this dilemma? Is this a function of the policies of dour and prudent Finance Ministers and Chancellors who appear to prefer free spending to saving? Did he create an illusion of a successful economy which will go wrong once the credit boom stops? Or have we become, over the years, nations of spendthrifts unwilling, unable or unresponsive to saving? Why bother about a rainy day: the state will provide. Live for the moment; we do not know what tomorrow may bring.

All parents want their children to grow up money-savvy. They want them to understand money and use it wisely. They don't want misers or spendthrifts, gamblers or godfathers in the family. They want their children to be money-rational. And so they introduce pocket-money or allowance regimes at an early age to teach them about finance.

There remains some debate about when pocket money should begin and the rules that you might apply. Start around primary school; pay once a week, moving on to once a month when they become adolescents ; agree clear rules about what the money is for; encourage saving.

And you might teach them about the world of work through the time-honoured Saturday job, or the paper round, or a stint as a waiter/waitress. It's good for their social, moral and economic development. It is how they are integrated into society and learn to become upstanding, responsible citizens.

But all parents know and dread the power of the peer group. They worry about their children falling among thieves; about getting in with the wrong crowd; about being inappropriately socialized by ne'er-do-wells who become no-hopers.

We know that binge drinking and drug abuse in young people is heavily influenced by peer groups. But what about economic behavior, such as saving money?

A Canadian study published in the *Journal of Economic Psychology* (2005, vol. 26) looked at the effects of peer groups and the experience of work on young (aged 12–24 years) people's saving behavior. The researchers were able to describe four clear youth subcultures. First there is the fun, somewhat *delinquent,* subculture of hedonists. This is populated by "drug-gies and partygoers". Opposite them are those in a *studious, academic* subculture. They enjoy school, work hard and have a rich extra-curricular set of activities. They have been called "brains and nerds", depending on the values of the observer.

A third group is populated by "loners and nobodies". They are *uninvolved*; *non-groupies.* They are not part of teen culture and little involved in any groups. They may not be influenced by others very much but can appear rather lost; inconspicuous outsiders who don't get accepted.

Finally the "jocks and populars" come from the play-hard, work-hard, well-rounded culture that is both peer-oriented and adult (achievement-oriented).

These subcultures dictate how young people speak, dress, spend and play. They relate to all aspects of their lives, from how hard they try at school, to whether they take on part-time jobs, and how they spend and save their money.

The results of the study confirmed the researchers' hypotheses. So the "brains" and "populars" (nerds and jocks) saved, while the "partygoers" and "loners" did not. Those more conscious of the adult world (the formal reward systems from school and work) saved more than those who paid more attention to the peer-oriented world (the informal reward system of short-term fun and acceptance).

Interestingly, those young people who worked were more savings-oriented than those who did not. Sure, they had more money to save, but the results suggest they sought jobs in order to save.

It comes as no surprise that youth culture powerfully affects young people's attitudes towards, and the use (or abuse) of money. Being a member of a group affects their reputation and their normative behavior. They are usually highly sensitive to how their peers behave, and gain acceptance from emulating it.

The young people who through their parents' and teachers' encourage-ment, or through their own choice, become deeply involved in extra-curricular activities such as team sports, book clubs or the performing arts soon begin to develop a more adult outlook, with adult responsibilities. And this includes being sensible with money. So all the good work put in over a long period with pocket money advocators can easily be undone by feckless, hedonistic, peer-group pressure. Equally the carefree, feckless young person can, with the right peers, learn to become a grown up quite quickly and be eminently sensible with money.

Losing the moral compass

Business ethics are only really interesting when you see something like an Enron in action. It's a bit like going to a Formula 1 race and waiting for a crash. Perhaps ethics can really only be understood when it all goes wrong: when companies really lose the ethical plot; when their moral compass loses magnetic north.

The problem with ethics committees and business ethics is that it is often assumed there is one (and only one) correct moral ethical position. This is clearly nonsense, because there is a myriad of different ethical/moral codes/systems that lead to quite different conclusions. And ethics can be tricky, subtle and relative. It is indeed a moral maze when making judgments about what is good, right and true.

In the business world there are checks and balances. There is the law, procedures and precedents, guidelines and recommendations. Some actions are pretty clearly wrong – ethically, morally and legally. Others less so.

But how and when and why do dubious and doubtful business practices become dangerous and duplicitous? Blame cannot be assigned exclusively to the avarice of individuals or the corruption of society. It is an organizational issue.

It seems that there are three factors that lead to a dark spiral of moral decline. They are recoverable, and there may be other factors that contribute. Yet case studies of a company's moral fall nearly all identify the same ones.

1. Impossible, unrealistic, unachievable targets
What gets measured gets (mis)managed. Measuring things changes them. They become more than a metric of success. They become the total focus of the whole enterprise. Soon the clever people start planning how to "fix" the stats or "bend" the figures to suit their strengths. The focus is exclusively on making the data look good. The more measures the better, to keep people straight. The more objective or observer-based rather than self-report, the better. But that is rarely the case.

Everyone has resisted measurement, from the "spy in the cab" objected to by lorry drivers in the 1960s to university lecturers, who were surprised and annoyed to find the "unlearned" would be encouraged to evaluate "the learned" via questionnaires.

There are different metrics in business, and some are more important than others: the share price; growth in pre-tax profit; market share; turnover;

net present value. Some are supplied by the company. Some have hard measures. Some statistics can be judged more easily than others.

Everybody loves a winner. A CEO who turns around or maintains a company's outstanding growth; someone with the magic touch. But there is always pressure and challenge to hit targets, increase market share. It is the bottom line that focuses all the attention. Its targets at all costs; the ends, not the means. And is it precisely this dissociation that causes the problems.

2. Corporate culture

This is little more than the implicit rules of how to behave – or the way things are done. All the text books call for an open, achievement-oriented, win–win culture that encourages communication, comradeship and a sense of community.

But many organizations' cultures are the very opposite. Closed, punishing and secretive, they are characterized by fear, back-stabbing and blind obedience to leaders.

There are acid tests: how bad news is dealt with. If no one wants to deliver it; most are concerned with covering it up; more interested in finding and punishing those who are responsible, you might be in trouble.

3. Groupthink

Identified more than fifty years ago, groupthink describes the behavior of teams (cabinets, boards) that get into serious trouble. These behaviors are specifiable and include such things as belief in the superior moral cause of your own position; a tendency to frequently belittle the opposition, and therefore be over-confident in your decisions and approach.

More importantly, there is strong pressure to appear unanimous behind the great leader, and to repress and self-censor voices of doubt or opposition. Indeed, mind-guards or whips are appointed to ensure that all sign up to the group's position.

There is, therefore, no serious debate. The group is coy, sycophantic and pusillanimous. That quiet, still voice of conscience never gets heard. The doubters are labeled traitors. They bow to the group or are terminated.

Watch out for companies under pressure to achieve with a dysfunctional culture and a group-thinking board. It will not take a lot to toss out, one-by-one, any ethical principles, so easily trumped and discarded to make everything look good.

Loyalty schemes

To be loyal means to be unswerving in allegiance. It means being faithful to a cause, an ideal or a custom. Loyalty is binding. Loyalty means overcoming doubts and temptations.

The stark reality of the definition makes a mockery of so-called loyalty schemes such as store cards or frequent flier programs.

Have you ever tried booking a flight using your loyalty-driven air miles? Ever worked out how much you have to spend on your supermarket loyalty card to get a "free" bottle of drinkable claret? Ever wondered how many times you have to stay at a particular chain of hotels to be "upgraded" to the executive floor with its small private lounge and free canapés at the cocktail hour?

Marketing people certainly know about, and strive after, loyalty. They know that the cost of holding on to customers – the so-called loyal repeat purchaser – is a fraction of the cost of finding new ones. So they try to lure you in, then handcuff you with schemes that, at least to the cynical, are a very bad deal.

The word loyalty seems wholly inappropriate for some schemes. Loyalty, you see, is a two-way process. Further, it is about honesty and trust and honour. How different from reality.

Take frequent-flyer air miles, a scheme invented in the 1980s and used (should we say abused?) in the 2000s by over 100 airlines. The promise is simple – if you fly with us we will reward every mile you fly. You can bank these as a sort of investment and then redeem them at your leisure. A good deal, it seems. The airline gets your repeat business and a wonderful database so that they can target you (sorry, market to your personal needs) more easily.

But the reality of these loyalty schemes is rather different from this simple and honest-looking proposition. *First*, you don't get air miles on some flights. It's about revenue rather than distance. So you might have to buy expensive and uncompetitively priced seats to gain air miles that are not worth the effort. A mile is not a mile. The currency is rather odd and not based much on geography. It seems based more on greed than on real distance.

Second, redeeming your investment is a nightmare, leaving many customers angry, confused and frustrated. Some allow for upgrades, others don't. Some routes seem embargoed. Others are, curiously, fully booked fourteen months in advance. Some require you to fly business class, eating up your miles more quickly. No wonder there are over 10 trillion unredeemed miles in the system.

The same is true of many other schemes, be they store cards or coupon-collection strategies. Occasionally, people calculate how much you have to spend to get some tangible reward, and it's a ludicrous amount.

So should loyalty schemes be labeled handcuff programs or bribe systems or a tax on the stupid and gullible? Is it just old *"caveat emptor"*? The product's promises and the stark reality are poles apart. Read the small print, shop around. Do your sums. It is not rational behavior.

But these schemes will continue – however bad they are for the average customer – for three reasons. The *first* is that, for certain products such as business-class travel, people do not generally pay for their own tickets. So it's no big deal paying way over the top for you to get air miles redeemable for a personal holiday. It's very different when others pay.

Second, the human condition accounts for a lot of these problems. Avarice, greed and vanity play their part. Getting something for nothing is as old a belief as it is naïve. Free lunches and all that! And then there are gold, platinum and diamond-studded membership cards, which discretely show your power, wealth and status. Loyalty schemes paradoxically pander to our basest and most banal needs.

Third, the marketing boys are often a step ahead. They do have real special offers. They do go into partnership with other organizations, creating a sort of new tax-free, electronic currency. To maintain status and appeal they re-brand, re-advertise and re-name frequently.

But it has very little to do with loyalty. Bribery yes, but faithfulness never.

The central question for the company is to define its objective. Is it to attempt to maximize customer retention; or to collect valuable data, or simply to make more money? And who precisely is the company aiming at: its elite, top-end customers, or those lower down the food chain. Do you know how customers perceive your offer, and their motivation for taking it up; or, of course, refusing it.

You want loyalty; repeat business; to be thought of as a supplier of preference. Sure, but so do your competitors. The question is how and whether your scheme does it better!

Magic links

Since the early 1990s there has been good evidence of a positive link between the work satisfaction rating of employees who have customer contact, and customer satisfaction. Happy employees are nicer to customers, who are then more satisfied with the service they receive. So companies have invested in programs and processes that monitor (and, they hope, increase) employee satisfaction.

But, as ever, it is a bit more complicated than that. Other factors play a part to strengthen or weaken the job satisfaction/customer satisfaction relationship. One German study published in a recent issue of *Psychology and Marketing* (2005, vol. 22, no. 5), tried to unpack the particular conditions under which salespeople work that result in job satisfaction and lead to stronger customer satisfaction – that is, how to strengthen the magic link.

Ideas for this magic link originated in balance theory. This suggests that a lack of balance causes both tension and a drive to restore balance. There are three elements in this model: are employee, customer and company. If the employee likes the company and the customer dislikes the company there is imbalance, which is solved by the employee "helping" the customer to like the company. Equally, when the employee's work satisfaction is low and customer satisfaction high, either party might change its satisfaction to ensure balance.

However, most assume that changes in customer satisfaction are more likely to change than employee job satisfaction, which is more stable and resistant to change.

This satisfaction relationship has been demonstrated across a wide range of industries including finance, hotel, security and retail sectors.

But what of other factors (called moderator effects) that strengthen or weaken this effect? The German study quoted above looked at three salesperson characteristics and three customer characteristics.

The first of the salesperson characteristics was *empathy* – the ability to express interest in, evaluate accurately and reflect another's thoughts, feelings and experience. This is both an intellectual and an emotional activity. Low employee empathy means lower-level customer interactions and hence lower customer satisfaction.

The second is *expertise* – quite simply knowledge about the company's products and services as well as a good understanding of its procedures. Expertise means efficiency; being good at solving problems. Customers like staff who are "on top of the job". Happy staff make an effort to learn the ropes.

Third, is *reliability* – which means that promises are met. Naturally, this means being (reasonably) honest and informative, and trying hard to honour implicit and explicit pledges.

And what of the customer? What features of the customer might strengthen the magic link? The first examined was *trust*, defined as perceived confidence in the supplier company's reliability and integrity. Trust means customers find out more about the salesperson and the company. The second was *price consciousness*. Those who are very price sensitive are probably less interested in other things (quality, sales, advice, reputation) and therefore don't tend to notice (or much care about) the salesperson's job satisfaction. Those who know the price of everything, as we know, understand the value of nothing.

Third, there was *product/service importance*: that is, how much the customer values and looks for a "quality interaction" with the sales staff. The more customers value it, obviously the more they look for it. This study interviewed over 200 sales staff and customers from very different areas (including automotive, banking, chemical and electronic sectors). The researchers were able to confirm their hypotheses. The most powerful of the customer factors was price consciousness, and the most powerful salesperson characteristic was empathy.

What does it all mean? If the average customer for the product/service is highly price-conscious, little interested in quality or service and somewhat distrusting of the organization, there seems to be little point in investing heavily in salesperson satisfaction. But if the reverse is true, to increase customer satisfaction dramatically, it seems particularly important to seek out warm, reliable staff who learn quickly.

In the world of sales "the customer is king". Sales managers worry about customer loyalty and satisfaction a great deal. For some, the cost of keeping customers is far less than finding new ones. One obvious implication is to invest in staff morale and satisfaction. If you have customers who value good service and are prepared to pay for it, this is a seriously good investment. The link really is magic then. A satisfied work force; happy, loyal customers; and a successful business.

Managerial versatility

Versatility is an Aristotelian virtue. It was thought of as the ability to perform in different, even contrary, modes. Versatile people are flexible, multi-talented, conceptually ambidextrous. The etymology refers to the easy of turning from one task to another, often its opposite.

Great strengths often belie great weaknesses (that is, developmental opportunities). Fortunate people discover their strengths early on in life. The number tumbler becomes even more mathematically sophisticated, because their facility leads to more experience and exposure, and hence more to greater expertise.

People usually become better at what they are good at. They also seek the company of like-minded individuals. And so we have silos of creatives and IT experts, data miners and people specialists. Diversity is unnatural; homogeneity much more comfortable and comforting.

The great virtue of versatility is that leaders and managers have the ability and skill to know when and how to switch into different modes. Consider three: some call it *task versus socio-emotional*; others structure versus consideration. Leaders have clear tasks – many of them, often complex, are usually not well formed. They have to keep the show on the road, beat the opposition, increase market share. But they also have stakeholders to consider, including employees and their families.

Decisions are made by both the head and the heart. One is influenced by the other, and they are often difficult to disentangle. The task-driven leader is supremely logical, action-oriented and focused, while the socio-emotional leader is caring, perceptive and trusted. The fault of too much task-orientation is to forget, neglect or minimize the human dimension in the whole process; and the fault of too much socio-emotional, morale-riented stuff is not to take tough decisions.

The best leader can turn to either mode at the right time. Be clear about the task then encourage people to do it. Or fire them up, then clarify the goal. Its not a matter of first one, then the other, but both, always.

Next there is the *strategic–operational distinction*: the big picture versus the day-to-day. Yes, leaders have to be visionary and imaginative. They need to anticipate, even create, the future. They need to keep an ear close to the railway tracks, hearing what is coming down the line.

The blue-sky stuff is important. It's future-oriented, strategy work. But there is also the here-and-now. That is ensuring efficiency, alignment and effectiveness in the daily operation of the business.

In some businesses, everyone works at one level below what their task requires. Directors manage, managers supervise, supervisors work. They find the transition from the operational to the strategic too difficult.

Equally, occasionally you find a strategist, possibly plucked from a smart business consultancy, who neglects the present for the future. Because he or she is so excited, or concerned, about "what the morrow might bring", any sense of his or her role in day-to-day affairs is lost.

Third, there is the dichotomy between the *forceful, commanding leader* and the *subtle, enabling leader*. Some managers, through force of intellect or charisma, or simply positional power, direct by giving orders and instructions. There is clearly a time and a place for this style. Many of the led like it. It's nice to know who is the boss, and what is to be done.

But there is also a role for enabling: working through others. Dictators, tyrants and demagogues don't enable, they order. And so they destabilize organizations when they go. There is nobody to take over. Nobody has been empowered, enabled or helped. There is a time to be forceful and a time to enable. But they seem related to rather different managerial characteristics.

There are other dimensions. There is the hands-on and the hands-off; the micro-managing and the distant monitoring. Many of these traits are related. So hands-off managers are often strategic and task-oriented.

But the moral of the story is simple. And the rather misleading metaphor is that it's about being left- or right-brained. The Jungians talk about a shadow side. Others talk of complementarity.

The truth is that great strengths too often belie great weaknesses, because it is too difficult to switch to the opposite mode when required. It seems for many as unnatural as writing with the non-preferred hand. Yet, adaptation to different tasks is pretty important in business. After all, the opposite of versatility is inflexibility.

Managing with heart and head

There are two types of people in the world: those who believe there are two types, and those who don't. Similarly, it is possible to divide management training: the cognitive and intellectual versus the emotional and affective; the hard versus the soft; the task versus morale.

All management training, allegedly, is aimed at producing better managers, who in turn yield better bottom-line results. They manage change and encourage better creativity; they don't buckle under pressure and are proactive. They know how to motivate themselves and others. They have better insight. And they have the courage to own problems and even to try to solve them.

As well as having the heart and the head, we have the visible and the hidden in organizations and their leaders. The formal, rational, objective organization is on display. Mission statements hang on concrete walls; there are sexy PowerPoint presentations about strategy. But there are hidden factors and forces. The visible is formal, rational and concrete. The hidden is informal, a-rational, often irrational and very abstract.

There are complex, subtle interpersonal processes and dynamics in every group, especially the board. And even those with self-awareness and insight might not be able to understand the unconscious motivation and intra-psychic conflicts of others. Hence the failed, derailed, incompetent manager. Those conflict-avoiding types who need too much to be liked; the lowly manager who is a tyrannical bully because of his inability to charm persuasively; the micro-managing perfectionist; and most of all the vainglorious narcissist: self-centred, pretentious, grandiose and haughty.

All leaders need help to become better at the task. They may take on a personal coach, or a small group of consultants. They may be able to diagnose their own developmental opportunities, or not. But they need to pay attention to the issues of the head *and* the heart.

They need to understand the big picture, have a helicopter view, see the trends. In short, they need to understand strategy. And they need good, old-fashioned courage to make the right decisions, even if they are difficult or unpopular. They need to be morally and interpersonally courageous: they need to be assertive in their daily lives – neither aggressive nor passive. Quietly but clearly assertive.

And they need to be warm, but no pushover. To be empathic, but not a softy. To be agreeable without being weak. They also need to be optimistic, positive and upbeat. They need to see the glass as half-full and to be able to see an opportunity in every drawback.

And, of course, they need to be aware of group dynamics. Call it teamwork or board processes, leaders need the psychological nous to be able to understand how to build, sustain and motivate a team.

Some call it *emotional literacy*. This really involves two things: being perceptive and being flexible. The emotionally literate manager understands his or her emotional life: what causes them tension and stress; where their emotions come from; and, most crucially, how to manage them. The manager might have taken anger or anxiety management courses, or he or she might be a natural. Managers need to understand, not deny or be frightened of, their own emotions.

Equally importantly, they need to be able to read others' emotions. They need to know what triggers powerful emotions in others, and how to recognize when this happens. They need to be able to read people well – body language, euphemisms and so on. And they need to be able to change emotions. Good actors, good speakers, good politicians know about the power of timing; of words of comfort or defiance or apology. They know how to work an audience. That too is emotional literacy. It's all the work of the heart.

Managers need the energy of youth, but the insight of maturity. Perhaps most of all they need self-insight or self-awareness, to be able to peep into the theatre of their inner world.

Many are called, but few are chosen for the role of leader. To be an architect and builder. To be both charismatic and sensible. To be focused but not a micro-manager.

To get the best out of oneself and others is certainly the key. To stretch people, giving them a sense of pride in their achievements and their organization. People do best when they have a strong sense of doing meaningful work, among people who have a sense of community and where, quite obviously, they are having fun.

Managers as masters

The concept of the master-class is regaining popularity. Once the domain of the great musician, many kinds of "experts", from sales people to television presenters, now offer expensive master-classes. These look suspiciously like repackaged seminars, perhaps with fewer people but at a higher cost.

One way of educating and training people in an important, often sublime, skill is through the apprentice relationship. Here, the master and the pupil workout a pupillage of, say, three years, while the master gently, firmly and wisely both imparts his/her insights and skills and also teases out the unique strengths of the learner.

It is a slow but well tried practice. And it remains to this day. Plumbers, electricians and mechanics still retain the concept, if not all the practice. It is certainly true in music. And it is the model for a Ph.D. – the supervisor is the master, and the graduate research student the apprentice. The aim is to make them equal, or at least equivalent in their skill base and outlook.

There are many more modern words for those who perform this service, of which the worst is "coach". Perhaps it's the mid-Atlantic fake enthusiasm associations that make it jar so much on European ears. Coaches are for teams, masters are for individuals.

A master (like a dog) is for life: masters leave an indelible impression on the outlook, skills and preferences of their pupils. The "hand of the master" can be seen in the pupil long after the relationship has ended. They live on through their pupils, who may in turn pass the baton to theirs.

But this does not happen by accident. Both parties spend some time finding each other: sniffing the other out; thinking about the relationship. Psychiatrists often have "preliminary" meetings with potential clients to see if they believe they can work together. It's about values, temperament and outlook.

Not all apprentice relationships work out. A good number "terminate" early. Some stagger on for ages. Others conclude but never fulfil. Masters develop a well-deserved reputation among peers and pupils for their abilities and care, but also their idiosyncrasies.

So what has this all got to do with management? Well, everything actually. Even in the largest companies, managers do their own hiring, with or without the assistance of HR. And it is not difficult to see that some are rather better at it than others. Further, having found the right person, they are able and willing to teach, groom and develop him or her. Third, they know when, how and why to let a person go, to everyone's benefit.

Perhaps these managers should be thought of as master managers: those who understand and meet the requirements of the apprenticeship system. They are a wonderful resource. They save the company a fortune. They increase morale and decrease turnover. They "seed" the organization with talent.

So how can the organization benefit from them? The first trick is to identify them. This can be done by using both official statistics from the performance management systems (PMS) and the grapevine, which always knows. This can yield plenty of data: the percentage leaving voluntarily or involuntarily; the percentage in the top band of the PMS system (that is, high flyers); and how quickly people climb the ladder successfully. The second is to find out how they choose – what they look for, what they do. The third is to watch and try to unpack the ingredients in their apprenticeship model. In short, to duplicate them.

How do master managers have a "third eye" in the selection process? Is this "mere intuition", "psychological-mindedness"; or a skill acquired by course-attendance or book reading? It is not at all clear. Nor is it obvious how they get the best out of their hires.

Those master managers spot something and really develop it. They are not alchemists. They find real gold and burnish and shape it till it gleams. And most enjoy the activity. Their legacy, their progeny, their contribution.

If you have a master manager or perhaps a raft of them responsible for pivotal jobs in the organization, your success factor must increase. The hiring factor does not decide the fate of the apprentice alone, but it does account for a great deal of the variance. Talented people left to wither on the vine or battle office politics soon go elsewhere.

It may not matter what you call these master managers, though the PC police will probably object to the sexist, neo-colonial, un-egalitarian concept. Good hiring managers, development managers, coaches – these are too bland and do not sum up the true essence of the activity. But don't sweat the small stuff on the title. Get looking for these people. They may be the best saviours of the company you ever have.

Meals at work

It used to be "a family that prays together stays together". Now it's a family that eats together is happier, healthier and stable. Many types of professionals recommend the multiple benefits of the traditional family meal: counsellors, dieticians, doctors and educational psychologists among them.

This is not just the Sunday roast, redolent of sepia pictures of the proud pipe-smoking and cardigan-clad head of household carving a steaming joint of best beef while a domesticated and dowdy mother flanked by perfect Enid Blyton children look on approvingly. This is *every* evening meal, and even breakfast.

Mealtimes encourage sharing. Sharing food, thoughts for, and of, the day, and problems. It encourages family talk; inter-generational interaction. It teaches skills, insight and knowledge. And it usually encourages better eating.

A therapeutic family meal does not consist of a whole family gulping down take-aways while staring at the TV. It is a media-free time of concentrating on others while sharing food. It may be in decline, but has been recognized belatedly as psychologically and physically important.

But what about meals at work? Certainly school meals have long been an important political and social issue. They are seen to have a significant educational impact from many points of view.

Despite being aware of all this, how many educated middle-class people eat with colleagues at work? Most gulp down a deli sandwich at their Dilbert desks while goggling at Google-found websites. And why? Well, there are the usual three reasons: not enough *time* (the pressure of work, deadlines and so on); the pressure of *money* (the canteen was closed; affordable diners aren't available); and the pressure of *convenience* (people prefer to eat different food at different times and in their particular way).

Yet we do go out for a meal together on high days and holidays: someone's birthday, Christmas, celebrating a promotion or a retirement. And, by and large, even without any excess, these occasions are really appreciated.

But is there any evidence that shared meals at work are good for *morale* and, dare one admit it, *profit*? The answer seems to be yes. Some organizations have experimented with "the works canteen", whatever it is called. They have done so in many ways, including radically changing the menu, outsourcing the whole thing, even redesigning the rooms. Some have tried to drive down costs in the belief that meals provide little bottom-line advantage, perhaps just the opposite. Others see it as a great investment to increase worker engagement and decrease alienation in addition to obvious advantages of better health (absenteeism) and mood (customer relations).

There are many advantages of eating together at work. *First* there is the physical stuff – ensuring people eat so that their work is not adversely affected by hunger. Whether it is hard physical, intellectual or emotional labour, we know people perform better when stoked up appropriately. It's a nutritional fact that people are less tired, make better decisions and take less time off if they eat meals at regular times.

Second, there are communication advantages. Meals encourage interaction, interaction leads to friendship and understanding and understanding to better, faster, more honest communication. Eating together is a primitive, but probably all-important, activity, known in all cultures, all religions and all time-periods. No doubt the socio-biologists can tell us why.

Third, it often helps morale. Food is seen as a benefit, and a nice place to eat it is a fair compensation for a cramped office. Conference organizers will tell you that feedback shows that the meals are considered to be more important than the speakers.

Studies have shown that staff morale in a chain of supermarkets was a function primarily of the canteen. It was the food, the ambience and the cleanliness that really contributed to morale, and its positive and negative indicators, such as absenteeism and turnover, productivity and good time-keeping.

But in hard times, when the cost-cutters appear, the canteen looks an easy target. The cost-reduction many occur step-by-step: certain things off the menu; hot food replaced by cold; reduced staffing; the enterprise outsourced. Or else it's quick and dirty or just closed down.

It is not easy to quantify the benefits of meals at work any more than to prove that advertising works. But those who have looked into the matter often feel the cost–benefit analysis suggests a good canteen is well worth it in terms of moral and job satisfaction. All organizations, not just armies, march on their stomach.

Office politics

Politics is a bad word. To many people, politicians come between used car dealers and estate agents in terms of trustworthiness – or indeed untrustworthiness. A heady mix of hypocrisy, spin and hubris means we have lost faith in politicians to do much for us. Everywhere, except where compulsory, we stop voting.

And yet, as Churchill remarked, we may not have a perfect system in democracy, but it is perhaps the best there is. Our politics are a *relatively* clean, transparent, uncorrupt operation. We have the rule of law, checks and balances, an open press.

We have national politics and local politics, but we also have office politics. What is this? Office politics seem to be a catch-all, supermarket trolley of wickedness: "He plays politics all the time"; "Office politics caused the failure"; "She was only promoted because of office politics" and so on.

It is certainly not easy being a politician. It probably never was except, of course, in totalitarian, one-party states where you don't have to bother too much about what people think. Or indeed about being re-elected.

Politicians have to be verbally enormously skilful. No doubt that explains why most politicians started life as lawyers and teachers. They have to be able to dodge questions, and read and interpret figures so that they suit their purpose. They have to inspire people to vote for them. And they have to make tough decisions. But to be "political" is nearly always a negative concept. At best it means shrewd. It means taking into account all the features of a situation, and all the shareholders, and doing a fine, persuasive balancing act to leave them satisfied with their decision.

What are the key features of the concept? *First*, perhaps, is the secrecy, the covert agendas, the underhandedness of it all. Politics conducted in smoky rooms, behind closed doors, in private clubs, on the golf course. There are the insiders and the outsiders. The players and the pawns. Those in the know and those in the dark. Politics are exclusionary. Office politics are about processes, procedures and decisions that are not meant to be scrutinized. Politics are about opaqueness, not transparency.

Second, there is impression management. Another word for this may be hypocrisy. Office politicians (all unelected) speak with forked tongue. The clever ones understand the difference between sins of omission and commission. The others just dissimulate. What you see, hear and read is not what you get. Internal communications (except those carefully encrypted) are half truths, little more than management propaganda. Office politics are about censorship; about disguise.

Third, office politics are about self-interest. They are concerned with power and all the trappings, such as money and prestige. About select groups high-jacking activities, processes and procedures to secure their (and only their) interests. Covert groupings of individuals based on clan, ideology or simply greed, cooperate with each other to obtain an unfair share of the resources of an organization. In this sense, office politics act against long-term organizational interests, at least from a shareholder perspective.

The negative view is clear. Politics cause distrust, conflict and lowered productivity. People do not openly share; they are guarded. They spend too much time and energy ingratiating themselves with the in-group and try to work the system. The in-group are as much concerned with increasing or holding on to power as steering the company. The opposition is internal, not external. Office politics are dysfunctional.

But there is another perspective, and it's much more positive. Office politics are about building and strengthening networks and coalitions. About getting together movers and shakers prepared to do the hardest thing of all – make change happen. About driving through necessary but unpopular strategies. About identifying those with energy and vision – those who command various constituencies.

Yes, politics are about power – the power to influence, persuade and cajole. Most organizations seek out and admire a CEO who is well respected and connected. One who knows how to "play the game"; how to get people (investors, journalists, and "real" politicians) on side. In this sense, being political is about being shrewd, pro-active and strategic.

CEOs have to present a positive picture of their organization. They have to align, steer and change the organization. And they need help. They turn to those who have a reputation for doing so.

You can't outlaw office politics. You might want to blame everything from personal failure to falling share price on office politics, and there is no doubt that some offices are dysfunctional places to be. But better to study and try to understand management power than to condemn it.

Optimal ethics

The topic of ethics is no longer restricted to rather dry courses in philosophy and theology, learning the meaning of big words such as consequentialism, deontology or utilitarianism. Moral philosophers and psychologists write a great deal about ethics, though they may use synonymous concepts such as integrity, justice and social conscience. They may even prefer more old-fashioned words such as virtue, or charity.

All businesses are confronted by ethical questions such as:

- Should a company place the interests of its shareholders before those of its employees or of the environment?
- Should a company be responsible for all the social consequences of its operations?
- When is regulation necessary, when excessive, and when counter-productive?
- What does a corporation "owe" its employees?
- To what extent should an organization be accountable for its products?
- Is there an ethical difference between tax avoidance and tax evasion?
- Is the only social responsibility of business to maximize profits?

And most say they adhere to various fundamental principles such as:

- Be honest to stakeholders.
- Stick to values despite financial loss.
- Fulfill commitments.
- Avoid conflicts of interest.
- Respect the rights of others.
- Take responsibility for actions.
- Treat stakeholders fairly.
- Avoid unnecessary harm.
- Act benevolently.
- Obey the law.
- Protect the environment.

A radical alternative to the emphasis placed on business ethics was proposed by Friedman (1980), who argued that businesses should concentrate on producing goods and services efficiently and legally, in open and free competition and without deception and fraud, and that socio-ethical problems should be left to concerned individuals and government agencies.

Others argue that organizations and the business community do have some responsibility to act in what they see to be the interests of society, and to pursue and advocate ethical positions.

The late Robin Cook introduced, and then swiftly swept under the carpet, Great Britain's *ethical foreign policy*. Now hospitals, schools and universities have *ethics committees*, whose job it is to assist with just, fair and principled decision-making ... and to avoid litigation. Ethical concepts are bandied about in business schools, and there are now semi-serious academic journals and books all about *business ethics*. And, of course, we now have *bio-ethics*.

Those who really know something about this area know that there are different, distinct and often contradictory ethical positions. Thus some have distinguished between principle, social and rule-following conscience. If you prefer, you might use the terms virtue/value ethics, utilitarianism/ consequentialism and deontological/law-based ethics. The different principles of the different systems lead to different answers.

Thus an ethical committee of deontologists looks more like a group of lawyers, while one of virtue ethicists looks more like a group of (highminded) philosophers. They would come to different conclusions because they apply different ethical principles.

But perhaps the most interesting feature of ethics is the concept of optimality, not linearity. In the world of business, people look for human virtues, rather provisionally called competencies. So recruiters and selectors look for team-players with analytic minds able to take a helicopter view. They require their leaders to be innovative and creative, cool under fire, great at communication, and much more.

But recently there has been some interesting work, mainly born out of psychiatry, which suggests that there is a dark side to nearly every competency. The dark side lies essentially in excess. You can, very simply, have too much of a good thing. Being too creative may mean also being seriously impractical; being too analytical may mean being prone to decision paralysis. To be a great team worker may hide an inability to think for yourself, and taking the global view may too often make you blind to local circumstances.

And the same applies to ethics. The ancient Greeks listed the great and distinct virtues, but they knew too that virtue can all too easily also be a vice. So let's take a few of the well-known virtues and unpack their meaning, and indeed dangers.

Remember prudence? Not a maiden aunt living in Eastbourne, but having good sense and good measure. The prudent are wise, cautious and mindful of the rights of others. Prudent people are discreet and circumspect. Too much prudence results in over-cautious timidity, while too little results in impulsive recklessness. To be prudent means to be canny and exercise good judgement. Hence, perhaps, Prime Minister Gordon Brown's love of the word.

And what of fortitude … such an old-fashioned word. It means patient endurance; calm in the face of calamity; courageous in dealing with adversity and setback. Too much of this virtue and one might find dogged, zealous stubbornness, combined with a callous disregard for danger. Too little and there is weakness, laziness and a lack of moral fibre.

Temperance: a virtue for ever linked to the anti-booze lobby and one of the most disastrous social experiments of all time. It means to be moderate in all things, particularly in the indulgence of the appetites. The temperate are self-disciplined and self-controlled; they are patient, restrained and modest. The intemperate are those who do excess, indulgence and emotional outbursts. They are often impatient, impulsive and childlike in their "nowness" and their indolent indulgences.

And faith? Meaning trust, loyalty and commitment. The over-faithful are naïve, perhaps even gormless. But "ye of little faith" can be cynical, skeptical and angry. Those who had, then lost, their faith can indeed be dangerous people.

And so it goes on with the other virtues: hope, love, justice, charity. Too many people are worried about not finding enough evidence of a virtue. The wise are equally concerned about finding too much!

Reference

Friedman, Milton and Friedman, Rose D. (1980) *Free to Choose: A Personal Statement*. San Diego/New York: Harcourt.

Organization ASBOs

We are people of the head and the heart. We are ruled, we like to think, by our heads. We like to believe, particularly at work, that we are cool, rational, cognitive beings, but deep down we are not. Irrational and affective forces play a big part in what we do, and how and why we do it.

We are emotional beings. Emotions serve a function. We have positive and negative, bright and dark emotions. At work they are triggered by rude customers and caring friends; by achieving or failing to achieve our goals; by praise from a boss; by help-seeking behavior from a colleague.

They matter most because, essentially, we all have two things to do at work. It used to be called task versus socio-emotional, now it's called task versus contextual. What it means is that we have core tasks in our jobs. These are often skill-based, technical and knowledge-based activities for which people are trained. Pilots are trained to fly aircraft, surgeons to operate on bodies, salespeople to sell the product.

But there is a second, softer aspect to any job. It's the way you do it. It's the soft stuff. It's how you tackle tasks with energy and optimism or grudging unwillingness. It's about playing the game, obeying the rules, going the extra mile. It is about what you say about the organization outside work – defending, endorsing, even selling the brand. It's about volunteering and being cooperative.

In short, it is about being a good citizen of the organization. All those old-fashioned words such as courtesy, civil virtue and conscientiousness.

The thing about this critical but not core stuff is that it can come in good and bad forms. Nice or nasty. Cooperate or complain. Bright or dark. The soft stuff is not usually found in the job description.. It's shaped by personality and emotions, and is not often a cause for sacking or disciplinary action. Unless, of course, it gets really bad.

There is now a real concern about dysfunctional, antisocial behavior at work. Aggression, bullying, deviance and violence happen in both the playground and the workplace. The yob culture, public rudeness and general incivility has spread to the workplace.

Nasty, uncivil contextual behavior has been called counter-productive work behavior. It means that while people might technically fulfill the task requirements of the job, the way they do it is frankly appalling. This can range from a mild interpersonal rudeness to an intention to damage the organization and the people in it.

The milder forms are that everyday discourtesy: not being greeted or thanked; abrupt, demeaning, demanding orders and emails; infantilizing support staff; fouling public areas with no attempt to clean things up; malicious gossiping; invasion of private workspace; keeping people in the dark. It's the behavior of the angry and alienated; of the disaffected and disillusioned; of those with the "whatever" attitude.

Some people spread a virus of cynicism about the place they work in. They are critical and cynical, disparaging and disgusted. They continually attack the integrity of the organization, often very publicly pointing out hypocrisy, unfairness and betrayal. They argue again and again that their organization is opportunistic, expedient and deceitful – quite the opposite of what it publicly says about itself. Some do serious sarcasm. Others simply withdraw into a lethargic "don't care" state.

But there are bad behaviors that are much more serious, even illegal. These include theft, sabotage and abuse. Fortunately, these are a minority sport.

The easy route for the organizationally uncivil cynic is that long list of small everyday behaviors that grind everyone down. The abuse of power; the busybody; micro-managing interference; the incessant back-stabbing. It is no wonder that all those books on how to manage a boss from hell sell so well. They list the types – asshole, bore, bully, and discuss how to deal with them.

Perhaps we could have the idea of an OASBO – an Organizational Antisocial Behavior Order. A recognition of destructive nastiness in certain individuals. A sort of yellow card.

Is this all too big-brother, nanny-state-ish? Is this a Peter Pan or Disney vision of organizations that never existed, or can never be created? So what is all the fuss about the soft stuff?

The answer is that it really does matter. The everyday organizational civility shapes and maintains the culture and the climate of the organization. It is a mood and emotion regulator. It affects deeply all the social and relational issues in the organization.

To be surrounded by energetic, supportive and appreciative people really makes a difference. They can ward off and reduce all the stress at work. They make the workplace warm and safe.

The incivility of everyday life, the yob culture with its self-indulgent, cynical rudeness has invaded the workplace. People don't help each other like they used to. Politeness, helpfulness and support seem lost. And they do make a difference. Anti-social behavior spreads like a virus.

But is the solution the work-place ASBO? Doubtful. Yet it could signal the simple, but important fact that the organization values the soft stuff, that some workers are really more trouble than they are worth; and that managers simply will not tolerate rude, belittling and uncooperative staff.

Organizational philistinism

In business, there is much talk of values. CEOs chant mantras about their (carefully scripted) personal and organizational values. These may have been suggested, approved, improved or moderated by the PR, HR or even industrial relations (IR) people.

This usually means a list of bland, positive words or phrases that are not (perhaps never could be) wrapped up into a coherent philosophy. So we have integrity and courage and innovation, and other world ideals.

Philistinism, always used pejoratively, is, in essence, a specific set of values. Philistines despise (all but the most simplistic representational) art; they are anti-intellectual, dismissing many issues as "merely" academic questions; and they don't do spiritual anything. Philistines favor materialism over spiritualism; to have, not to be; to have toys more than friends. They appear uncritically to accept the conventional social values of their time and group. Dictators like philistines.

In the nineteenth century, the philistines' enemy was the bohemians. The latter were usually seen as avant-garde, bourgeois people with an "artistic" temperament. Philistines have been called barbarians, vulgarians, boors and anti-intellectuals.

So be it. But, though they would hate the label and the accusation, could most, or at least many, well-known organizations be described as philistinistic? Take four components of the concept and see how they apply:

- *Conventionalism*: Most organizations are terrified of being different despite all that PR/HR speak about innovation. That is why they do "benchmarking". They want to be the best at what everyone else does. They would like to have new products. They love to differentiate themselves from their competitors, but in terms of issues such as staffing, outsourcing, and so on, they are often conformist straight-down-the-line. Most organizations were very pleased to see the end of the dot com pretenders. They really were bohemians in what they thought and did and aspired to. Deeply threatening young people who got their just "comeuppance".
- *Materialism*: If the organization is in manufacturing or finance it is most certainly materialistic in many senses. Only material things are real and important. They believe money is a powerful motivator. They assume job satisfaction is a function of office size, or furnishings: that

car parking facilities are as crucial as friendship networks; and that power, status and money are the ultimate aphrodisiacs. Western countries have certainly become materialist societies. For many, to possess luxury goods is seen as the main goal of life. That's conventional now, even more in the Second than the First World. If you don't quite understand the concept of philistinism, watch a few shopping channels.

- *Anti-intellectualism*: Intellectualism is about curiosity; about questioning. Intellectuals want to know how things work; what is the philosophical underpinning of various policies. Some enjoy pointing out the contradictions, and even hypocrisy, in organizational life. Philistines despise intellectuals as time-wasting, meddling, unproductive wasters. One organization makes a policy of never hiring those with a PhD. because they believe holders of such degrees are not only over-educated, but also imbued with the university ethos of intellectualism. The anti-intellectuals like to see themselves as practical realists. They tend to do black-and-white, not grey. How many organizations are bookless zones? How many think blue-sky research time-wasting twaddle? Consultants who try to introduce new thinking or produce models that try to understand complex processes are despised. Many well-qualified people in philistinistic organizations have to hide the evidence of their degrees or learning. It's too threatening to others, and against the ethos of the organization. And as for asking theoretically-based questions in meetings: that is all evidence of a career-ending strategy.

- *Aesthetic values*: Although it has been acceptable to waffle on about spiritual intelligence (indeed, everything intelligence) it is considered suspect to talk about beauty or art or meaning. Talk of authenticity is more about egocentrism than anything else. The Nazis talked about decadent art. Most organizations are prepared to spend thousands on rebranding, logo changing and the like. Ever seen any challenging art in an organization? That's not necessarily modern art. Look at screen-savers. The epitome of kitsch: those photographs of idyllic nature scenes with some trivial line about team work or customer service. How about a Cubist or surreal painting of the board; how about a difficult customer pickled in formaldehyde? Andy Warhol has become popular, but he did the unthinkable and unacceptable in his time.

Do you work for a philistine organization? Scrape away the PR gloss and look at the place. Is it an art-free, anti-intellectual shrine to materialism, wrapped up in the conventional values of our time? There are, of course, exceptions: corporate sponsorship of the arts is a serious issue, but cynics see this is compensatory and clever advertising and little more.

Score each of the four dimensions on a ten-point scale where 10 is high. If the score is over 30, but you like the values of the organization, some wastrel of a dangerous pinko might suggest you are a philistine in a philistine organization.

Overcoming mediocrity

To be mediocre means to be conspicuously lacking in distinction or imagination. It means to be average: neither good nor bad, yet it is usually used as a seriously pejorative adjective. Mediocre is worse than run of the mill: it implies not good enough; in fact, bad.

There are certainly mediocre workers. But most are made mediocre by mediocre management practices. You often see and experience this most dramatically when a restaurant changes hands. It can go from five stars to one star in weeks. Many restaurant reviewers delight in puncturing the pomposity of restaurateurs whose dull menus and unimaginative cooking are matched by surly service in sepulchral surroundings.

One of the oddest characteristics of mediocre organizations is the extremely naïve belief that you can, or indeed should, try to abolish or prevent mediocrity not by primitive denial, but rather through trumpeting hypocritical mission and vision statements about "number one", "leading", "organization of choice." Perhaps that sort of hubris is itself a good index of mediocrity?

What are the signs of mediocrity? Perhaps the clearest causal factor is related to alignment. Individuals, teams, groups, sections, silos or whatever you want to call them are not pulling in the same direction. This is partly because they do not know which direction to pull in. That is, there is no clear strategy, targets, key performance indicators (KPIs), key result areas (KRAs), etc. Either the top management do not know, or fundamentally disagree about, what business they are in. Or else they have not really communicated it to their staff.

There are two other clear indices of poor alignment. The first is that various specialist groups (Accounts or HR or Marketing) are more dedicated to their own ends than to pulling their weight in the organization. They see their peers or other departments as competitors for resources. They enjoy power play. They rate how they are doing by social comparison with other departments. This is divisive competitiveness.

Groups lose sight of their central tasks. They lose sight of their real customers. They lose sight of their true competitiveness and competition, because they are competing with each other. Group self-interest and plain egocentric, egotistical self-interest are the order of the day.

Worse than maladaptive and misdirected competitiveness is the urge to sabotage the efforts of other teams. Not content just to beat them, in some organizations they are actually undermined.

The alignment issue begins with some pretty simple performance management ideas, including seeing that individuals and teams have explicit and well-defined objectives. Next, performance is measured and related to rewards. Managers without these systems often become, and are certainly perceived to be, whimsical, subjective, biased ... or worse, not really that concerned with performance.

Strong, successful organizations have structures and processes aimed at fulfilling its core tasks. This means that strong personalities, pet projects and professional preferences (and jealousies) are unable to distract people from their central tasks. Focus, energy and resources need to be directed towards theses central tasks, not towards self-advancement or running down colleagues.

Yet the cult of the superstar, the Übermensch, the saviour of the company, is often perpetrated by those at the top. Intoxicated by power and influence, they come to confuse organizational success with individual success. They sacrifice long-term for short-term goals, and the well-being of all stakeholders for their personal agenda.

Of course, it's about more than structure and process. People need to be well-selected, properly trained and motivated. But mediocre managers can feel deeply threatened by hardworking and competent employees. So either they don't get selected or they leave the company, disaffected by scheming, political and unproductive managers.

And so a culture of mediocrity originates. Mediocre organizations are not uncommon in the service sector, partly because service organizations have never been good at performance management. Local councils, government departments and state-run industries used to be the very epitome of mediocrity. Performance was never seriously measured, sacking was next to impossible, and selection was a sham.

The major change strategy for the mediocre organization is the shock therapy of real performance management to replace the bureaucratic service ethic.

First, clarify the overall goals, targets and tasks of the whole organization. Avoid the flimflam, hollowspeak of mission statements.

Second, do the same for teams and groups, and make sure they understand how their effort contributes to the whole. This means getting the structure right; not just the wall chart. It may involve a bit of pruning or re-engineering. But get the links right.

Third, ensure that the productivity of individuals and groups is properly assessed. And rewarded.

Fourth, set a good example of openness, cooperativeness and hard work. Walk the talk. Don't do ethical talk when you don't mean it or show it.

Fifth, celebrate success, and reward effort. Do this openly, regularly and conspicuously when, and only when, it is totally deserved.

Sixth, understand the difference between the spirit of the law and the letter of the law. So don't go too hard, too quickly, on imposed procedures and policies. Remember that form-filling, cover-your-back processes are the hallmarks of mediocrity.

Seventh, get those involved in the change to have some say in how it is introduced. Beware terrorists, cynics and snipers – but use them to expose the weakness of the old system.

Eighth, don't waste money on all that ephemeral feel-better stuff (new furnishings, conferences, climate surveys). Productive, above-average companies have better engagement, and better employee relations, as a result.

Ninth, make a big thing of those who embrace the new culture and bypass those who are sentimental about the squabbly past.

And *tenth,* get on with it: mediocrity leads to organizational death.

Post-modern management

Just before we enter the post-post-modern era, it's perhaps worth worrying whether this radically new philosophy can help the faddish world of management. Post-modernism certainly influenced all the arts. From poetry to painting, and especially philosophy, literary criticism and many of the social sciences, the doctrine of the post-modernist has swept all before it.

So what precisely is it? Well, that depends on who you read. It is characterized by the following ten trends:

1. A rejection of grand ideologies, often called "meta narratives".
2. A skepticism towards fixed values and any sort of certainty.
3. An erosion of the distinction between high culture and popular culture.
4. A belief in decentralized control.
5. A rejoicing in pluralism and disunity.
6. A deconstruction of the fundamentals of all knowledge.
7. A fragmentation of identity and the real self.
8. A rejoicing in transnational consumerism and globalization.
9. A recognition of the powerful role of the media to both re-create and transform reality.
10. A deep disillusionment with the faith of the Enlightenment.

Oh dear; not sure that helps a lot. Put more simply, post-modernism is an "anything goes" philosophy. There is no good or bad, right or wrong, better or worse, saved or damned, us or them. There is no bedrock, no shining path, no best practice.

But this is not a case of "it all depends"; it's very complex. It's a rejection of the spirit of the Enlightenment. It rejects empiricism as a way to the truth.

Can it, has it, will it, influence management thinking? Well yes – and no. To some extent there are post-modern themes in modern management writing. All that talk of *empowerment* is about the decentralization of control. Equally, the obsession with *diversity* is a recognition of, and indeed rejoicing in, pluralism. Talk of *global brands* and one-world markets is a recognition of the limitations of nationalism.

And certainly management knows about the power of both the old and the new media. This is much more than simple advertising. All executives have to undertake media training. A careless "Ratnerism" can have multi-million-pound consequences (Gerald Ratner was the CEO of a jewelry business who unwisely made jokes about the poor quality of his own products and in doing so brought down his whole multi-million-pound business). We know that the media create heroes and villains, by creating, transforming, underlining and distorting reality. We have always known that. But new businesses are exploiting the idea.

But (fortunately perhaps) much management speak and writing is the very antithesis of the post-modernist agenda. Rather than rejecting faith, certainty, specific (albeit old-fashioned) values, business chappies champion them. You want the "new faith" in a post-Christian world? Try good old-fashioned materialism. Business people, be they writers or trainers, consultants or gurus, always write with certainty. They peddle silver bullets, ideas for magic potions, concepts and techniques that solve all problems. Read the Quality Circle, Business Re-Engineering or Emotional Intelligence books. This is not a world of doubt, skepticism or cynicism. This is not a world of relativism, where any technique is equally good or bad.

Business does modernism, indeed rejoices in it. It is still a Brave New World. In fact braver, newer and shinier than ever. Post-modern management? A bit like business ethics, military intelligence and social science. A touch of the oxymoron!

If you read business books you could not get further away from the post-modernist vision of the world. They assert all sorts of things anathema to post-modernists. These include:

- Universability – the formula works everywhere for all people.
- Managerial control – the formula rightly gives managers extra control.
- Changeability – people can, should and want to be changed for the betterment of the organization.
- Simplicity – good (silver-bullet) management techniques are simple, straightforward and behavioral.
- Individualism – individuals, not groups or society is, or should be, the focus of management.

Professional stress

Is it the stress industry that is responsible for the constant stream of reports of stress among our professionals? The clergy are stressed, so are policemen. Civil servants buckle under it, and transport workers can, it seems, no longer take it.

But it is people in the health and educational sectors who now seem to be complaining of stress as never before. Is this just fashionable griping in an attempt to get some compensation, or a very genuine response to changing circumstances? A good case could certainly be made for the latter.

Many doctors and nurses, lecturers and teachers are finding that resources are down, more closely rationed, or monitored. It is also clear that, in society as a whole, respect for professionals is lower. Their roles no longer automatically command admiration or confer status.

The media seem to exaggerate this problem by highlighting professional misconduct, incompetence and general slackness. There are too many Dr Shipmans and not enough Dr Kildares; too many St Trinian's teachers and not enough Mr Chips.

At the same time, government control at all levels (call it interference) has greatly increased. Added to this, customer expectations and assertiveness have increased. The ever-litigious clients seem increasingly ready to try to punish professionals if they are disappointed with their advice or service.

At least there used to be early retirement. Now the government who started the problem wants them to go on enduring this nightmare for even longer ... ideally, dying before retirees put pressure on pensions.

It's easy to understand why certain groups complain about stress. The hours and responsibility of the junior house doctors; the challenges of the inner-city teachers dealing with "feral" children.

The trouble with stress is that it leads to vicious circles. Stressed people often use inappropriate coping methods, such as alcohol, which actually increase stress. Stress leads to anxiety and depression, which lead to poorer decision-making, memory and concentration, and which in turn lead to both accidents and absenteeism.

There are, of course, various predictors of stress: individual personality and coping style; work–life balance; age and stage and other commitments; the wisdom of the career choice; and whether it's a good fit.

Sometimes the personality factors that lead to early success lead on to failure. The perfectionist with high standards can easily become very stressed as a result of being unable to meet them. Self-criticism that acted as a motivator early on easily turns into immobilization and doubt. The benefit of high self-esteem can develop into a paradoxical narcissism.

To experience stress is not uncommon or unusual. But how individuals cope with it is very important. Avoiding the problem by denial or distraction does not help. Nor do prayers, booze or litigation. Getting fit, calling for social support and tackling the problem logically work best.

Doctors need their own doctors. Teachers need to be taught how to recognize and respond to stress. Both need stress management techniques and career counseling.

At the simplest, but perhaps most parsimonious level, consider two factors that lead to stress: demand and discretion. *Demand* is the quantity and quality of workload. This is easy to measure. We are all encouraged to do more work with less support and fewer resources. Demand refers to how much: how many patients we are required to see in a day; how many students we have to get through their exams; how many peer-reviewed papers to write. Not enough demands and we get bored, but too many and we get stressed.

Demand is a killer if we are required to do many important (life-or-death; succeed-or-fail) things, rapidly, faultlessly and to a tight deadline. Demand can easily overcome supply. There is an optimal amount for everyone. But politicians, senior managers and others do not like to hear that.

Along with demand there is *discretion*. Another word is *choice* or *control*. This is the ability to exercise some personal control as to how, when and where the work is done, and what the outcome is. All low-discretion jobs are miserable: cleaners have low discretion (but often tolerably low demands). Assembly workers have low discretion, but arguably have high demands on quality and quantity or output.

Those with low demand and high discretion could be seen to be in ideal, hobby, post-retirement sorts of jobs, though they could be prone to boredom. But high-demand jobs – those of lawyers or doctors, for example – can be made tolerable by high discretion: give me choices, give me control, give me options and I can deliver.

But this is the rub. Professionals in the high-demand, high-discretion box have found that they are being pushed into the *very* high-demand, but lower-than-before discretion box. They are asked to do more with less, whether they like it or not, at a particular place, within a particular time frame, and in a particular way. Quirky, idiosyncratic approaches are frowned on.

No wonder our professionals are taking early retirement in droves. No wonder there is a shortage of doctors and teachers. Things ain't what they used to be ... and stress is on the rise as a result.

Pro-retirement

To retire is to withdraw, retreat, recede. You can retire from work and retire from the world to become a recluse. You can retire into yourself, becoming uncommunicative and unsociable. You can retire well, both at cricket and from a job. But you can retire hurt, retire angry, retire unwillingly and unhappily.

In the old days people retired to live a last few years, often in poor health, before they died. The image was of the individual with declining power, prestige and influence. Sucked dry, spat out, of little use to family or society as a whole.

Retired people were old people. Some seemed to adjust pretty well. They reorganized their life-style and their priorities. Others focused on a few satisfying leisure activities. Some disengaged, withdrawing to pipe and slippers.

Poorly adjusted retired people can look angry as well as apathetic. They become passive-aggressive snipers. Others become depressive, believing they have nothing more to give and that nobody cares about them any more.

Some retired people try to "hold on". They appear defensive, unwilling to recognize or admit that they have retired. They keep busy; they drive themselves hard. They find hobbies that replace their jobs in everything but salary.

Now retirement has a positive image. But there are caveats. Happy early retirement requires several things:

- Good physical and mental health.
- Adequate finances – which is, indeed, a moving target.
- A vibrant and largish social support network.
- A structured, intrinsically motivating activity.

It is the last point that is perhaps the most interesting and paradoxical. Happily retired people need a sort-of job or occupation. They need something to give them a sense of purpose, in co-operation with other people, which they find interesting and valuable.

But now people retire earlier and live longer. They might have thirty years of life after retirement. So things have been changing. *First,* because the one-job-for-life era appears to have passed, people now retire more than once. They may retire many times, becoming serial retirees. There may be retirement villages, but there are also retiring occupations.

Second, employers rather like these young-old retirees. It used to be believed that you should never trust anyone over 30 years of age. Now it is the opposite. The older employee is seen as more conscientious, more socially skilled, more trusted and more trustworthy.

Third, the clear distinction between working and retirement is now increasingly blurred. There are volunteers who do unpaid work with all the appearance (and benefits) of work, but no salary. There is a wide variety of part-time jobs, from the well-heeled non-executive director to the shop assistant who works morning only.

Retired people may be called back to work at a time of crisis to be an interim manager, a position they really enjoy. They feel valued, important, pleased to help out. Certainly, professionals who retire are often very different from the less skilled. They like to keep their identity and title. Hence Emeritus Professor, or Captain Smith RN (Retired). And their years of education make them adaptable and eager to learn.

Many volunteer organizations are heavily staffed by retired people who were brought up with the motto *pro bono publico*. Both managers and volunteers benefit from the experience.

So, has retirement become a dirty word? People in the City all want to make their millions by the time they are, say, 40 . . . and then have a "real" life. All they are retiring from is the grind, the stress, the tedium of those deeply extrinsically, but not very intrinsically, motivating jobs.

The boundary between work and leisure; between vocation and vacation; between career and post-career is blurring. And so it should be.

Many people are more amused than relieved at getting a bus pass or a special heating allowance. They eschew pipe and slippers, rocking chair and daily paper, the allotment and the homely image of retirement that their parents had.

Retirement is a state of mind; not a calendar date. It's not the end phase of the journey, but another phase of the journey. It's nothing to be ashamed of. But it needs repackaging. We now have senior citizens, oldies, retirees and veterans – but none of this renaming really captures the nature of the beast.

The cost of this to any country and its citizens means we shall have to keep going longer. But many of us do not look at this with fear and dread. Yes, there are jobs that probably no old (or young) person relishes – traffic warden, dustman, for example. And there are jobs where one has to be fit, dextrous and alert enough to do well, which may well put a ceiling on age.

But there are many jobs in the burgeoning service industry that can give a retired person something to do, a structure to the day, a little pocket money, a group of friends, and a sense of purpose. In this sense, jobs prolong, not shorten, lives.

Psychometric flimflammery

Bewildered by the choice of psychometric tests on the market? Confused by test publishers and consultants? But eager to look professional and delve below the superficiality of the interview?

Here is a simple test of the worth of any psychometric measure. Test 1: Go to any test; it's easily done online. Don't read the questions, but randomly tick or click yes or no; agree or disagree; often, sometimes, never ... whatever the test requires. Do this at least three times on the same test. Then ask for the feedback, either from a computer-based test engine or a qualified feedback provider.

There are three things to look for in the results. *First,* how easy is it to differentiate the three "readings". If they appear to be fairly similar, "we have a problem, Houston".

Next, look at the bland, non-specific positivity of the findings. One famous personality theorist and textbook writer did exactly this. The following is the sort of feedback he got.

- You hate to miss out on what is going on around you.
- You strive to be authentic and genuine, and you communicate well with others.
- You want to be liked and admired by others.
- You are interested in new ideas.
- You dislike bureaucracy.
- You enjoy learning new things and have good self-discipline.
- You have a great deal of charm and others genuinely like you. At times your attention span can be short. While you can be intellectual, serious, and all business, you are also capable of flipping the switch and becoming childlike.
- You always try to tell the truth to those around you.

This feedback is bland, positive and true of most people. It's called the Barnum Effect – people naïvely believe things are specifically true of them, when they are probably true of everybody (or wished to be true).

The *third* factor is related to the second. Real tests have to deliver tough messages. They have, where appropriate, to point out that you are neurotic or a psychopath; dim or well below average; emotionally unintelligent; or deeply uncreative. But people don't like negative feedback and find it easier to shoot the psychometricians and reject the test than accept the findings.

So bad tests do one of three things to cope with this problem. *First,* they don't measure crucially important facets of personality – such as adjustment – simply because it's too problematical to give feedback under certain conditions. *Second,* the feedback is rarely done in cold clinical numbers (for example percentiles), but is wrapped up in bland, non-specific, culturally acceptable platitudes. *Third,* while positive feedback is specific, negative feedback is general and cloaked in a positive shroud. So scoring low on a creativity test you are not "very uncreative" but "very hands on and practical". You are not "disagreeable, unempathetic and ruthless", but a "shrewd, focused business person".

The problem for the test consumer is threefold. *First,* the cost-to-market investment to produce a passable test is low. Despite attempts to regulate this market, the internet and other issues make it impossible. Those with an eye to fashion, the Zeitgeist and a quick buck will have a test on the market as soon as they spot an opportunity. Bestseller business books and super-confident and garrulous CEOs are a great incentive.

Second, being non-specialists, it is difficult for consumers to differentiate between tests. There is no simple "Which? guide" with all those little stars that provide both the criteria worth applying and the test ratings. How do you decide between one website and another? Between a Jungian, Cattellian or Eysenckian test? Many consumers fall for the smart packaging (literally), their consultants' (possibly biased) advice, and the oldest trick of all – personal validation. Test sales people ask you to take their tests, give you all that bland, positive, true-of-everyone guff (see above), and then you buy.

Third, what do you do with the results anyway? In many ways the process is circular. You tell the psychologists how you behave and they then put a label on that behavior. The question, of course, is where these preferences came from and how easy or not (desirable or not) it is to change. On the one hand, the testers want to give the message that we have a particular profile (or type) that "explains" our behavior, while on the other the message is that it can be changed.

There are numerous highly-predictive psychometric tests. Ability tests are probably better than personality tests, but because they cause so much controversy they are (unwisely) less used.

Want to test the validity of a personality questionnaire? Try the above semi-vandalistic approach – answer randomly; look for how the negative is encoded; ask for evidence of test validity. But if you just want to complete those "Are you a saint or a demon under the duvet?" quizzes so beloved of lightweight magazines, then have fun. Just don't assume they have any characteristics of real tests. A good psychometric test takes long-term and expensive R&D. It's not cheap and quick to market – and it does give tough, veridical feedback.

Quirky decisions

There are lots of words one may associate with good decision-making: judicious, timely, wise and so on. Good decisions are considered fair and just. They are also efficient, balanced and well thought through.

Certainly, most of us are familiar with the antonyms of good decisions. Many of us live in, and with, dysfunctional organizations with daft managers and disaffected staff.

Managers make decisions primarily on the basis of their ability, experience and personality. Of course, the corporate culture does play an important part. And we must recognize that many important (and less important) decisions are made by committees rather than single individuals.

Yet it certainly is the case that people have stable and characteristic ways of making decisions. And it is often our pathologies that influence both the decision process and the product of those deliberations.

Psychiatrists have described a number of *personality disorders* that are stable but dysfunctional behavior patterns which have an impact on, and impair, a person's personal, social and working life. Most people have heard about – although are unlikely to truly understand – "psychopathic", "narcissistic" or "paranoid" personality disorders.

While the psychiatrists like to think in typological terms – one is, or is not, borderline or obsessive-compulsive or schizoid – psychologists have long argued that these constructs should be thought of rather as dimensions. Thus one is not tall or short, but a certain number of centimetres high. In this sense, one can be more or less on each dimension. Furthermore, while having a touch of narcissism or paranoia might not be such a bad thing, at work these tendencies can be a real problem when under stress. We revert to type; we regress when anxious, stressed or pressured. In this sense our disorders "inform" our decision-making style.

Robert Hogan, a well-known business psychologist and writer, has pointed out that one's personality traits and disorder profile can give a good indication of how one makes decisions, particularly under duress. The idea is that we all have a dark side, as well as bright one. Most of the time this dark side does not affect our behavior at work. If it did, surely, one would not be in a position to be senior enough to make important decisions. Alas, this is clearly not the case, as it pays to be disordered in some organizations.

The dozen or so identified personality disorders cluster into three groups, which tend to have characteristic and often unhealthy behavior patterns.

The *first* cluster are often called the *odd* or *eccentric* disorders. Those in this cluster tend to be highly skeptical and reserved, but also just plain peculiar.

The argumentative, paranoid, vigilant type of manager is trustful of (all) others all the time. Because these people are so sensitive to threat, betrayal and danger, their decisions are based primarily on keeping them safe and secure. Decisions are intended as a warning. They are not about growth or profit, or long-term planning; they are about safety.

Some of their cold-fish, solitary, reserved colleagues are disastrously low on EQ, warmth, social skills and empathy. They are people of head, not heart. They pride themselves on their cold logic, and they certainly do make clear decisions. But they appear not to understand or care about how others react. Feelings, morale and social impact just are not part of the process. And it shows. They seem not to understand how others may react.

Another part of the group is the frankly quirky idiosyncratic who might have a reputation for creativity and imagination. These individuals certainly think outside the box; a bit too much for most people. And many rejoice in their reputation to the extent that some make decisions deliberately aimed at startling, surprising and entertaining people. The idea of a decision being measured or thought through or balanced seems to many of these types ludicrous. Decisions are advertorials of their quirkiness.

The *second* cluster contains a medley of dramatic, emotional and erratic disorders. First there are the excitable, mercurial types who are always impulsive, unpredictable and unstable. They can be anxious and jumpy, with an unfounded sense of urgency. Hence they are prone to hasty, unconsidered decisions designed primarily to reduce their anxiety, rather than to solve problems.

Next there are the bold, self-confident, arrogant types, whose decision-making styles and products are merely part of their personal publicity agenda. Their decisions are high-risk, based on both overestimating their own, but underestimating their competitors', abilities and strengths. The real aim of a decision has nothing to do with the welfare of the company shareholders. The aim is almost exclusively to enhance the decision-maker's personal prestige and status.

Next there are the mischievous, antisocial, adventurous types, whose recklessness was once thought of as courage. Their decisions flaunt convention, rules, rights ... and frequently the law. They cut corners, test limits, distort facts and hide information. They believe decision-making is aimed exclusively at fulfilling their own personal, selfish agendas.

Then there are the drama queens of business. Those theatrical, attention-seeking, self-dramatizing types who believe all others are attracted to, and compelled by, their personalities and management styles. Naturally, an underlying feature of all their decisions is the aim not to be reasoned, strategic or balanced, but rather to generate interest in them personally. Decision-making is seen as just another attention-seeking device.

Lastly, there is the *third* cluster, of the anxious and fearful. These are the avoidant, dependent or obsessive-compulsive types. They are cautious, conservative and risk averse. They do not like being criticized, as the process is anxiety-provoking. They are terrified of making mistakes. So they make short-term, cover-your-back decisions that are more concerned with minimizing costs and risks rather than maximizing rewards.

Some are eager to please others too much rather than making the right, or best, decisions. Their decisions may be concrete and practical, but they rarely take tough, confrontational decisions when they are required. They seem to have an aversion to "kicking ass" even when it is strongly required.

So, yes, personality does influence decision-making style – and more so when the decision is a big one and the decider is under stress. But at least knowing a person's disposition makes the style reasonably easy to predict. And it helps when thinking through who one really wants (and doesn't want) on committees that make really important decisions.

Recognition and recall

It's often quite fun watching television advertisements in a different country. A great deal of time, money and thought go into creating thirty or sixty seconds of images and messages that have two strong aims: to get viewers to remember the brand; and to go and purchase it. Advertisements can be funny (ha-ha, peculiar or pathetic); they can be quirky, both visually and verbally; they can even be really aesthetically pleasing.

But they are somehow dreary at home, mainly as a result of repetition. Repetition, as we all know, enhances learning, so advertisers repeat them so that you can get to know (and love) the brand. And they measure their success by next-day recall. That is, the day after a target and/or group of ads were aired, people who said they watched the programs during which the ads were aired are asked to recall all they can about them.

Marketing experts are very clear about whether they should use recall or recognition as a measure of an advertisement's success. *Recall* is about remembering (retrieval/reconstruction) when given minimal cues. Thus, "Can you remember any ads that were shown during 'Emmerdale' last night?" *Recognition* shows people the original ads, plus others, to see if they can pick out (recognize) those they have seen. So, for recall, the viewer or listener must describe all/any aspects of the ads (brand name, strap line, actors, scene) they can remember, while for recognition they must merely identify the ad as being the one they saw/heard.

Recall is the gold standard: it is the real thing. If you can't recall the ad, it has been pointless. But the fact that people can (relatively easily) recognize what they can't recall means that something has been stored.

The call for using recognition has various supporters. They argue that viewer involvement (attention) is inevitably low during ads. Recall is an appropriate measure for high-involvement stuff; recognition for when there is low involvement.

The old left-brain/right-brain people claim that recall is left-brained and recognition right-brained. And television viewing is a right-brained activity, with all its visual, emotional and musical components. That is where the memories are stored and should be located.

Others distinguish between intentional and incidental learning, the former purposely and best measured by recall, the latter "accidental", and best measured by recognition.

Many in the advertising industry have been skeptical about recognition measures, paradoxically, because they seem to demonstrate how effective advertising is. They claim evidence of a sort of *false memory syndrome*.

However, researchers have tested bias in recognition quite carefully. Here is how it is done. First, get a bunch of ads and divide them into short (say 10 seconds) and long (say 30 seconds). Then air them for a varying number of times – say one, two or four times. In testing people's recognition, either have a few (say four) or more (say eight) distractors – that is, irrelevant ads. You might also check if they can recall the product category (for example, detergent, aftershave, beer), or brand name or major claim (strap line), or visuals.

Studies like this show four things. *First,* the most powerful predictor of recognition is *always* the number of repeats: the more repeats, the better remembered. *Second,* the length of the ad has a very significant effect on the more complicated stuff like claim recognition, but not brand or visual recognition. It is possible to communicate these aspects effectively in a short time. *Third,* having few or many distractors (false ads) in the recognition test does not make a big difference. *Fourth,* alas, but as ever, the results of different studies do not always agree: they sometimes give contradictory results.

So ... what is the bottom line? It seems that learning can be measured in situations where using recall would indicate that learning has occurred. So you can have reasonable accurate recognition with almost zero recall. But you must not cheat. It depends on how hard you make the recognition list, what is recognized, and how long after the ad is shown.

The problem is that advertisers' success is measured by their recall/recognition scores. They have a vested interest in efficacious awareness claims, and are clued up as to what measures put them in the best light. They need to be monitored by disinterested outsiders.

But this research can have enormous benefits for media planners. It can indicate the optimal length of an ad. You can get over the brand name as effectively, or perhaps even more effectively, in a 10-second commercial as in one lasting 30 seconds. And, while more repetition is good, you can work out the value after a certain number – the law of diminishing returns.

Does all this worthy research help copywriters, visual artists and designers? Are some shapes, colours, images or words simply more memorable than others? No doubt.

Yet nothing much matters unless, when passing those shelves of high-stacked, multiple products, consumers pick out the one they have seen on the telly because it is their preferred brand.

Recruitment and selection psychiatry

If you think recruitment and selection are easy, then look at the divorce statistics. On a personal level, most of us conduct a quite extensive, if amateur, recruitment campaign. We also amass a good deal of data on our preferred candidate. But somehow we miss some crucial facts: their attitude to money; their natural state of (un)tidiness; their roving eye at dinner parties, perhaps, until it is too late.

The selection business is too serious to be left to amateurs. Try getting rid of a quick-to-litigate, narcissistic, second-rater. Try to understand why *wunderkinder* labeled talented, fast-stream high flyers crash and burn just when they are supposed to be taking over the company. And what to do about the IT engineer who wants a senior management job, but quite clearly cannot even manage himself?

So recruiters and selectors, like all of us, fuss and fret and fail. And they become ill and suffer a range of specific, specialist problems that might require treatment:

1. Habitual *ability test* inhibition
This is the terror of using intelligence tests, known to be the best discriminator in both the positive and negative senses of the word, lest some under-powered individual takes revenge via lawyers, the press etc., claiming unfair practice.

2. Premorbid *application form* fixation
The idea that application forms need to be redesigned, formatted and generally fiddled with despite the fact that it remains quite unclear why some pieces of information are sought and others ignored, for curious historical reasons.

3. Unconscious *assessment centre* complex
This is the idea that, despite their cost, assessment centres offer by far the best real look at candidates – particularly aspects such as how they eat their lunch, get tired and touchy, or deal with each other. They are definitely the Big Brother of selection.

4. Psychosexual *head-hunter* obsession
This is the sorry abrogation of real selection responsibility to highly polished and professional individuals who exude as much confidence as aroma of aftershave. They appear to have no doubt about their choice, irrespective of a very checkered history.

5. Developmental *internet advertising* disturbance

This is the constant worry that the whole business has, should or must become web-based, but not being not quite sure what to do, or what implications this might have for oneself, one's department, or indeed the whole profession.

6. Bipolar *internal promotion* disorder

This problem manifests itself in blowing at once hot and then very cold on the whole business of internal selection. It's much harder, paradoxically, because much more is known about the internal candidates. It is also suddenly that they are so second-rate, and yet it was you who chose them in the first place.

7. Episodic *job analysis* fetish

The books say always start with a job analysis, which leads to a competency list, which leads to a job spec, then ad and finally interview. Trouble is, the process is both difficult and boring. And anyway the job is in flux. Further, the task is to select talent which transcends one particular job. The problem is manifest in sudden, unpredictable and unsustained bursts of enthusiasm for the activity.

8. Atypical *person specification* abreaction

This is the obsession of describing the characteristics of the desired person in sexy, unique and neo-psychobabble language. This involves disguising aspects of the job, such as how much ambiguity, change and stress they will have to deal with, while sounding upbeat, forceful and optimistic.

9. Post-traumatic *psychometric test* malady

This is a dependency on personality, motivational and other "tea leaf" tests that miraculously reveal the real person underneath, warts and all. The disturbance follows a well-known pattern: naïve enthusiasm, hopeful dependence, skeptical anger, out-of-pocket fury, and then good, old-fashioned bewilderment as to why it all went so badly wrong.

10. Abnormal *reference check* dependency

This is manifested in two opposite forms. The first is engaging in a lot of paranoid checking-up on the individual by constant telephone calls, detective work and testimonial collections; while the other is not to believe anything that others write about candidates, and to eschew all warnings and advice from others.

11. Undifferentiated *structured interview* compunction

This is the semi-theatrical need to have a script for the interviewer, who is required to proceed through a tightly constructed series of questions that supposedly do a better job than any preferred, gut-feel stuff that most interviews prepare. The script includes the "killer question" you have preferred from the past.

12. Intermittent *talent search* impulse

Once there was a talent pool, then a war for talent, then HR became talent management. Despite the fact that no one quite knows what "it" is ("I know it when I see it"), "it" is now seen as the saviour of the company in years to come.

13. Substance-induced *chemistry/fit* obsession

This is a wonderful old-fashioned approach using phrases such as intuition, chemistry, fit and so on. The idea is to answer those first-rate 1950s questions: "Could you do business with this gel?" or "Could you bunk down with this chap"? It has the advantage of simple yes/no answers.

14. Delusional *real motive* psychosis

This is a paranoid worry about the amount of the iceberg under the surface, and candidates' real motives. It may be caused by reading one or two psychological detective novels, which, of course, always demonstrate that things are not what they seem. So the task is to find the applicants' real motives for wanting the job, the title and the package.

Remembering the brand

Marketing and sales people have relatively simple objectives. First, notice and be aware of the product – make sure people see and hear about the campaign. Next, more than notice it, remember it and feel good about it. And, third, go and get it; follow up the message with action.

We are flooded with advertisements. People give you flyers in a street that is already awash with billboards, shop-windows and posters. The supermarkets now do radio-style ads. Letter boxes are crammed full of catalogues you never ordered.

Can you name one advertisement you saw yesterday on the television, heard on the radio, saw in the paper or on a billboard you pass every day? Think of memorable advertisements. What made them so? … and can you be sure of the brand?

But nothing works unless you notice the product and brand. More than that: you need to make sure people remember it. They have to process and store the information. And they need to feel good about it.

How, then, to ensure the brand is recalled? The consultancy group *Mountainview* has looked at research from neuroscience to psychoanalysis to try to understand how, when and why people process and then remember information.

They found four factors that make a difference. The *first* is co-creation. It's about involvement. The television people worked this out some time ago. It's about interaction – pressing the red button. It's about active problem-solving. The Silk Cut ad also did this. Each one gave people a problem to solve.

There is nothing quite as successful as an ad where people rehearse or imitate (and then repeat) the strap line. Most people recall "reaching the parts other beers cannot reach". How many people tried to be a tenor to sing "Just one Cornetto". Induce people to talk about, mimic or even joke about an advertisement and it is effectively replayed. Further, it becomes more and more memorable for the co-creator.

Co-creation is not a new idea. We all know its easier to persuade your boss to do something if he feels it was his idea in the first place. Get people to work at the ad, playfully, and you vastly improve brand recognition.

You can use humor or gimmicks or music or tick-box interaction. It may not matter much. But doing often leads to feeling, which can lead to thinking and thence to action … namely the desirable goal of brand purchasing.

Next, use metaphors. Metaphors are figurative language. They make wonderful vehicles for ideas. And they suggest all sorts of further possibilities. A brilliant metaphor is worth a hundred expensive words.

There are visual metaphors and verbal metaphors. But you need to think carefully about your choice. Too abstract, subtle or clever, and the general public don't get it. Too simple and they feel patronized. Best is to be quirky and allow people the idea that they have "worked it out for themselves".

These ads should not need explaining. The best are clear, multi-faceted, amusing and therefore memorable.

Third, tug on the heart strings. Evoke good memories. Through smells, music, old songs people can be transported immediately to their idealized childhood, first Christmas, first love.

Stores have for a long time tried "in-store environmental modification" to change people's moods. At Christmas, they play "Jingle Bells" and pump in smells of spice and pine. In summer, they offer "The Sleepy Lagoon" and smells of sun-tan oil. Certain products redolent of an era "can bring it all back". Witness the huge success of *The Dangerous Book for Boys* (published in 2006, and basically a compilation of articles from boys' magazines of the 1950s and 1960s dealing with many topics of interest to adolescents of the period).

But do the positive memories. Target a cohort – for example, affluent people in their thirties – by thinking what happened in the late 1980s. Clips of old films or old ads have tremendous appeal.

And *finally*, and perhaps most important of all, wrap it all together in a story. We are programmed to attend to, appreciate and remember stories. Call them yarns, sagas or vignettes – it's the same thing.

Even on a billboard, in a 45-second commercial or in a magazine it is possible to use the story-telling format. We need a beginning, a middle and an end. It's good to use tension, to surprise and to be personal. It's OK to repeat phrases, themes and storylines. Make the pictures fit the words and the music.

Think of haiku poetry. Amazingly succinct but very powerful. So bring it all together. Get the audience involved as co-creators of the story. Explore some salient metaphors. Stir those emotional memories as part of the story-telling. And Joe Public will be more likely to recognize *and* recall the product and the brand.

Reference

Iggulden, Conn and Iggulden, Hal (2006) *The Dangerous Book for Boys.* London: HarperCollins.

Rules

Over a hundred years ago, Max Weber noticed that all organizations became more rule-bound over time. He believed that this was a good thing, because rules are aimed at increasing efficiency: he was, after all, the father of bureaucracy. Rules, like laws, make for an orderly, predictable, fair organization. A naïve view?

It is important to distinguish between laws, rules and customs. Politicians love laws and taxes: this how they force their will on the people. But laws do, or at least should, have a purpose. It was Cicero who pointed out that we are in bondage to the law so that we may be free.

Rules in organizations are *explicit* directives. They can imprison or liberate. They are supposed to ensure good, efficient behavior. They are, said the advertising guru, David Ogilvy, for the obedience of fools but the guidance of wise men. If (and only if) wisely conceived, implemented and (regularly) revised, they are extremely important in organizations.

Corporate culture, on the other hand, is *implicit.* It's about appropriate behavior at work. It's about etiquette, but there is usually no guide-book. You have to "pick it up" by observation, by gentle hints, and often just by breaking the convention.

Rules are often there to coerce. If managers don't conduct their requisite appraisals, rules are drawn up to encourage, then to force them. Likewise for organizational misconduct, such as being absent, stealing and sexual misbehavior. Of course, people will always find their way around the rules. More rules have to be drawn up to combat each clever or devious way people have found to get around the existing ones.

The increase in tax laws is a nice example of this problem. Accountants poach tax inspectors who know the system and its foibles, peculiarities and loopholes. A clever, new tax-efficient scheme is found, so another law has to be enacted to stop it.

Not only does the number of rules grow, but they seem never to be revoked either. Laws and rules are more likely to be added than removed. Rules are drawn up to govern all sorts of behaviors, often aimed at miscreants, deviants and incompetents who won't play the game.

So innovation becomes stultified. A best-seller published in 2003 was called *First, Break All the Rules.* It suggested that you have often to confront the popular wisdom that has led to rule growth. But there are inevitably critics, rivals and the politically correct police eager to squash any possible threat to the status quo.

Consider which parts of an organization are most rule bound. Of course, some areas must adhere to legal requirements. Accountants, engineers and human resource people, for example, have to comply with the law.

But we are talking about organizational rules. About following pre-scribed and proscribed behavior patterns. Often unthinkingly.

Every so often the rules are challenged, not by sour, alienated or anarchic staff, but by those eager for improvement. Many of the "great" business ideas of gurus start by challenging the rules. *Process re-engineering* aimed to do things differently – very differently. Dr W. Edwards Demming, the American engineer, advocated giving up targets, quotas and appraisals to reduce variation.

And *lateral thinking* is the essence of rule challenging. Edward de Bono said it helps us escape from fixed patterns of behavior. It encourages us to challenge assumptions, generate alternatives, and jump on new ideas.

The popularity of a single tax rate, for example, lies partly in its simplic-ity. Tax complexity benefits only accountants. The Italians have a specialized police force dedicated entirely to dealing with tax issues.

The problem is straightforward: it is easier to introduce laws and rules than to revoke them. Further, there are those who favor rules as a primary method of influence. Perhaps they have a strong need for order, regularity and predictability, which they also try to impose on others. Maybe they just don't do charm or interpersonal persuasion.

So we have people in their more-or-less rule-bound silos. The account-ants, engineers and health and safety people are probably rather rule-conscious, while the sales and advertising people are somewhat less so.

There are the rule-followers and the rule disobeyers. There are those who are natural rule-makers and those who more naturally challenge rules. Some see rules as liberating, others as imprisoning.

But there is, quite clearly, a rule about rules. They grow remorselessly and exponentially. They can asphyxiate the very activities they are trying to breathe life into. Weber knew this paradox.

So here is a suggestion. For every new rule that is introduced, one (how about two?) needs to be abolished. There should be a rule-challenging com-mittee tasked to examine rule-bound behavior. No rule lasts more than three years: after that, they have to be approved anew. The committee's mission is to decide whether it is still adaptive. And they should be given the permission and encouragement to challenge the rules continually.

Reference

Buckingham, M. (2003) *First, Break All the Rules*. London: Pocket Books.

Selection superstitions

There is a famous story that illustrates what psychologists call "superstitious behavior". An animal psychologist had a lab full of pigeons he was using to explore the implications of behavior theory. Pigeons demonstrated they had shape and colour discrimination, and quite a bit more. They had become quite used to the old food-for-a-correct-answer routine.

One weekend, the researcher went home but forgot to turn off the time feeders for a row of birds. So, after half an hour the machine dispensed a tasty helping of feed. Naturally, the birds observed this acutely and assumed they had been rewarded for what they were doing. And then they repeated the behavior every 30 minutes, and out came the reward.

Thus the pigeon-fancying researcher was both amazed and astonished to find that every so often the birds got ready to do their thing. Some pecked at their cage, others lifted both wings, some pirouetted at the bottom of the cage, others cooed appreciatively. The food came unconditionally, but the pigeons had "seen connections" and causal links and believed they had brought about their just reward.

Daft birds? Well, what about sports players and their "lucky" socks or boots? Students and their equally lucky charms, pens, mascots? Can a pair of socks affect the outcome of a game? Of course not. Perhaps the less control we have over life and the more unpredictable it seems, the more we believe not in luck, chance and good fortune, but the operation of fantastical powers.

A good place to observe all this is, quite paradoxically, the selection interview. Selection is important but complex. Neither selector nor selected is being totally honest and natural. Things are left unsaid; others embellished. Failures are forgotten, while victories are recalled clearly.

All selectors would love a simple but powerful test that revealed all – the real person. Hence the maintenance of interest in the pre-scientific, totally discredited set of "ologies" such as graphology.

But some selectors believe they have a few nuggets of psychological gold hewn from the mine of experience. They have noticed what they believe to be causal connections. They have witnessed the cheating preferences of untrustworthy employees, low on integrity. They have pondered similarities in the recreation preferences of those prone to absenteeism. They know, they believe, the "Da Vinci Code" of personal strengths and limitations.

Naturally, therefore, they are eager to use these insights at the job interview. Nothing trivial appears to have escaped their attention. Something as petty as sock preference "says it all", they believe. The person who wears white socks with a dark suit has the impetuousness and lack of polish of a market trader; while on the other hand those 1950s-style diamond Argyle patterned socks show change aversion. Nylon is a good indicator of low intelligence, but wool is an indicator of conservatism.

Women might notice dress issues more than men, but the latter seem to attribute greater meaning to them.

Apart from dress there are other aspects of physical appearance that appeal to the selection-superstitious sleuth. Men with beards excite comment. Body language is, however, one of the best areas of psychological speculation. Fiddle with your wedding ring, watch, cuff-links or pen and you are saying all sorts of things about your hidden motives, your deep desires and your embarrassing passions.

Touch, eye contact, gestures, posture, orientation – they all tell the knowing observer a great deal about traits, motives and the like. Experts – that is, the real ones who have studied the topic – talk about idiosyncrasies, about establishing base-rates, about state rather than trait indicators. But that is all too cautious.

Some people have wonderfully simple taxonomic theories that help them group others into little boxes. The boxer Muhammad Ali, in a famous speech to Harvard students, said he believes there are very few different sorts of people: they are pomegranates, prunes, walnuts or grapes. The scheme is based on fruit that may be both hard and soft on outside and the inside. Some people are as they appear, hard on the outside, hard on the inside (pomegranates). Others are softies throughout: grapes. But the confusing ones are those who appear soft but are hard (prune) or appear hard but are soft (walnut). Quite interesting, but I am not sure how much further this whole thing takes you in the business of selection.

Most people remember the theory X/theory Y distinction of Douglas McGregor in *The Human Side of Enterprise* (1960). Theory X people were hard-bitten cynics who believed that (all) people dislike work and thus have to be controlled, cajoled or threatened before they will perform. The theory Y people are Rosseauians, believing in the inherent goodness of people who, under the right conditions, will give their all to their employer.

The funny thing about selection is that everybody believes they are good at it. This despite the divorce statistics, which appears to illustrate that, as noted earlier, considering it is one of the most important selection decisions of our life, we do rather badly at it.

Perhaps there is a paradox here: the more you believe in your selection ability, the less you have of it.

Reference

McGregor, D. (1960) *The Human Side of Enterprise*. New York: McGraw-Hill.

Self-actualizing

There seem to be a few things that everybody knows about psychology: Freud thought everything was about sex; money is a hygiene, not a motivating factor; and we all have a hierarchy of needs.

In the early 1940s, Abraham Maslow drew his famous triangle to support his theory of motivation. The idea is pretty simple. We have a hierarchy of needs – basic ones need to be fulfilled first. Then we move up the ladder. Thus we have pretty basic physical needs (food, water), then needs for safety and security. Then we need to belong to social groups, because we are social animals.

Most of us do OK up to that point. It's the next two we struggle with. The fourth level is the need to feel confident, competent and strong. These are the esteem needs. Most of us would like to feel able, valuable and worthwhile.

And if you achieve that, then you can self-actualize, realize your potential and function at full capacity. You are one of the very few lucky ones who are not still fully involved with needs at a much lower level. But how do you know you are; how do you recognize a self-actualizer? Maslow came up with fifteen characteristics. Some look a bit dated now, others a bit apple pie, and some a bit ethnocentrically North American.

But they still make a good checklist. Consider these as a list of competencies to look for:

- *A good grip on reality*. Maslow called it an efficient perception of reality. It means that, quite simply, you see, accept and face things as they are and not through a filter of ego defence mechanisms such as repression, denial, and so on. This means that self-actualizers can detect spin, deceit and deception in others. They are fake-sensitive, clear perceivers of others.
- *They indulge in almost fatalistic acceptance*. They admit their own and others frailties, mistakes and shortcomings. They don't hide, conceal or talk-up these problems. They are part of who they are: part of the package, part of life. Like natural disasters, they are the result of the roll of the dice.
- *They have an unaffected naturalness and spontaneity*. It can look simple and childlike. It may have to do with wonder, or fascination, or being easily engrossed. Maslow said the self-actualized tend to trust their intuitions and impulses.
- *They are profoundly problem-focused*. They differentiate between the wheat and the chaff; the petty from the important. They get interested in

and involved with the bigger socio-political, economic and ethnic problems or issues of their society and their time.

- *They can be alone, and have an affinity with solitude.* They are comfortable being alone. Solitude does not mean rejection, failure or boredom. It may be seen as a benefit, a useful time to recharge the batteries, ponder the big picture, get things into perspective.
- *They are not swayed by fad or fashion.* They are independent of cultural swings, preferring to follow their own inner voice and self-determined interests. This makes them both potentially out-of-step, and enduring at the same time.
- *They have an open, fresh appreciation of things.* Maslow called it a beginner's mind. He said they seemed to be able to find awe, pleasure and fascination in the mundane.
- *They have frequent "peak experiences".* These are sort of orgasms of the mind. Maslow called them "oceanic feelings" and they are difficult to describe, but very meaningful to the individual. They are clear, insightful, almost visions of understanding (grounded, remember, in reality).
- *They are empathic, caring, kind.* They manifest a deep and genuine desire to help their fellow humans. This is a sincere, even passionate, desire to make things better for others.
- *They have deep, profound private relationships with others.* But relatively few. They trade off width for depth, preferring to spend most of their time and energy with a select few.
- *They respect and value all.* They treat people as individuals, not as representatives of their group. Maslow said they respect democratic values. It means seeing through the stereotypes.
- *They can differentiate the means and the end; the destination and the journey; the process and the product.* They can enjoy the activity for its own sake, as well as always being goal-oriented.
- *They have a philosophical sense of humor.* That is, they do not define a sense of humor as the keen appreciation of the foibles and failings of one's enemies. Rather, they find the foolishness of the whole human condition funny.
- *They are creative, because they can see the connections between things.* As a result of the freshness of their perceptions and ability to ask the naïve questions, they can be genuinely innovative.
- *They resist the conformity of the crowd.* Maslow called this "resistance to enculturation". It means being detached from the culture-bound rules of the group.

There are quite clearly themes in this list. There is something about inquisitiveness and curiosity; something about honesty and self-awareness; something about kindness and caring. They really do seem attractive people – liberated from all those struggles about feeling liked or loved or lovable that lesser beings stuck at lower levels experience.

Self-actualizers, as spelled out by Maslow, seem both authentic and wise; calm and energetic; both people- and problem-oriented. Too much to ask for in a CEO? Probably ... but worth the search.

Selling ethics

Have the Enron, cash-for-peerages and Berlusconi scandals rekindled an interest in that old business school oxymoron, business ethics (BE)?

Ideas about concepts of corporate responsibility and business ethics have changed considerably since the start of the twentieth century. The Depression, the Second World War, the consumer movements of the 1960s and the renewal of aggressive capitalism in the 1980s all influenced what individual workers and managers believed to be the social role, if any, of their organizations. There is now a considerable literature on business ethics. Thus there are concerns and learned papers on human resource ethics, marketing ethics and the ethics associated with performance management systems. And new developments in science have led to new dilemmas, such as the ethics of genetic testing in the workplace.

For some, the concept of *caveat emptor* (let the buyer beware) was enough. It was, so many believed, the duty of companies to serve their shareholders, employees and customers by maximizing profits and staying within the law. But since the early 1990s, for a variety of reasons, businessmen, academics and writers have been considering in more detail the relationship and responsibilities between companies and society. As a result, the sub-discipline of business ethics has appeared.

Business ethics questions apply at very different levels:

- At the *societal level*, questions concern the ethics of dealing with certain countries, the desirability of capitalism versus socialism, the role of government in the marketplace. At this level, the discourse is about societies and principles.
- At the *stakeholder level*, questions concern the employees, suppliers, customers, shareholders and those related to them. Ethical questions here are about the company's obligation to these various groups.
- At the *company policy level*, the ethical questions are about how people in the organization should, and do, behave towards each other.

Business ethics are concerned with values, rights, duties and rules. To a large extent, companies are interested in the definition and application of rules covering such things as keeping promises, and mutual respect for persons and property. Many organizations even try to enshrine their ethics in the company mission statement.

BE have a sort of aura – part sanctimonious, part pc, part unchallengeable. Like praying and research, they are thought to be a good thing, but people aren't quite sure what is involved. We used to have an ethical foreign policy (conveniently dropped) and we have ethical investing, and ethical farming.

Complete nonsense, of course, because "ethics" is plural. There are different ethical positions, sometimes diametrically opposed. Each is based on ethical principles, just different ones. The conclusions derived from different principles are seriously different. Amen.

So what about sales ethics? Will "caveat emptor" suffice as an ethical principle? Is it workable or wise from a business perspective? Probably not.

Selling organizations live in a risk environment. They have to understand and make decisions about short-term and long-term reputational, regulatory and market risk. Countries, corporations and regulator bodies often favor a legalistic, rule-following approach to "ensure" ethical behavior. They hope to impose justice, integrity and morality. But this often undermines the very essence of the whole enterprise – namely doing the difficult thinking for oneself.

Ethical dilemmas are just that – dilemmas. Sales ethics involve resolving the explicit, implicit and deeply conflicting issues and interests of different stakeholders. In sales, these can be the customers, sales staff, suppliers, the after-sales support staff and the senior management.

The independent financial adviser (IFA) scandals illustrated this nicely. The whole industry paid dearly for the dissimulating activities of a few agents in search of a quick buck. For short-term gains perhaps, but they led to massive damage to institutions, and the role of IFAs as a whole. IFAs are now viewed with more suspicion than journalists and estate agents.

So what to do? Ethics are about deciding and applying principles or fairness, integrity and justice to everyday selling situations. They are the stuff of the moral maze.

Point number 1: Ethical decisions are not simple. All parties have rights, but also duties – to tell the truth with no errors or omissions, or commission. Principles and guidelines need to be articulated in full.
Point number 2: Ethics is best taught by case studies. These are memorable, complex parables.
Point number 3: BE are a journey, not a destination; a chemistry textbook, not a recipe book; a messy muddle, not a crystal-clear formula.

So ethics are difficult and discomforting. For the dogmatic, deductive thinker and those intolerant of ambiguity or the fundamentalist, BE have to be boiled down to rules and regulations. All this debatable, relationistic stuff is confusing. But alas, the world is like that.

You reduce, but never eliminate, all those selling scandals by spending time on BE in training programs. Sales courses pay scant attention to BE, believing the subject to be a sort of fancy "add on" to teaching the recruits all that stuff about "closing the deal".

You need to put BE on the table at least: raise the issues, hear different voices, look at the data. What are the consequences of a short-term, caveat emptor, sort-of-follow-the-regulations approach? The answer these days is probably a flourishing website dedicated to exposing and destroying the organization.

And the consequences of enjoying a reputation for fairness and integrity? Customer loyalty, which drives profitability. And sales ethics don't have to be anti-ethical! You can have highly successful sales people with an ethical sense and moral compass. Some would argue it's the only way to have a long-term career in sales. Perhaps that, in part, explains the amazing attrition rate in sales staff. Ever thought that BE plays a part in staff retention? Worth testing?

Selling to children

Marketing products and services aimed specifically at children is becoming more and more of a hot potato. Toys, fizzy drinks, snacks and so-called junk foods are clearly in the sights of all kinds of groups. Selling to children is more about politics than marketing nowadays. Most would love to ban the products, but start by imposing advertising restrictions.

There are many myths about selling to children, especially advertising products on television. Thus, it is argued:

- Children are intensive consumers of television and are therefore massively exposed to advertising. But facts suggest that they spend less than 5 percent of their waking time watching television.
- Children are gullible, and unable to differentiate ads from programs. Two-thirds of six-year-olds are able to do this, and many question the credibility of ads.
- Advertising leads to unnatural wants, and thence to parental pester power and psycho-terror. Comparatively few parents who have healthy parenting styles and habits report this.
- Children are never critical of advertising. This is patently not true by the age of 10.
- Parents are powerless to influence what their children see. Precisely the opposite: they are the most powerfully influential factor.
- Television is the main factor influencing a child's diet and food preferences. Wrong: it's the family, by a long way.

How long will it be before the tobacco story is repeated for convenience foods? First, restricted television and radio advertising, then swingeing taxes, and finally health warnings on every product. How many people blame the childhood obesity crisis on crisps, soft drinks and deep-fried fast foods? Some would love to see your standard burger priced at £6.99 ($10.00) with a health warning on each wrapping.

The legislators all argue that they are protecting children and their parents. The former because they are naïve and gullible, the latter because they resent pester power. So they want rules about public advertising, products in schools, product displays in supermarkets. They want to demonize and legitimize their socio-political position through legislation.

But anyone who has tried to sell to children knows they are far from naïve. Most are exceptionally "cool" and "savvy", albeit highly capricious and whimsical. Today's "must have" becomes tomorrow's discard, making life for the manufacturer difficult and unpredictable.

Some brands and products endure almost without change. The *Beano* and *Dandy* comics look very familiar to 50-year-olds who read them forty years ago. *Barbie* still flourishes with modifications. But other products - such as those once ubiquitous silver scooters - are long passed. A flash in the pan, but a very profitable flash for manufacturers and retailers while it lasted.

So, for the marketing specialist, understanding children's and adolescents' values, wants and purchases is pretty important. Young people have serious spending power. The average 16-year-old may have a disposable income of anywhere between £5 and £20 ($10–$40) a week, and many have much more than that.

What is abundantly clear is that the idea that media commercials cause "false" product wants in the simple-minded is wrong. Young people are much more victims of peer pressure than of any advertising campaign. They follow the crowd, and gain acceptance by being cool, having the gear, the gadget and the brand.

But what drives this peer pressure? Should the media be implicated here? Parental values do play a part. They determine how the children are raised. They regulate, often through house rules, how much money and free time the children have to spend, and their access to the media. Some homes are media-saturated, with oversized TVs in every room that are always on. Family meals are, in this sense, spectator occasions, not times for discussion.

In other homes, the media are rationed but also critiqued. Parents comment on products and advertisements. They hope to bring up media-literate and economically literate children. And, of course. they try to influence the sorts of peers that their offspring mix with. Parental hobbies and beliefs dictate their spare time activities and peer group ... and all of this naturally affects the children.

Rather than being a marketing "pushover" the average adolescent is amazingly brand-sensitive, discriminating and well-informed. They certainly do not believe "what it says on the tin". They are skeptical, often cynical, about advertising. They do know their brands, often have strong preferences, but are very capricious. As noted above, what's in today is out tomorrow, for all kinds of reasons. That's the nature of the "*Sturm und Drang*", up and down, moody adolescent.

The first impulse of the legislators to ban, control and tax has little effect because of the changing nature of the world; it probably never had much effect except to satisfy the political instincts of certain groups. The web and word-of-mouth are ten times more powerful propagandists for brands than 30-second television commercials.

Young people, indeed all people, like choice. They are influenced by role models and price, and what the marketing people call "value-proposition".

All the evils in our society – sloth, violence, crime and so on – are not caused by greedy multinationals, nor by cynical marketing people. When politicians and parents are frustrated by their inability to influence others as they would wish, many look for easy targets to blame, but never themselves. Alas, the problem, dear reader, lies not in our ads but in ourselves.

Selling to laggards

It's curious, quaint even, but sometimes also a little pathetic, to see people deeply wedded to products long since updated and improved by technology. Letters-to-the-editor writers to certain newspapers bash out their fury on old manual typewriters and have eschewed all developments for thirty years.

Others find kitchen, gardening or motor equipment which they started to use as a teenager comfortingly familiar and quite sufficient for their purposes: thank you.

In a celebrated work called *Diffusion of Innovations* (1983), now in its fifth edition, Everett Rogers divided the market for new products into five groups. *Innovators* (around 2.5 percent of the population) found out about and obtained products even before they were properly on the market. *Early Adopters,* who, it is claimed, make up around 13.5 percent of the population, are first in line to purchase, use and even champion new things. About a third of the population are the *Early Majority*; that is, they wait until the product or process is fairly well known and there may be different brands available before they commit. The *Late Majority* (also a third) are just that. They don't ride the enthusiastic wave. Cautious, conservative, techno-phobic, even skint: there may be many reasons why they take their time trying out the new.

And then there are the *Laggards,* supposedly around 16 percent of the population. It is only when it becomes a legal requirement (for example, to wear a helmet, or a safety belt) or on the total withdrawal of their favored product that leads them, "kicking and screaming", into the fierce, fiery and frightening world of modernity.

Rogers, in his book, now forty-five years old, but many times revised, pointed out some of the more common characteristics of each type:

- Innovators – venturesome, educated, have multiple information sources, a greater propensity to take risk.
- Early adopters – social leaders, popular, educated.
- Early majority – deliberate, have many informal social contacts.
- Late majority – skeptical, traditional, lower socio-economic status.
- Laggards – neighbors and friends are main information sources, fear of debt.

The argument was that, to adapt a new product or process you first needed *knowledge* of the innovation. Next you need to be *persuaded* that it has virtues worthy of uptake. Then the decision has to be taken to buy and use the product or process; then to actually put it to use. Finally, acceptance needs to be confirmed by repeat usage.

There is a S curve to innovation: a slow start, moving to steep curve. Of course, the nature of technology may prevent innovation or severely disrupt the pattern.

But the fascination for most people are the laggards: those anti-change, anti-innovation types.

Of course, it has been fashionable to look on laggards with a mixture of pity and contempt. What is wrong with them? Can't they keep in touch? Are they a sausage short of a fry-up?

But if you think of them as the ultimate in *product loyalty* and the early adopters as *fickle defectors*, it all looks rather different from a marketing perspective. It may be all very well praising innovators and adopters for their curiosity, courage and conscientiousness, but they are unlikely to be product- or brand-loyal. Their interest is in novelty and creativity. They like new-and-improved formulas, and gadgets which, as they get smaller, can do more and more. So they quickly move on and discard perfectly serviceable products. In this sense, they could even be seen as environmental polluters – unless of course the appeal of the new product is its bio-degradability.

Innovators and early adopters certainly get through electrical goods. Dumps are full of computers barely a couple of years old. Late adopters seem happier to let products wear out before replacing them.

And laggards? Think of them as loyalists, and sometimes good environmentalists. They probably started using beloved products when they were young. They have powerful associations. They function just fine. Loyalists know there are things that are faster, supposedly more convenient, possibly healthier.

Old fogies who like fountain pens and the like may be loyalists, but it is often more of a game and a political statement. We know it's much more expensive obtaining new customers than it is keeping old ones. So don't pooh-pooh your best customers, who are not tickled, tricked or enticed by new fangled stuff. Keep giving them what they like. And get one in the sales and marketing team to represent them.

Too many young gadgeteers brought up on computer games go into marketing and assume, as we all do, but quite wrongly, that everyone is like them.

And the counter-argument? These so-called loyalists are expensive to service and far from cost-effective to court, because they usually want repairs and not replacements. They can take up a disproportionate amount of staff time (for example, they won't use email) and drive your company into a costly corner. Do you really want to be the only remaining specialist supplier of needles for wind-up gramophones? Abandon them all to small, outsourced specialists and make no further investment in them. Thank you and good day!

Reference

Rogers, E. M. (2003 [1983]) *Diffusion of Innovations*, 5th edn. New York: Free Press.

Service orientation

Most organizations have some "competency" around service orientation. It may be called "customer responsiveness" or "service quality". And, paradoxically, a reasonable number of those in the service industry, particularly in government organizations, have service orientation fairly low down on the list.

But what is service orientation? How can we define and measure it? Can it be taught? Are there biographical markers of it?

It is essentially a disposition to be considerate, helpful and thoughtful. It's a non-technical, non-cognitive emotional and social skill. The service-oriented person is consistent, emotionally aware and co-operative.

For the personality psychologist there seem to be four dimensions that make up this disposition:

- Agreeableness/Likeability: This means empathic, kind, warm, unselfish.
- Stability/Adjustment: This means not prone to stress, moodiness, anxiety, depression or hypochondriasis.
- Extraversion/Sociability: This means seeking out, enjoying and relaxing around social activities.
- Emotional Intelligence: This means being aware of, and sensitive to, your own and others' emotions, and knowing how to manage them.

Various other components have been suggested. One is the general desire to make a good impression. To worry what other people think of you; to monitor yourself and others. Another is the habit of being able and willing to take responsibility for your actions. That's pretty important in service-oriented situations, where staff are always extremely eager to "shift the blame", whatever the problem.

It seems that a general desire to get on – called need for achievement – is a good thing. It means being ambitious but self-disciplined; orderly, hardworking and conscientious. After all, it can be a tough job.

And then there is a generally sunny disposition, someone who experiences general life satisfaction. This is more than stability or adjustment. It's the gift of seeing the glass half-full. About being positive, optimistic and enthusiastic.

Some organizations seek out those who have had some, albeit casual or short-term, service or sales experience. Pulling pints, serving burgers, selling clothes, working a market stall all test an individual's service orientation.

Some customers are plain rude, others time-wasters. Many are ungrateful, and a very large number seemingly very demanding. For every charmer there may be ten bastards.

It's not intellectually demanding work. Being able to add up is about the limit of the skills required in that department. You don't have to master difficult technology – perhaps a till and a credit card machine.

The skill is in the interaction with people. You have to be able to take the role of the other and really enjoy helping people. The joy should be the same as for the good salesperson. Not in the commission per se, but closing the deal. People need to be seen as a source energy, fun and stimulation, not as demanding, difficult and demeaning.

More women seem to be in service jobs than men. Yes, it does depend on the sector. Some say it's because it's too badly paid for men. Others say women have the disposition for the job more than men. It's got to do with women being genetically nurturing, supportive and helpful: their biological role. Still others reject any evolutionary idea, arguing that it is the way we socialize our male and female children that leads to these differences.

There certainly seem to be personality correlates of good service orientation. The sanguine seem best suited to the role – stable extraverts with a middle-class socialization.

But are there biographical markers? Coming from a large family; having parents in the business; having been brought up in a strongly religious household; or having parents ambitious for their children?

Many of these ideas have been tested and there are some weak, but not always replicable, links. Most people who are good at, and enjoy, service jobs tend to gravitate to them early. Often at school. They might have had good models in peers and parents.

They get a real buzz from helping others. So people in the caring or teaching professions often show a service orientation.

Can it be trained? Sure, but only if you have the disposition. Neurotic, disagreeable introverts cannot be trained for it. Resting actors often do service jobs. They understand that service is partly theatre. It's called emotional labour. But it's more than just acting. You can fake kindness, helpfulness and responsibility – but only up to a point. So it is true that "Hell is other people"? If you agree and you are in the service sector, then almost certainly you are in the wrong job.

Seven habits of super failures

There is something magical about the number seven. We have the seven seas and the seven days of the week. We even have a seven-year itch because we are not in seventh heaven. Psychologists say that lists should contain seven (plus or minus two) items for maximum memorability.

A famous bestseller by Stephen Covey, *The Seven Habits of Highly Effective People*, first published in 1989, set out to list the simple, crucial but all-important habits of very successful people. Note that they were *habits* – not abilities, traits, motives, needs or values. Habits you see, are acquirable. They can be trained. The list was succinct and parsimonious. The book was positive, upbeat and inspirational. That sells.

But for those who see the glass as half empty; for those who think optimism a branch of naïvety; for those who have been knocked around by capricious, egotistical bastards, what about the dark side? Surely there is worst practice, as there is best practice? Surely there is a list of habits that cause derailment, failure and doom? There are, in fact, a growing number of business books looking at Executive Failure. They may not sell as well, but they are probably much more useful and honest.

Indeed, there is a paradox here. The personal qualities or habits in business leaders that lead to doom and destruction are often seen as strengths, and in moderation may indeed be so. But they contain the seeds of their own destruction. So, what are they?

1. Delusions of power, success and pre-eminence

The problem with success and power is not that it is intoxicatingly addictive, but rather that it leads to overestimating one's actual control. Success in business is a result of many things. Economic, political and social forces completely beyond one's control have devastating effects. Failed leaders are not fatalistic. In fact, precisely the opposite is true. They seem to believe they have almost magical powers; that they are special, that they (and they alone) have the secret. This is seen as a heady mixture of narcissism, complacency and a disregard for those in their organization who really do the work.

Many think they have special insight: the answer to the difficult questions. They know the formula: they can understand, control and predict when others cannot. Hence they have an increasingly worrying tendency to underestimate difficulties, hurdles and obstacles. Worse, they pour time, effort and money into failing projects which they alone caused to fail in the first place.

2. Blurring the boundaries

Various corrupt dictators apparently think the national bank and the country's reserves are theirs alone. They see no distinction between what is theirs and what is ours.

The potentially failing leader certainly does not do work-life balance in any sense of the word. They identify so much with the company and its success, image, power and influence that they are not figureheads or even patron saints. They *are* the company. Decisions, therefore, are based on their needs. Headquarters are moved to suit the educational needs of their family. Things are renamed and rebranded to reflect them. The personality cult of the president.

3. Obsessed by PR, spin and media power

Bad press hurts; good press is elixir. Everyone knows that the charismatic, articulate and, if possible, good-looking boss gets interviews and invitations. His or her performance can affect the share price dramatically ... and, of course, this can explain the boss's generous remuneration package. Much media interest may be ephemeral, shallow and trivial, but the narcissist in the potentially failing CEO notices its effects. So the PR department is doubled. Image consultants are hired. Media training occurs.

The image-obsessed CEO can, after meeting pop stars and icons, begin to behave like them. They prefer soundbite to analysis; the big picture to operational details. Everything is spin: from financial statements to organizational restructuring. Every communication gets the PR treatment. This is not simply to ensure consistent media branding or writing clarity. It is to present (censor, distort) the facts to suit the image.

4. Repeating the old formulas, letting go

It's very easy to fall back, to default, to replay old strategies that worked in the past. It's difficult to let go of old skill areas and deal with the really important and urgent issues.

Things change: laws, customer expectations and technology which worked in the past may have precisely the opposite effect today. The older the CEO, and the longer in post, the more prominent is this habit.

We all want to believe and live in a just, predictable and orderly world. Those who fear or do not understand change look back for the secret of success, not forward.

5. Watering down the conscience

Even in this world of fuzzy relativism people need to know the difference between right and wrong, good and bad, legal and illegal. Yes, it's fun to have concepts like "tax evoidance" which is the fudge between tax evasion (naughty) and avoidance (skilful).

There are grey areas. And there are lots of temptations . The CEO who fails either always had a little or a deaf conscience, or a very faint "still small voice", or lost it. People with power and influence have to exercise considerable moral restraint. They need to resist numerous very tempting offers that cause all of the seven sins. Sex and money are just two of the things on offer for the executive whose integrity is not up to scratch. Many are called, few resist. Some fall, confess and repent. That's natural enough. It's those who sin but don't care and spend all their time hiding their moral turpitude who are the really dangerous ones.

6. Hypervigilance, paranoia and distrust

Things go wrong. People let you down. Competitors triumph. Such is life. But some CEOs become ever distrustful, ever vigilant and ever sensitive to what they see as the scheming, lying crooks who are out to get them.

Their energy is spent in trying to understand others' real motives. And they are quick to misinterpret innocent actions as some kind of plot against them. They are, in short, paranoid. Nobody can be trusted; all messages are potentially intercepted. They lose the plot because they invest all their time and energy on hunting imaginary enemies rather than doing the job.

7. The perfectionistic, stubborn obsessive

Setting high standards and getting things right all the time is a desirable characteristic in managers. So is obeying the law, enforcing the rules and maintaining the standards. But one can go too far ... and become an obsessive perfectionist investing all one's energy into what is essentially trivia.

The perfectionistic manager often can't let go; can't delegate, can't be sure other will do it right. So he or she overworks and often get exhausted ... and depressed. Such managers are always overwhelmed by detail and never able to so the strategy and tactics thing. They are, as the Freudians have observed, anal: they are rigid, stubborn, obsessed by time, money and cleanliness, and unable to function unless things are done according to their exacting standards.

These seven deadly habit rarely exist on their own. There is nearly always what clinicians call evidence of co-morbidity. This makes diagnosis far from smooth.

Normal, healthy people under stress may reveal some of those behaviors. But that's the point: these are not habits. When they become so, the problems begin.

Reference

Covey, Stephen (1989) *The Seven Habits of Highly Effective People*. New York: Simon & Schuster.

Sex, violence and car chases

Does sex sell? In the mid-1990s, Calvin Klein jeans launched a rather controversial and highly sexual advertising campaign which doubled their revenue. So is it a good idea to use sex (or violence) to improve sales? There are four questions here:

- Should one sex-up products using names, images, innuendo?
- Should one ignore the product and attempt to sex-up the ads for it?
- Should one leave the product and ad alone but advertise in sexy programs?
- Should one do all three: sex-up the product and ad, and put them in a sexy program?

We have recently learnt that the "Hello Boys" Wonderbra ads that seem to be noticed more by chaps who liked superstructure than women who have it, are to be changed. A rather more coy and more functional approach appears to be in the offing.

There are various ways in which one can "sex-up" a product. Obviously, one can use sexy ads. They may use highly attractive, scantily clad actors or subtle innuendo, or not-so-subtle, culturally understood images. Most of us remember speeding steam trains rushing into tunnels; the girl biting the chocolate flake ad and the music of 'Je T'aime' and so on.

Another way is to embed the advertisement in a sexy program. There are many post-nine o'clock watershed programs that deal with all aspects of sex … but not always sexily. And do you get more value for money if you put a sexy ad in a sexy program or in an unsexy program?

The idea of commercial advertising is pretty simple: people see, listen to or read an advertisement. They recall the brand, its strap-line and the product. They later recognize the product in shops, on the web or elsewhere, and buy it. They trust products more that have been advertised. Good ads lead to great sales.

But how to get the ad noticed and remembered in the first place? Psychologists have known for half a century that memory for anything is dependent on how deeply it is "processed". People have to notice the ad, pay attention to it, understand the central message of it and integrate it into their personal "knowledge bank and system" – the more the advertisement catches your attention and interest, the more you are likely to devote energy and capacity to processing it, and the stronger the memory trace will be.

Processing goes through various stages: notice the ad; pay attention to the pictures, the words and the benefits; understand and comprehend that message and then integrate it into your knowledge bank, commercial schema and so on.

So ad agencies use drama, humor, sex and violence to make the ads more attention grabbing, interesting and memorable. They try to elicit emotions and mood states that enhance memory, although recall may depend on that mood state being experienced again when the shopper is buying.

People seem to like humor, some like sex, fewer like violence. But the job is selling products. Once the ad is made, the question is where and when to show it. Various factors effect this decision, including costs and (for television) viewing figures.

But assume you have a choice. You are marketing a food product. And you have made an outrageous, near-to-the-line sexy ad. Do you slot it in a food program ad-break, of which there are many, or in a car program or a gardening program? Assume the same cost, the same viewers, the same readership. In other words, should you maximize program/advertisement congruity or incongruity?

A few American studies have looked at whether putting an advertisement in a violent or sexual program improves or impairs memory for it. Three groups watched either a violent, sexually explicit or neutral TV program that contained nine standard advertisements. Afterwards they were asked to recall the brands and identify them from pictures of similar brands on supermarket shelves. The next day they were each phoned and again asked to recall the brands. The studies showed that those watching the neutral program remembered most. Irrespective of their sex or age or how much they liked the program, the sex and violent programs seemed to impair memory for the advertised products.

It may be that people attend more closely to sex and violence, so they inevitably have less attentive capacity for other stimuli like the ads. Also it is believed that sex and aggression in the films stimulate sexual and aggressive thoughts, which further limit interest in and attention paid to the ads.

So the moral lobby of parents, priests and pundits might not stem the flow of sex and violence on the box, but the advertising lobby which effectively subsidizes and therefore pays for the programs certainly will if these results are to be believed.

Shopping habits

Apart from endless queues at checkouts, perhaps customers' biggest gripes with their local supermarket happen when a clever new manager does a spot of rearranging. Pesto moves from sauces to the pasta section; and eggs that were in baking are now to be found in the dairy section.

Some believe in a "goes with" pairing idea. So crackers are near the cheese; tea and coffee next to the biscuits. Others do a purely categorical classification: all biscuits go together, be they sweet or savoury, exotic or local, cheap or costly. Still others, so the conspiracy theorists believe, put the "essentials" such as bread and milk farthest away from each other and farthest away from the store entrance to maximize our walk through the store while indulging in a spot of impulse buying.

The next most important and frustrating supermarket event is to find that they are suddenly out-of-stock of that crucial and irreplaceable special ingredient. It has to be sour, not sweet, dried cherries. Only one type of cheese really works. There is no substitute for a special or favored product. You know where it should be, but the shelves are bare.

These two very common frustrations illustrate the fact that, when it comes to supermarket shopping, we are creatures of habit. Read the marketing literature and we appear to be attentive, discriminating consumers motivated on the one hand by bargain-hunting and on the other by a murky mix of sins – avarice, greed, pride and sloth. We are supposed to pay attention to marketing messages; process them; seek out particular brands, and become happy, brand-loyal advocates.

But in fact we are rules by our habits. Habits are repetitious behaviors: they seem difficult to give up, particularly bad habits such as biting your nails, eating chocolate for breakfast, or smoking. Habits represent automatic routinized behaviors that do not involve conscious decisions. How many times have we returned nearly panic-stricken to the house with no memory of ever locking it up? It has become a routine and an unconscious habit.

Curiously, both Freudians and Skinnerians (that is, psychoanalysts and behaviorists), argue that the best predictor of future behavior is past behavior. You tend to do what you have done in the past. But while the former look for deep unconscious motives to explain the origins of behavior in the first place, the latter seek our behavior shaped by the environment. And this is where the supermarket comes in.

Some radical marketing theorists argue that purchasing behavior is not dependent on the personality or attitudes or feelings of the consumer. These are anyway merely hypothetical constructs that exist primarily in the minds of psychologists. What determines behavior is prior experience of the environmental rewards and sanctions.

But the science of behavior is easy to apply to sales. People have a learning history; a habitual pattern; a personal story of likes and dislikes that have been shaped by experience. The ways people move around shops are typical of them: the purposeful, hunter-gatherer male eager to get back to the cave; the browsing and dithering couple who always shop in pairs; the list-dependent automaton. Where they go, how they pay, how they arrive at the shop are all soon clear patterns based on prior positive and negative experiences. Given the choice, they park in the same place, choose the same type of trolley, walk the same aisles, take the same routes, pay in the same way. People buy the same sized products from the same shelves at the same time of the week. Confronted by a new product (on their usual route) which they may have seen advertised, some will have a go at trying it. If it's easy find, good value, rather nice – or in a positive reinforcement as the behaviorists claim – they are likely to repeat the behavior till it becomes a habit and on the list, as it were.

There are three things, and only three things, we need to know about consumers to predict (and understand) their behaviors: their learning/consuming history; the setting or situations in which shopping occurs; their response to a particular project (positive, negative, reinforcing, averse). Consumer habits occur because people get used to particular set of positive outcomes. They are – in the jargon – contingency shaped to repeat the behavior.

Reward types are many. One reinforcement is approbation or status recognition from buying things that publicly attest to a person's economic attainments. Toys for the rich. Another powerful reinforcer is hedonism – enjoyment for its own sake. Others get a thrill out of collecting or accumulating: token-based buying.

Do consumer experts understand this? They sure do. First, through loyalty cards they can learn your entire shopping history. Next, the clever ones really understand the importance of the in-store experience. Third, notice how many times you are offered tastings of try-outs, be it food products, alcohol, perfumes or the like.

Fourth, note how in the supermarket advertising they are offering a major, but rather general, reinforcer. It's fine quality, or value for money, or greenness or whatever.

So drop your focus group, give up on your deep-motive researchers and instead watch your customers' behavior. Reward them for what you want them to do. Understand it's as much about the shop and the shopping experience as the brands. And make it a habit to study habits.

Staff and customer satisfaction

It is now around 20 years since the Profit Service Chain Model was published in the prestigious and ever-popular *Harvard Business Review*. It was called a chain because it documented various logical links between management style and practice to profitability.

The model proposed that perhaps the most important proximal factor driving profit was customer loyalty. The repeat customer; the brand evangelist; the loyal supporter. And what drives loyalty? In large part, satisfaction with the brand. And if that brand is a service product, it is largely about the service experience. Happy customers are loyal and drive up profits. So what makes service customers happy? Happy, contented and motivated staff. *Staff morale drives performance, which drives loyalty, which drives profit.*

Put another way, unhappy sales staff often express their negativity and low morale to the customer – surly, unhelpful "jobsworths", who refuse to perform the "emotional labor" associated with all service jobs. And the resultant dissatisfied customers take it out on the organization: they never return, they bad-mouth it, possibly even acting as brand terrorists.

Companies have certainly taken on board the customer loyalty message, even if they only try to tie customers in with loyalty cards and schemes. If you can't easily differentiate the product (for example, gasoline), or location (supermarket), loyalty is encouraged by rewarding points, which mean prizes.

It is questionable whether loyalty schemes are really about loyalty as properly defined. They are designed to tie the customer into a repeat purchase scheme which offers meager benefits. But the idea really spread. So many organizations went for the idea that we now have generic loyalty cards that record and reward purchases from a specific group of retailers.

But what about the equally important idea that it is staff morale and not the loyalty scheme that is the best driver of customer loyalty? If this is true, why did senior managers not take the issue seriously, investing time, effort and money in understanding how to ensure and maintain staff loyalty?

It may be because, despite its popularity, they simply did not believe it. Another fancy model dreamed up by impractical, expensive, other-worldly consultants and academics who have never done a real day's work in their lives?

In fact, there have been various rigorous studies carried out that have proved the causal link between sales and service staff morale and customer satisfaction. More interestingly, big companies often had sophisticated systems that recorded and tracked that information.

But it is one thing to have the data and another to interrogate it. Is the data mined? If not, why bother to record it? Who is responsible for this? It's not a difficult job to devise and test a causal model if the data are available. So why do companies spend money collecting this data and then ignore it?

There are many possibilities. *First*, it's nobody's specific job or responsibility to look at those different data sets and do this sort of analysis. Maybe it is thought of as an academic question irrelevant to the day-to-day workings of the organization. *Second*, it could be that different departments (Finance, HR, Marketing) collected the data and it was encoded or stored in different places. Possible, but unlikely.

Third, line managers have enough on their plates keeping the show on the road, without testing fancy management theories. They may believe their resources are best used elsewhere. Of course, on the other hand, they may not have the analytical skills.

Fourth, the grown-ups (the senior management) may not feel it is really important. Many say they have little time or inclination to read business books or magazines, and they may be wise not to do. Puzzling, though, is the lack of curiosity is levering one's unique database. All strategy should be data- and theory-led, shouldn't it?

Fifth, even if the data they have is mined and modeled, and the causal path established, it would show that staff morale is important, but not necessarily how to improve it.

People are difficult, loyalty schemes are easy. But there is increasing cynicism about all those cards and points and air miles. After a few miserable-staff-driven customer experiences, customers cut up their card and try a different brand.

The moral? Morale matters. And it matters most among sales and service staff. You have a CEO and a CFO; why not a CMO: chief morale officer. Their job is to monitor, uphold and improve staff morale through the bad times and the good. It is not an easy job. Is the concept too elusive? No more than corporate culture. Surely.

Morale is a function of organizational policies, rules and procedures. It's a product of the nature of work people do – how much control, autonomy and challenge they have. It's also a large part of the function of management: how people are managed. Are they set clear, stretching, but attainable targets?

Are they given all the technical, informational and emotional support they require? Are they given accurate feedback on their performance?

Managers themselves have the greatest impact on morale. The question is who ensures they personally have good morale to model it to others. Step forward the CMO with a flexible and sensitive performance management system that does just that.

Status anxiety

We strive both in life and at work with two conflicting drives: to get along with others but also to get ahead of them. We do a lot of social comparison. Indeed, many things such as pay satisfaction are entirely dependent upon it.

There are many indicators of status and rank in society. The first, of course, is social class. Despite everybody denying that it exists and claiming that everyone is now middle class, we have lots of words to describe people at various levels. At the bottom is the slave, or lower – or underclass. They are the proletariat – or worse, the lumpenproletariat. Then we have the middle class – upper and lower middle; the bourgeoisie or petite bourgeoisie. Above them are the upper or ruling class; then the gentry, the old money.

And how do you tell one class from another? Yes, there is education and occupation; income and wealth. But there are more subtle signs, such as language and costume, and grooming and manners. While many rejoice in their "working-class roots" they also celebrate their upward mobility.

But status at work is also terribly important to people, particularly men. Your grade, job title, size of office, car parking space, are all little, but terribly important, indexes of rank, status and power.

Only a very few people are not concerned with rank and status. Hence all the fuss about job titles, uniforms, company cars and office space. These are public statements of special status, not only at work but also beyond the workplace.

And what should we make of the "cash-for-peerages" scandal, that first appeared with Prime Minister David Lloyd-George in the 1920s, and has recurred at the time of writing under ex-Prime Minister Tony Blair? What will people pay to be called My Lord or *Sir* Humphrey?

But let's not be moralistic. We have more admirals than ships in the British Navy. And universities have created dozens of types of professors for those longing for that once grand and important title. We have *ad hominem*, special, titular and visiting professors, in addition to the Regius professors and Endowed Chairs.

It used to be the case that you simply inherited status, through titles, wealth or sinecures. And there were socially approved signs of that status. Through clothes and ceremony, through make-up and gesture, you knew your position. A fair skin and pointy shoes meant you did not do manual labor in the sun, and indeed might not work at all.

The top hat, the bowler and the cloth cap were simple class and status markers. Now that is all another world. But there are still symbols – just harder to read. Inherited status made for a stable, predictable, structured, but probably unfair, world. Your birth determined your rank and status, and kept everybody in their place.

How do we achieve status today? This in part depends on what you do. Business and political animals show their status in many ways. All have an entourage, who accompany them everywhere. They have special advisers. They have security personnel. More status – more guards, more cars, more people, bigger planes. They become a travelling circus requiring all these people to minister to their needs.

They need stylists and cooks, translators and PAs. They carry nothing. Those who look as if they travel light in fact travel very, very heavily. Consider what it takes to enable an HRH, a prime minister, or best of all, a Saudi prince or African potentate to travel abroad. It's part of the status thing now.

Creative people acquire status in other ways: through their quirky genius. We want them to be extraordinary, unconventional. They acquire status by their talent, but the public are fickle; and they also speak with forked tongue. They want their actors, musicians and writers to be ordinary but special, one of us but better-than-us. And, as artists and actors often long for status, they appear to eschew it once achieved.

Those of us who are neither megastars nor Masters of the Universe have to acquire status among our peers. We used to be able to do this through hard work and effort, by gaining educational and professional qualifications, or by good works.

But in our meritocratic society we have, it seems, been empowered to acquire status. So we worry about it. We can do something about it, so we fret – we have the new disease: *status anxiety.* And it becomes something that we trade in.

Stereotypical truths

There are lots of jokes about people in different professions: the unstable marketing type; the introverted, inadequate actuary; the arrogant, big-picture-obsessed strategic planner.

Think of the stereotypical creative director. Pony-tailed and called Donatella he/she (for that fact is not always clear) is famous for personalized "fashion statements", quirky use of language, attitude to management, and inability to control budgets. From the newspapers they read, to the food they prefer, this type are well known.

Stereotypes are situation-based. There are marketing types and HR types. There are engineering types and legal types. There are definitely health-and-safety stereotypes, as well as the dreaded administrative types.

And what of the IT manager and engineer? They are easy to caricature in their short-sleeved, slightly old-fashioned dress when they pitch up at meetings. The usual picture of them is this: these chaps (for they nearly always are) are "techies" confined, it seems, to self-imposed exile in their functional bunkers.

They are inwardly focused, speaking their own language. They seem trapped in their own imaginary world, quite unable (or, worse, unwilling) to communicate with the outside world. They call their customers "users" and have a helpline staffed by people who frankly (and obviously) despise callers. This attitude leaks from every pore. Significantly, they are unable to understand political agendas. Even the top performers are hopeless at selling, persuading or charming the board into supporting them.

The greatest problem, according to the stereotype, is their complete lack of *psychological mindedness (interest and awareness of psychological phenomena)*. They simply don't do people. Indeed, that is how they become IT or engineering specialists in the first place. Faced with uncertainties, social rejection and confusion in adolescence, they remained at their computers, in their dad's tool shed or with other like-minded adolescents, turning themselves slowly into "geeks". They loved technology, logical problem-solving and, yes, innovation, but strictly within their sphere.

They find people a mystery; capricious, emotional and needy. They understand their own clan and how to speak to them. But others are a puzzle. Their managerial approach is command and control: issue orders, check responses. Communication is best done through email or formal presentation.

The words that never seem to be applied to our stereotypic IT engineer are: ability to empathize; good at motivating staff; excellent communicators. They may have passion and vision, but it is very much confined to their system, their 'toys', and their (small but important) part of the business.

Hence they are difficult to promote, because they are essentially not very good people managers. They don't really like or understand management, unless it is of a small group of homogeneous, like-minded pals.

But enough of stereotyping. Is there even a kernel of truth in it? Two business school academics, Lesley Willcoxson and Robina Chatham, have recently published a paper in *Information and Management* (2006, vol. 43, no. 6) that explored this stereotype in 130 senior IT managers. This is what they found.

The leadership style of the IT managers is task-focused: they give instructions, follow orders and stick firmly to final decisions. They are extremely reliable, they meet deadlines and they believe that they gain legitimacy through specialist knowledge, skill and proficiency.

Burrowing a little deeper, they are comfortable working alone or in groups of various sizes; and they are relatively little concerned about inclusion by others, with no super-sensitivity to acceptance or rejection.

However, they do have a strong need for control and recognition, having a preferred way of sharing responsibility rather than having sole responsibility. But they do have doubts about their ability and seem fearful of (public-task-oriented) criticism and failure. Interpersonally they are rather defensive, yet quite needy with respect to gaining affection.

So how are they different from the general manager? Willcoxson and Chatham did a nice compare and contrast table which made this pretty clear. General managers are people-focused, offering a lot of encouragement, support, feedback and communication. The IT managers are task-focused: with structure, deadlines, clear instructions. General managers believe they gain legitimacy through commitment and loyalty rather than proficiency alone.

In a sense, the senior IT managers had fewer of the deeper skills. They were essentially specialists, while general managers were just that: generalists, better at influencing, and less technical.

Evidence that the stereotype is true? Partly. But don't you want people who work for you to follow instructions, meet deadlines and rejoice in their technical proficiency? You bet! But wouldn't it be nice to have a spot of emotional intelligence thrown in as well?

Surprise me

You don't have to be a tree hugger to be seriously annoyed by junk-mail. Pity the poor postman who "let on" how to prevent it. He was sacked. Junk mail is really big business for the Royal Mail.

But why all the fuss? One answer is that junk mail generates a comparatively (the word is used advisedly) good customer response. Telephone cold calling generates a response rate of around 5–10 percent, while direct marketing, catalogs, emails, postcards and radio jingles get a response from those who received, saw or heard it, of only 2–5 percent. For advertising in newspapers and magazines, response rates drop below 1 percent.

So advertising hardly works? True, but it does not have to be like that. The reason is that most advertisements go unnoticed, unprocessed and ignored. If you don't get the product and the brand into basic awareness, you have failed at the first hurdle.

So how to be noticed, whatever the sales media? *MountainviewLearning* have developed an approach that is appealing because it fits with our knowledge of neuroscience, our experience and advertising research. In their model, step one involves *surprise*. You are noticed (and recalled) if you use images that are different, quirky, funny. It's the unusual that gets people off their guard.

Sometimes, the image or the message is shocking. Shockingly frank, shockingly rude, shockingly un-PC. Imagine the organization that boasted it was number 2 or 3, and not number 1. Imagine the Germans or Japanese boasting about their exploits in the war.

The surprise can be in the message, in the image; or even in the chosen medium. So why not give up billboards for sky or cloud writing? Why not try graffiti advertising?

The first question, then, is whether the brand or the message *stands out* from everything around it. Is it just another ad for another X with the same old promises?

The great ads of all time had this quality. The Rolls-Royce ad that proclaimed how quiet the car was (the loudest noise was the ticking of the clock); the pregnant man; the car stuck to the billboard. Guinness was a master of the genre. Agencies such as Saatchi & Saatchi, and gurus like Ogilvy certainly preached the message: *Stand out, get noticed, cut through.*

Standing out means being different. Having incongruous symbols; people saying the opposite of what they mean; showing the unfamiliar in a familiar light, or vice versa. There are many factors one can use to stand out including colours, sounds and movements. Silence is noticeable in a world of noise; black-and-white in a world of colour.

So you have the audience's attention. Now speak to them. And more to their hearts than their heads. We are, after all, people of both affect and cognition. Of emotion and reason. And perhaps as a result of our education, our upbringing, or simply tradition, we seem to prefer the head.

So we try to persuade people to buy something because it is good value, or reliable, or has more bells and whistles. Luxury goods never bother with this nonsense. They go for some pretty powerful human needs: to belong, to be recognized and respected, to feel proud. Cosmetics sell hope; sports cars sell power; diamonds sell love.

Understand your product and your audience. Understand their needs and values. Where are they coming from? Who are they? Aim it at them ... and no one else.

Then touch the heart-strings, awaken the soul. Be brave; don't be too British. Admit we have feelings, often strong ones. We feel pity, but get compassion fatigue; we feel guilt, and anger and pride. Advertisements can touch and legitimize these emotions. Emotional advertising often features a transference from one state to another: from disappointment to optimism, conflict to peace of mind, shame to pride, boredom to excitement.

You can use cute children or animals to help the emotional messages, as well as powerful symbols. The idea is to stimulate memories that change moods, just as they do in shops when they use mood music or pump in smells to attempt to trigger memories. Many memories are emotion-laden, be they of people or events.

Try emotional heart plucking. But get it right. Do your research. And speak to those simple but important needs we all have: for self-respect, and friends, and security. And yes, there are the "Disgusted of Tunbridge Wells" who like complaining. But you don't have to offend to be noticed. You simply have to be clever. You need the head to understand the heart. And there is a strong feedback loop. Touch feelings and you might have the Midas touch.

So be targeted, be original and be affective. Affective is effective. And get their attention, otherwise you might be left in the starting blocks.

Tall poppies

People will always take a pop at the person on a pedestal. But are some individuals or some nations particularly prone to hubris pruning?

People in Australia and New Zealand have a concept for this activity. It's called cutting down tall poppies. The idea is to equalize, to prevent individuals or groups showing off their ability or success. Stand out, shine too much and you get the chop.

It is sort of reverse snobbery: a rejection of the naturally superior concept. Some see it as a resentment of others' success, while others see it as a useful mechanism to attack those who take themselves too seriously or flaunt, with arrogance and hubris, their success.

In fact, an Australian psychologist, Norman Feather, has devised a scale to measure it. Here are some of the statements you may like to inspect:

- It's good to see very successful people fail occasionally.
- Very successful people often get too big for their boots.
- At school it's probably better for students to be near the middle of the class than to be the very top student.
- Very successful people who fall from the top usually deserve their fall from grace.
- Those who are very successful ought to come down off their pedestals and be like other people.
- People who are "tall poppies" should be cut down to size.
- Very successful people sometimes need to be brought back a peg or two, even if they have done nothing wrong.
- People who always do a lot better than others need to learn what it's like to fail.
- People who are very successful get too full of their own importance.
- Very successful people usually succeed at the expense of other people.

It is, however, unclear whether it is excelling at some endeavor that is the problem, or glorying too much in success. Clearly, it is bad for any endeavor to encourage people to be average; to punish the successful, the talented and the hard-working.

But is it equally unwise to discourage the lauding of tall poppies? The question probably hangs on two issues: who in fact recognizes and celebrates the talented; and what form the praise takes?

Most organizations, be they schools or businesses, like to hold up, as examples, those who do a good job. They set an example, showing that it can be done. They may have their photos published in the in-house magazine, or be given special awards.

What, however, is not acceptable, is for them to go about trumpeting their success. Humility, not hubris, is required. Just as at the Oscars, the award-winners must thank many people and point out that, essentially, all their success is due to others. Cocky show-offs are "tall-poppied" … and so they should be.

Thus success is good; being outstanding is desirable, but others should recognize and reward this. No pushing yourself forward; no self-nominated aggrandisement.

Second, the recognition and the reward. Being top should be its own reward. The simple knowledge that you are the best is, or should be, enough. You don't want to reward people for an innate ability. It makes them smug and complacent. You do, however, want to reward them for effort. That is why the person who doggedly finishes the race, albeit in last place, receives as much applause as he or she who came first.

Is it healthy to have the tall-poppy-cutting instinct, or is it essentially unhealthy? It is suggested that there are fundamental differences in how Americans and British people react to the success of others. The Americans supposedly admire success, believing as they do that it can be achieved (easily) by everybody. Success is the product of effort and ability, risk and good judgment. Those who achieve success deserve it and, equally, deserve acclaim and approbation.

The British, on the other hand, are jealous and vicious towards the successful, somehow believing that they do not deserve their success. They use words like "opportunistic" to imply luck rather than effort. The British press has the powerful urge to pedestalize and then pooh-pooh. They are as fast and enthusiastic at putting people on a pedestal as at knocking them off. The more so if those pedestalized show any trace of hubris.

Perhaps the most important thing about the tall poppy syndrome is that it should encourage equality of opportunity. All Americans believe they can, if they wish, become president. Being a tall poppy through the luck of birth is deeply undesirable in our egalitarian age. Being a tall poppy through some other inherited ability, such as body shape or brain power is also frowned on. But being a tall poppy through effort – self-discipline, deliberation or hard graft – that's a different story.

So it's OK to be really good at something; to stand out above the crowd, as long as it is through your own efforts; it is others who ordain the tall poppy status and that the reward is the accolade alone.

Targeting sales

First, we had the grey vote and the grey lobby. Then we heard tell of the grey panthers and the grey pound, and the gay lobby and the pink pound.

Suddenly, sales and marketing people are becoming aware of, and interested in, many kinds of hitherto forgotten or ignored groups that are ripe for a spot of serious targeting. So they have discovered ethnic and ethical shoppers. Some have tried to target highly specific religious groups such as Catholics or Muslims. Americans know the power of the Evangelical lobby.

Originally, marketing was interested only in demographics: information about our gender, age, stage and job seemed to be sufficient to understand us and our buying habits. So the young mother, the busy executive, the early retired groups were addressed in various campaigns.

Then the VALS™ (Values and Life-Styles) marketing tool and psychographics came along. A person's interests, opinions, values and lifestyle were considered to be an alternative, even a better way, to segment the market. So we had the belongers and the emulators. Of course, people themselves did not use these words and probably never knew who their peer group was.

You can segment any market. One study of American housewives (Ziff, 1971) segmented them into six categories:

- Outgoing optimists;
- Conscientious vigilantes;
- Apathetic indifferents;
- Self-indulgents;
- Contented lows; and
- Worriers.

Another found the market for prescription drugs fell into four clear groups: Realists, Authority seekers, Skeptics and Hypochondriacs.

Then suddenly, like schoolboys who have found a sociology textbook, the marketers have discovered new minority groups, whose belief systems or social categories lead them to be easily definable.

Thus environmentalists or ethical consumers are defined by their sociopolitical beliefs. They might be teenage activists or retired bank-managers, but they share similar concerns which supposedly drive their consumption. The greenies don't like over-packaging, they like fairtrade stuff, and disapprove of vegetable air miles. Their concern for the planet, it is believed, shapes their purchasing in the high street. And it affects everything from where they bank to how they dispose of their refuse.

Equally, Catholics and Muslims and others of the Book (or other books) may be an identifiable group whose media consumption, food preferences (often highly rule-bound) and shopping habits are constrained by their religion. Their beliefs inform their morality, which dictates their life-style ... or something like that. Religionists favor other religionists. They shop with fellow believers at places owned by the faithful. They believe this is safe, sensible behavior.

But other people form groups as a result of their everyday preference or habits. Pipe-smokers are a clear, but dwindling, group. Cyclists are a growing group, as are vegetarians. And there are those whose group is imposed upon them by their skin colour or physical condition. You can go on and on, boxing, pigeonholing or grouping individuals. It's a fun hobby, but does it help the marketing enterprise?

What are the essential characteristics of a defined or definable group that merits targeting? Does it matter much whether the group members see themselves as part of this group?

What does matter is that the group is coherent, consistent and predictable. These people can only be targeted if they can be found easily. Do they "consume" different media? Are there specialist magazines, radio or TV programs that they watch? Or do they consume the regular media differently?

Next, do they require subtle or blatant messages. Think of targeting the greys or gays: what images, messages or strap lines facilitate their paying attention to, and then buying, the product?

More importantly, how affluent are they? Some identifiable groups are paradoxically rather anti-materialist. They might be well-off, but are put off by traditional advertising. Others are keen but poor. There's no point in pouring good advertising money down the drain.

It is certainly fundamental to all in the production and service industries to "know their customers". Marketers love the idea of getting under the skin of the customer, really understanding his or her needs, motives and drives.

Certainly, grouping them helps. But we are members of different groups at the same time. The gay, grey Chinese doctor may be a case in point. And they may either be ashamed of and try to hide their membership of certain groups, or not even see themselves within the category. Further, these groups and grouping go in and out of fashion in a state of flux.

It's hard targeting people if the target is fuzzy, moving and ever-changing.

Reference

Ziff, R. (1971) 'Psychographics for market segmentation', *Journal of Advertising Research*, 11(2): 3–10.

Ten Ps of management

Every so often a new CEO wants to know the value of his/her human assets. It's easy to evaluate the asset value of the stock, the plant and the shares. But what of the so-called "most valuable asset", the people? How good are they?

Have people become complacent, spoiled and smug during the good years? Have the right people been promoted, or is it essentially a "Buggins' turn" system? Can the top team take the pressure? Is there a realistic succession plan, with the right people in the right jobs?

Why not call in some experts to do a disinterested evaluation of the human assets. Put the stuff through some sort of assessment centre. Probe into their motives. Test their mettle. Then put them into a useful category that might determine their future. Good idea. What about the following tenfold classification for all senior managers?

- *Painful*: Almost too hurtful to witness. Washed up, underpowered managers with half the talent of those who report to them, struggling on a daily basis to keep the show on the road. Like an animal crying out to be "put to sleep".
- *Past it*: Personnel who cannot or will not "keep up" with the changes about them. Probably once labeled a "*wunderkind*" but now too reliant on stories about the glorious old days, of being promoted young, of early, long-forgotten triumph.
- *Peaked*: People who have been promoted once too many times; perhaps rewarded more for loyalty than competence. Perfectly OK really, but just "a bridge too far".
- *Pissed off*: Backward-looking, angry individuals who feel aggrieved at mistreatment. The result is an alienated, quit-but-stay jobsworth, who continually snipes at the organization. The enemy within – a terrorist worth dispatching.
- *Premature*: People who have been accelerated for good reason, but ever-so-slightly too fast. They may yet make it, but that remains uncertain.
- *Pressured*: Executives who always seem so stressed out that they cannot give of their best. They might not have the real ability or skill set for the job, or perhaps they are dispositionally unstable, the worrying type. Not good for them or the company to keep going.

- *Promising*: A good job history record, having the skills, the attitude and the hunger. Labeled perhaps as talented but not fully tested. The signs are good, however. Often young(ish), but not necessarily so.
- *Promotable*: Earned the spurs; clearly ready and able to face the next hurdle. Understands the job and the organization well. Able to learn fast, take on extra responsibility, do the business.
- *Proven*: A pretty unblemished track-record of success in everything that has been thrown at him or her. Able and stable with an enviable CV. The sort of person possibly on head hunters' lists.
- *Psychocase*: People who have lost the plot; had a "nervous breakdown": need a good shrink. They can be lethal in any business. But, as with the alcoholic, nobody knows quite what to do with them, and so they continue wreaking havoc.

Tests' revival

The fortunes of psychometrics go up and down in both the academic and the "real" world. There are periods when the critics seem to have sway, arguing that the jury is back. They report that tests are, at their best, very weak predictors of anything useful at work. At worst they are expensive, fakeable and unreliable. They discriminate against certain groups of people, who can be litigiously minded. One can easily be biased on all the sorts of "isms": ageism, racism, sexism. They give the gloss, but do not deliver the benefits of science. They are pushed by avaricious consultants, test publishers and old dons on the make.

The dark years for the academics were the late 1970s to the mid-1980s. It was received wisdom, based on one important book by Walter Mischel (1968), that factors outside the individual shape their behavior. So, at work, it has less to do with your ability or temperament and more to do with your boss, your company and your tools.

Psychometric consulting was boosted by three factors. The emergence of aggressive test-publishing firms; an increase in unemployment, which increased vastly the number of job applications where tests suggested an efficient and effective way of doing a good pre-sort; and one or two high-profile managers used, advocated and proselytized for the use of both ability and personality tests.

But there have been ups and downs. Big companies have been sued as a result of the test score criteria they used to reject applicants. And every couple of years an article appears ridiculing the whole enterprise, pointing out the ludicrous nature of some of the questions asked or the mundanity of feedback.

So the pendulum swings. The market is now more mature. Test buyers are, we hope, better informed. Journalists are bored with the story. And the researchers have been busy conducting good, disinterested and detailed studies on the one central, crucial issue for most test buyers. Do test scores predict bottom lines? A number of findings well known to the academic psychometric community are coming to light, and there is a new enthusiasm for tests.

The following factors seem to be among the most important:

- Different personality tests which measure different personality traits predict specific and different work performance criteria. Not all tests are equal. Further, specific traits (for example, neuroticism, conscientiousness) predict quite different outcomes (the former predicts absenteeism; the latter, diligence and dutifulness).

- Detecting fakers, liars and impression managers is pretty straightforward. Socially desirable responding has been over-emphasized. Those who dismiss all tests on this basis really need to look clearly at the evidence. Furthermore, you can't fake ability tests, except in one direction. And for those obsessed by this critique, what of the interview? It must be one of the most theatrical charades ever invented.

- Ability tests predict "can do" criteria; personality tests predict "will do" criteria. A simple, but important and effective, distinction. No amount of hard work can compensate for lack of ability. Equally, being extremely talented is not enough.

- This is the clear message of the EQ people: you need both IQ *and* EQ – the ability to manage tasks and people; to understand technology and emotions; to be talented but want to explore and exploit that talent. It means using both ability *and* personality tests.

- If you combine ability and personality test scores, your predictive power increases. The two give the full picture. The more complex the job, the more change that occurs in it, the brighter, the more stable and the more focused the person needs to be. He or she needs to be bright enough to deal with each new level of responsibility. But individuals also have to be able to take all the stress. And be tough. And hard-working. Tests give you the scores.

- If you add 360-degree ratings to ability and test scores, your predictive power increases significantly. This is the distinction between self-report and observer scores. Personality tests involve people reporting about their own behavior. But "other" ratings, by boss, peers, subordinates, clients, fill out the picture. Not everyone is particularly self-aware. People might tell you the "truth" about themselves as they see it, but others know better. Hence the use of references. But 360-degree reports are not platitudinous letters of uneven length. They are specific ratings on tight criteria known to be important.

What best predicts a person's output on the job? The answer is a job tryout of, say, six months. Obvious really, but frequently impossible if there are many applicants. Next, a two- or three-day assessment centre appointment, where you can have a really good look at them: give them many different tasks; have different individuals rate them; put them under pressure;

see how they react to others also seeking the job; watch how they are when off their guard. Most assessment centres also use tests. But they can be very expensive indeed.

What we do know is this. Most unstructured, unplanned interviews are next to worthless, as are references. Making the wrong and bad decisions can be very, very costly. If tests can reduce error and increase accuracy, they must be worth it. And, finally, they are surprisingly good value for money compared to all other methods of selection.

Reference

Mischel, Walter (1968) *Personality and Assessment*. New York: Wiley.

The ADHD organization

Being around an Attention Deficit Hyperactivity Disordered (ADHD) young person is enough to drive anyone to distraction. To say that they are hard work is an understatement. It is no wonder that parents and teachers believe in the wonder drug approach that renders those in their care almost reasonable.

For the fastidious, the definition of ADHD is this: "A persistent pattern of inattention and/or hyperactivity-impulsivity that is more frequent and severe than typical of individuals at a comparable level and age". And the clinical symptoms taken from the psychiatry text book are these:

Inattention

(a) often fails to give close attention to details or makes careless mistakes in schoolwork, work or other activities;
(b) often has difficulty sustaining attention in tasks or play activities;
(c) often does not seem to listen when spoken to directly;
(d) often does not follow through on instructions and fails to finish school-work, chores, or duties in the workplace (not due to oppositional behavior or failure to understand instructions);
(e) often has difficulty organizing tasks and activities;
(f) often avoids, dislikes, or is reluctant to engage in tasks that require sustained mental effort (such as schoolwork or homework);
(g) often loses things necessary for tasks or activities (e.g. toys, school assignments, pencils books, or tools);
(h) is often easily distracted by extraneous stimuli; and
(i) is often forgetful in daily activities.

Hyperactivity

(a) often fidgets with hands or feet or squirms in seat;
(b) often leaves seat in classroom or in other situations in which remaining seated is expected;

(c) often runs about or climbs excessively in situations in which it is inappropriate (in adolescents or adults, may be limited to subjective feelings of restlessness);
(d) often has difficulty playing or engaging in leisure activities quietly;
(e) is often "on the go" or often acts as if "driven by a motor"; and
(f) often talks excessively.

Impulsivity

(a) often blurts out answers before questions have been completed;
(b) often has difficulty awaiting turn; and
(c) often interrupts or intrudes on others (e.g. butts into conversations or games).

But what has this got to do with the world of work? Gurnek Baines from YSC, a London-based psychological consultancy, believes there is such a thing as an Attention Deficit Company. It has all the hallmarks of the syndrome and is a prototype response to pressure at work.

The problem is dealing with change. Lots of things have changed – technology, global competition, customer expectations, legal injunctions. Few organizations in the public or private sector have escaped (or will escape) these relentless forces. The trick is how to adapt.

There is the bury-your-head-in-the-sand approach. This is change-denial. It's more common in older organizations that have been successful, and characterized by over- confidence, and looking backward. But if you always do what you've always done, you will always get what you've always got.

Some are happy to manage a slow decline, watching everything from market-share to employee engagement drop year by year. They may increase their efforts at cost control, stream lining and the like, but the fundamentals remain the same.

It's easy to hark back to a golden past. Curiously, some change-averse companies were not that successful in the first place. They recreate a fictitious time, with happy workers and customers bringing in excellent profits.

The ADHD response is, however, quite different. The ADHD organization knows about change: it changes everything all the time. It does initiatives, restructuring, re-engineering, coaching and everything else that's going! Its competency frameworks are regularly rewritten, its organizational chart redrawn; its logo redesigned.

The ADHD organization is a guru fashion victim. Often, a succession of short-lived, over-paid CEOs initiate a series of equally short-lived, over-priced initiatives to "set the company on a competitive, profitable, sustainable footing for the challenges of the new millennium" ... and other platitudes.

Many forget where they are coming from, or worse, where they are really headed. In all the excitement and possibility of the new they can succeed in demotivating and confusing both their employees and their customers. They lose the plot, lose their way, and lose the confidence of the shareholders.

And their response? Fire the CEO, bring in another fix-it junkie and start some new initiatives. The same promises, same fanfare, same expenses ... and the same failure. There is so little follow-through: no attempt to think strategically and more importantly "bed-down" and attempt to sustain change.

The paradox for the lay person observing the miraculous effects of the drug Ritalin on the ADHD adolescent is that it is a stimulant. The reason is that ADHD behavior is driven by under-stimulation of the nervous system, not its apparent over-stimulation.

And the equivalent of Ritalin for the ADHD organization? Stimulate the stakeholders: all of them. Re-engage the staff by good management; reconnect the customer through good service and products. Good management is about getting the best out of people by setting clear goals, giving feedback and, more importantly, support. Help staff to feel good about their achievements; help them to get a sense of achievement and meaning at work.

The same applies to customers. Be consistent in delivering service and value. Sure, give them opportunities to try out new things. But give them predictability. And stay faithful to the real purpose of the organization.

Drugs for ADHD help people concentrate and learn. They help the person to develop and grow. The same is true of the ADHD organization.

The effects and effectiveness of advertising

Advertising effectiveness is concerned, quite simply, with making a tangible contribution to a company and its brand. It is essentially reducible to a cost – benefit ratio of the total cost of an advertising campaign divided by the incremental income generated from purchases of the product over a particular time period.

Wait a minute: that's simpleminded, black/white, naïve, "bottom-line" thinking, which does not and cannot understand the long-term achievements of the brand image in a complex, dynamic environment.

So that is why most researchers in this world study the advertising *effects* of an advertisement or series on consumers after a limited number of exposures.

So how do you measure the effects of an ad, or campaign? Three methods are favored: the first is memory. What, if anything, can they, the viewers remember immediately or sometime later after seeing the ad? Do they recall the brand? The "strap-line", or just the image? Do they remember, unaided, any propositions or product/service benefits? If they can't recall much we need to start again. The trouble is that there are very different types of memory. There is free response: "Name all the products you saw advertised last night." There is cued recall: "What brand of beer/soap/car was advertised during the news last night?" There is visual recall and verbal recall. There is product recall and brand recall. There is brand name recall versus strap line recall. They may give different results as a function of different ads.

The next is attitude or belief measures. This may be a "before and after" design, or more simply an "after" design, where people may be asked open or closed, but not leading, questions about the brand, the product and/or the ad. The aim of the ad is to increase a person's liking, admiration and preferences for that particular brand. You are supposed to feel warm toward the brand; that you want to own it; have some; use it. That it will make your life easier; that you will be a better, more attractive, even a more lovable person through having used the brand. The ad must say "have me". Third, there are action or behavioral measures, which are what you are really seeking. That is, do people really intend to choose or buy the product? Do they search out the brand? Do they look for shops that sell it? Do they insist on your brand and nobody else's?

So researchers talk about communication, attitudinal and behavioral effects. Another way of thinking about this is cognitive (the intellectual stuff), affective (all that touchy-feely stuff) and volitional (behaving, doing).

Ideally, an ad does all three: it is memorable, changes attitudes and encourages behavior. But that is a pretty tall order, and probably unrealistic. Thus some ad campaigns attempt merely to inform: to make a new brand "top of mind". Others, self-consciously, work on our emotions, trying to make us feel good about a brand.

Researchers in the area thus try to vary aspects of the ad and then measure its effects. There are many possible factors. First, there is the content of the advertisement. Should humor be used or not; foreign languages or not; and what about celebrities? Should the main characters be "traditional" or counter-cultural? Who should do the voice-over? Will the pictures do the talking? Should all ads for the same product, store or service echo the same strap-line?

And then there is where the ad is placed in the program, be it on the radio or television. How long is best? Better to have two 30 seconds long than one of 60 seconds. How long is the advertising block, and does that make a difference? If so, is it best to place the ad at the beginning, the middle or the end? Indeed, what program should surround the ad? And what time of day? Nearly all these factors have cost implications. But for the same amount of money you can get very different exposure ... and therefore a very different response.

It really becomes seriously complicated to answer even simple questions, such as: does humor work in ads? Well, it depends on the humor (sexist, verbal, aggressive); the brand; the actors; the slot; the surround; and how you measure it. That is perhaps why the results are so equivocal, and why it is not always easy to replicate studies.

The glass menagerie

We all know about the glass ceiling at work. Then we had the glass elevator and escalator. Now we have the glass partition. It refers to an unseen wall between the sexes at work which discourages and inhibits the development of any form of relationship.

It's an odd material for a metaphor, really. Glass is transparent but also very brittle. It is the material of light. Prisms and lighthouses, chandeliers and glasshouses all celebrate glass. Glass can be clouded and opaque. It is used to make mirrors. Glass can be dangerous. It can be made shatter-proof or laminated. It can be thickened and double-glazed. And the most beautiful objects can be made from glass.

The glass metaphor is all about sex at work, or should that be gender at work? It's all about the smoke and mirrors that go on in the modern office. It's about things not being what they appear to be. It's about unseen barriers that are nevertheless impermeable. We see, as it says in 1 Corinthians, 13 in the Bible, "through a glass darkly".

The increasing use of the glass metaphor is used to complain about subtle but pervasive discrimination in the workplace. It implies that there still remain many barriers to women rising to higher positions of power and influence at work.

The glass metaphor is, in essence, a conspiracy theory. And conspiracy theories appear to fulfill important functions for their holders. It seems often quite pointless to try to disprove conspiracy theories. There are those who "go in for" them. They are like hydra: sever one head and another grows in its place.

But the long shadow of the 1960s may now be receding. The sexual equality and liberation ideas might have seen their demise at the hands of the new crypto-sociobiologists who believe that men and women are from different planets.

Developmental and social psychologists now have the confidence again to speak about sex differences through the lifespan.

We know that there are observable, replicable and consistent sex differences in infancy. Boys tend to be more active and spend more time awake. Girls are more co-ordinated, more vocal. Boys are interested in objects, girls in people.

In the preschool period, boys like rough and tumble play and have a narrow range of boy-typical interests. Girls acquire language earlier and apparently more easily than boys. Boys are less communicative and use language more instrumentally to get what they want.

As they get older it becomes clear that certain tasks are easier for the two sexes. Boys are better at mathematical reasoning, finding geometric designs in complex patterns, and motor skills such as throwing darts. Girls are better at story recall, remembering displaced objects, and fine motor co-ordination. So the sexes differ in their confidence in their competence. Boys express more self-competence in sports and maths, while for girls it is in reading and music.

Boys pay a great price, however. They are more vulnerable to various conditions, from autism and ADHD, to dyslexia and dyspraxia. They maybe less empathic but they seem to be more sensitive. Boys are more affected by trauma, but tend to deny sorrow and loss. They are thus erroneously assumed to be tougher than girls.

In adulthood we know that men are bigger and stronger but don't live as long as women. They take more risks, are more promiscuous, and have better mapping skills. Females are more dextrous, empathic, nurturing, co-operative and linguistically sophisticated than men.

And so our preferences and skills determine our career choice and success. Most (over two- thirds) of language and drama teachers are women, while most science teachers are men. It still remains rare to have female pilots, snooker players or accountants. Unfair, foul play, discrimination?

Certainly, business organizations are male-oriented. Men have most leadership roles; hierarchies pander to male status and ego; competition is emphasized over co-operation; goal focus and performance management is male-achievement-orientation made manifest. And specialization fits male single-mindedness.

The sociobiologists tell us that culture is therefore working with biology. But they do say individuals can be either "too male" or "too female". Men can do with a bit of emotional intelligence. Women could learn a bit of task focus.

So the sexual division of labor is how things should be? Only the most courageous or stupid assert that. The problem is that all of the above findings are based on population statistics, that is, probabilities. Of course, there are extremely able female pilots or male counselors. There are tough, task-focused female managers and co-operative, caring male employees.

The task is to identify and encourage talent, not to have some ideologically imposed quota.

The inevitability of silo

It is called the "silo mentality". It is meant to be a bad thing. We are encouraged to destroy, reform and restructure to remove silo thinking.

Whence the metaphor? Is this the revenge of the California-based management consultants on the Mid-West grain farmers who glory in their silos as dramatic symbols of their wealth, success and power?

And what is the opposite of the silo mentality? Is it the matrix organization, flat-thinking or integrated networks – or any such organo-babble? And what is the evidence that silos are so bad and matrices so good? Is this just another evidence-free consultancy trend?

But why do silos exist in the first place? Are they natural occurrences? For the initiated, silos in management speak are groups of like-minded people who cluster together in biggish groups. The bad thing about them is that they are homogeneous and isolated ... and therefore easy targets and victims. They are bad because they seem anti-integrationist and the structure inhibits cross-fertilization of ideas.

But people are usually happy in their silos and reluctant to endure dotted-line matrix reporting structures. The question is, how silos evolve? It certainly is no mystery, as any vocational guidance expert will point out.

Relatively early in childhood, most of us discover we are good at doing some things and less talented at others. Further, some of these suit our temperament better than others. Thus through teachers and parents we may be introduced to a whole range of activities, from spelling competitions to swimming, from acting to arithmetic, from carpentry to computers.

That mix of ability and temperament works best doing things we are good at, at our own pace and in a preferred way. And then we discover like-minded people with similar dispositions. Thus those in the chess club tend to be relatively alike and rather different from those in the karate club. And it is fun to be around "like-minded" people who share our passion, world view and interests. We are, after all, social animals.

Over time we all invest time and energy, usually with pure enjoyment, getting better at the tasks and activities we thrive on. We are, in a sense, exploring and exploiting our gifts. Furthermore, we tend to shun those where our talents are not found. Hence we discover vocational interests and preferences.

While some people are multitalented and others apparently talentless, most of us by early adolescence have a good idea of our preferred activities.

This, in turn, leads to a particular choice of education "package" of disciplines at school and university, as well as in professional training.

There are many who get it wrong, for a variety of reasons, but they usually have opportunities to correct their misjudgment.

It is therefore no surprise that an actuary going to a marketing conference (and vice versa) is struck by how similar the delegates are, and how little the actuary is like them (and indeed *likes* them). They have different talents and preferences. Not better or worse, just different. And it is so much nicer, more comfortable and more productive being with "your own people" ... meaning, in your own department or speciality.

The Weber principle of specialization for efficiencies applies nearly everywhere. There are departments, sections, groupings of those in finance and engineering, marketing and production, IT and HR and so on. And they, for reasons of efficiency, have their own space; their own building even. This over time becomes the silo. Perfectly natural. Perfectly normal.

The danger, however, is that physical isolation and exclusive intra-group communications mean that the occupants of the silo become a special tribe with their own language and loyalties. They trust only their own chief and fight with those in the same organizational culture.

Silos mean balkanization, poor inter-departmental communication, little company alignment. The question, however, is what to do to prevent or repair this. How can you form people into happy, healthy, co-operative, interdependent teams when they are so multidisciplinary? One question is at what level this is best done. Board? Senior manager? Supervisory?

Clearly, there is a trade-off in the "de-siloing" of organizations. People seem to prefer them and soon build them up again after destruction. There are various "solutions" to the problem, be they architectural or engineering. But they do not work, bringing only lower morale and lower productivity unless the problem is understood. And there is a positive way to communicate with others and feel part of the bigger team.

The motive trilogy

The "depth boys", as the neo-psychoanalysts were called, used ink-blots and pictures or photos to peer into the murky pre- or unconscious aspect of individuals to try to reveal what they really felt and thought. They were interested in that fascinating and most puzzling of all concepts, motivation. What drives people to indulge in the oddest of behaviors?

Why would you want to be in the *Guinness Book of Records*? Why collect used bus tickets or beer mats? Why be an exhibitionist or a prohibitionist? The taxonomic chappies drew up long lists of needs such as abasement, dominance or succourance that seemed to fit into separate categories.

But it was one of the most influential psychologists of the twentieth century, David McClelland, who argued that we can understand all behavior, and particularly behavior at work, in terms of three basic needs: achievement; power; and intimacy or affiliation. These are powerful, fundamental drivers of behavior. All sorts of odd, possibly bizarre, behavior at work can be explained by these three basic motives.

1. The need for achievement
The drive to get ahead, be successful, be better. People with this need tend to like challenges and have curiosity. They like to be engaged. They are goal-oriented but enjoy the means as well as the end. In some sense, the reward is an index of achievement, and not the goal. The goal is to master a skill.

Those with this drive in abundance choose activities with optimum, not maximum, challenge. They choose things they believe they can achieve (with effort): neither too easy nor too difficult. They certainly prefer tasks where they can take personal responsibility for the outcome and those where they receive feedback on their performance.

The need for achievement is related to actual achievement. So can it be taught? Can you train someone to be entrepreneurial? We know that those with different levels of this need seek out different courses at school and university, put in different amounts of effort to attain goals, and react differently to both success and failure. They cope with ambiguity and uncertainty; they seek outcomes that involve personal responsibility; and enjoy problem-solving.

But is it inherited or learned? Some believe it's mainly inherited, indeed evolved. It has been proposed that, for many women, a happy family with good relationships is the real goal, while for men it's success at work. Thus men and women are on different "achievement trajectories" dictated by our caveman past.

Others see it as being all about childhood socialization – how parents encourage and reward independence, competition, skill-mastery and planning. They set tough but realistic goals and standards. They genuinely and regularly applaud success and celebrate accomplishments. They expect but don't dwell on failure, which is seen as a natural part of learning. They stress effort over ability; trying over gifts; motivation over talents.

The trouble is that these beliefs seem to be laid down young. You can teach an old dog new tricks, but it is difficult.

2. The need for power

This is the desire to have a serious impact on others. The opportunity to influence and control others and events is at the heart of this motive.

Those with this drive enjoy arguing, tend to be assertive and even early on like being elected to positions of influence. They like prestige, possessions, even choosing friends and spouses to enhance their status and reputation.

People with this strong need for power seek out work, and social and family situations that fulfill these needs. Naturally, this often involves positions of leadership, particularly political office. They are seen by others as strong, vigorous and commanding. They talk about wanting to make a difference. They are also perceived to be in a hurry, brooking no opposition and are sometimes control freaks.

The need for power is therefore associated with power-related careers, but less stable private lives. Those with this need in abundance do experience more stress, because they have increased frustration and conflict. Power-play costs.

3. The need for intimacy (affiliation)

This is the need for close, communicative, warm relationships with others. Those high in this need invest more time in relationships; report more positive reactions when being around people; smile, laugh and make more eye contact with interrogators; and communicate more via all media.

This is not just a manifestation of extraversion. Those with high intimacy needs prefer one-to-one interactions rather than parties, and they listen to others carefully. Others think of them not as "life-and-soul-of-the-party" or "outgoing, sociable attention-seekers" but rather "sincere and loving" and "definitely not dominant or self-centred". There is a difference between intimacy and social contact: close friends versus acquaintances.

We can therefore plot every individual on a three-dimensional profile. In many ways, good leaders are highish on all three dimensions, but it is important to see how the dimensions balance each other out. Power can be balanced by intimacy/affiliation, and achievement by power. Historians have tried to understand famous people, particularly American presidents, by an understanding of their need profile.

A person's drive for leadership and style as leader can be parsimoniously described by his/her need profile. Thus the leader who is highest on power and lowest on intimacy will have a very different style from one where these needs are reversed.

But the problem with the needs approach is that people either cannot or will not tell you about heir real, deep-seated needs. It has been possible to differentiate between *implicit* (versus explicit) *motivation* and *self-attributed motivation*. The former is manifest in people's behavior and reflects their largely unconscious desires and aspirations. The latter is what people *say* their motives are, but only if they have self-insight *and* are prepared to tell the truth.

Interestingly, we know that implicit motivation predicts long-term, life-course motives – the jobs people choose, how they do at them, the success of their personal and work-based relationships. Self-attributed (that is, questionnaire-based) motivation, on the other hand, predicts well in the (very) short term – that is, how they respond to very specific situations.

The moral of the story? Dig deep, look for behavioral patterns. Listen to the stories people tell. Profile them on these three fundamental needs. It may help you to predict the (odd) behavior of your leaders and understand it better.

The psychology of naughtiness

There are certainly as many negative as positive words to describe children's behavior. There are bad, evil and wicked children; there can be difficult, bullying, unrewarding and demanding children. They can be angry, destructive and disobedient. They can be, and often are, egocentric, moody and intolerant.

And they *are* naughty. The etymology of the word "naughty" is from "naught" or "nothingness": while it can mean "wicked", the dictionary talks of harmlessly mischievous, slightly improper, occasionally indecent. All children are naughty. They defy their parents and teachers; they rejoice in breaking rules. They answer back. They can be defiantly contrary. And they really enjoy subversiveness at many levels.

Naughtiness appears to be a childlike condition. To describe an adult as naughty always seems to imply a sort of forgivable innocence. People in the "Carry On" films were naughty. Saucy seaside postcards are naughty. But naughtiness is not only about sex. It's mainly about authority. Naughty people disobey the conventions; they challenge the great and the good; they frequently undermine.

Would you employ an adult if they were known to be naughty? What if you read a reference that described Carruthers as an amiable, likeable, able and/but naughty marketing specialist? Note the critical difference between "and naughty" as opposed to "but naughty". In the first sense, it can be used as sort of compliment; in the latter, definitely a drawback.

Is a naughty person a trouble-maker, or an innovator? Are they a nuisance or a breath of fresh air? Are they reactionary, un-PC, embarrassing problems, or essential challenges to the stuffy conventionalism of most businesses?

There is now overwhelming evidence concerning the adapted psychopaths at work. Most people think of the psychopath, sociopath or person with anti-social behavior as a dangerous axe murder. This personality disorder has various markers or criteria, but one of the most central is a lack of conscience. The Freudians believe such people have a very weak super-ego. They don't do regret, remorse or empathy. They feel no emotional pain and never hesitate to inflict it on others if it suits their immediate needs.

The really dangerous person at work has been described in a recent book by P. Babiak and R. Hare (2006) as a "Snake in a Suit". Beware the good-looking, educated, articulate psychopath. They are unconcerned about anybody but themselves, and lie convincingly to all and sundry. They abuse all those around them in their quest to achieve their own selfish goals.

The psychopathic manager is wicked. Most have criminal records. They have a personality disorder. They are unlikely to be thought of as naughty.

The essence of naughtiness is that it is self-conscious rule breaking. It is about challenging the conventions, often with humor. It is wilful. Naughty people break only some of the rules some of the time. Unlike the psychopath, they know and mostly respect the difference between right and wrong. They know and feel the consequences of their actions.

Perhaps there are two types of naughtiness in both children and adults. The bad kind in both is associated with problems with authority and impulsivity. Some people just resist being told what to do by anyone, about anything, at any time. It may have something to do with their parenting – certainly has something to do with self-discipline. And perhaps it has to do with empathy and taking the role of the other to whom the naughtiness is directed.

Naughty adults, of the poorly socialized type, smoke in places where it is forbidden, for example, jump queues, and attempt to evade many kinds of laws and restrictions. They are not very nice people.

But there is a form of positive naughtiness. Some naughty adults and children love puncturing the pomposity of those in authority. They mimic teachers and managers. They do humor and irony. Words are their weapon. Comics are naughty. Their targets are petty bureaucrats; their joy is found in testing the limits.

Does it take courage or self-confidence to be naughty? Partly both. We mentioned earlier the best-seller called *First, Break All the Rules* (see p. 151). It is not an anarchic tract. In fact, rather the opposite. It's about a positive psychology perspective on organizational life. It's all rather too worthy to be called naughty.

Children like naughty parents. Up to a point. They can be deeply embarrassing because they appear so unconventional. When the naughty adult gets a "black tie" invitation from a supercilious friend he may wear a black tie with a lounge suit. A naughty adult may make fun of a precious chairman … or, even naughtier the partners. A naughty adult disobeys the dictatorial and pointless injunctions from health and safety. Naughty adults go into marketing rather than PR.

But perhaps that's the point. Few, if any, organizations like naughtiness. The military and the security services may be the exception. But naughtiness in any form may be an anathema to the corporate world or local councils. Pity really. Important things can be expressed in a light manner by naughty people. If nothing else they can brighten the day of those less extraverted and confident when they break the rules so conspicuously.

Reference

Babiak, Paul and Hare, Robert D. (2006) *Snakes in Suits: When Psychopaths Go to Work*. New York: HarperCollins.

The self-esteem industry

A great deal of damage has been done by the self-esteem movement (SEM). For a long time, SEM advocates – often counselors, teachers and therapists – have seen low self-esteem (LSE) as the *cause* of most individual and societal problems and ills. So they set about designing feel-good, esteem-raising courses to help people gain pride and self-worth.

But has that simply turned many teenagers into egocentric and arrogant narcissists who are unable to accept negative feedback under any circumstances? The reaction of less-than-attractive and frankly talentless young people on various talent shows has revealed the damage done by the SEM.

The central question is whether self-esteem is a cause or a consequence of life success. A few years ago, the Association of Psychological Science in America commissioned a report into what the research really showed. In doing so, they shattered many of the myths of the SEM and called into question the usefulness of a lot of daft, simple-minded and misleading claims.

Half a dozen myths seem to have been perpetuated and need to be knocked on the head.

1. *People with high self-esteem tend to have many other positive characteristics, such as being kind, generous and self-controlled.* It is true that people with high self-esteem believe (say) they have many positive characteristics (that is, they feel attractive) but this view is not necessarily shared by observers. People with high self-esteem seem to inflate their virtues; a view not supported by those who know them well. In this sense, high self-esteem may be associated with low self-awareness. And the latter is an important predictor of mental health.

2. *Those with high self-esteem do better in school.* The SEM saw the correlation but incorrectly inferred causation. They assumed that high self-esteem caused greater achievement. Hence teachers were instructed only to praise; that all must have prizes; and that boosting self-confidence leads to exam success. If anything, careful longitudinal research showed the opposite to be true, in two senses. First, the causal direction was the reverse – academic success leads to high self-esteem (and not the other way around). Second, artificially boosting children's self-esteem by exaggerated and inappropriate praise in fact led to lower subsequent academic performance, especially if they were praised for their ability rather than hard work.

3. *High self-esteem in adults promotes job success.* It's basically the same issue. Results show that where job success is rated objectively (actual behavioral productivity) or by such things as supervisor (even subordinate) rating, the relationship between those ratings and how good people feel about themselves is about zero. If anything, the causal chain goes: able, hard-working people do well, produce more; this is then rewarded by salary, promotion, acclaim; this encourages greater work and more reward, and hence a virtuous cycle. No amount of feeling good can substitute for ability and motivation.

4. *High self-esteem individuals are more likeable, popular and have more friends.* And having the social support of friends, they are healthier, happier, more successful and better adjusted. Certainly the data shows self-reported self-esteem linked to self-perceptions about being popular. However, the bubble bursts when you get others to rate. Studies with students and schoolchildren show that they rate their peers reliably on likeability, social skills and so on, but that these ratings are unrelated to self-esteem, with just one exception. This was in initiating social contacts. So those with self-esteem are *not* more popular, skilled, charming or insightful, though they may well believe this. However, the self-confidence they gain from their delusion does make them more likely to strike up conversations with strangers.

5. *Low self-esteem increases the risks of a variety of anti-social delinquent or criminal behaviors such as alcohol, and drug abuse, underage or unprotected sex, or ASBO-worthy behavior.* In fact, the data shows the opposite. Those (cocky) youngsters with high self-esteem are uninhibited, risk-taking hedonists. Self-esteem is not a protective factor. Certainly, indulging in some of these activities, with their many unpleasant consequences, can lower self-esteem. Again, the causation is the other way around.

6. *Low self-esteem leads to physical and verbal aggressiveness.* The idea that aggression (that is, bullying) is simply a mask for self-doubt and insecurity. Again, the data show the reverse. Indeed, it is narcissists or those with a surfeit of self-esteem that are more likely to react with aggression when they don't get their way. Challenge their highly inflated view of themselves and they may very well thump you. Violent prisoners are often narcissists.

This is not to deny the importance of self-esteem. We know those with high self-esteem tend to be healthier and happier; more persevering to achieve goals, more socially networked and more confident to explore their talents. But you achieve it by helping people to do well at school, in jobs and in social contacts. Help them to achieve good grades, promotion and a great set of friends, and they increase in self-confidence. Give them essentially false or biased feedback and they can become both complacent and unable to face any sort of criticism.

The SEM has set young people back. It has infantilized them and wasted resources. They should have been encouraged and praised for the effort they put into learning, training and self-improvement, not for just being super, marvelous and wonderful people.

To go or not to go?

It all used to be so easy, so safe, so reliable. You toiled in the same vineyard all your life (if you were lucky) and at the age of 65 drifted off to pipe, slippers and potting shed. You might not have the gold watch, but perhaps were given some token inscribed tankard as a memento of a lifetime of graft, dedication and loyalty.

With your expectations of three score and ten, this left five quiet years of reflection before the grim reaper came out of the mist. You would be lucky not to be dogged by ill-health of mind and body. And that was your lot.

But now times are certainly "a-changin". It is not that unusual to find fit 50-year-olds retiring. It's also not that uncommon to find sprightly 70-year-olds or even energetic 80-year-olds working hard at full-time jobs because they could imagine no better alternative.

With increased health and wealth, we have quite simply much more choice. We live much longer, as worried politicians and pension managers know, and have wealth unimagined by our parents.

A further complication is the anti-age discrimination which makes it hard to give 60- or 65- year-olds the push if they don't want to go. So it is now much more a matter of choice. The question is, what influences the decision to go or to stay?

In a recent study by Leo B. Hendry, with M. Kloep, published in the *Journal of Occupational and Organizational Behaviour*, the researchers looked at the types of motives found among retirees and non-retirees. There seemed to be four major reasons to go (early). First, there was the simple "Had Enough" motive: people were bored or exhausted; overwhelmed by re-organization or changes; or quite simply honest enough to know that it was just too much effort to keep up. The game was not worth the prize.

Then there were those with an alternative plan. They had Other Things to Do: more interesting, more important. There were all sorts of things – especially traveling – that they now really wanted to do and had decided to do it. A sort of "now or never, life's too short, what-the-hell" attitude.

Some had, of course, health problems. They suffered from chronic or acute illness or disability, which meant to a large extent that the decision was made for them. Sometimes it was more psychological than physical: multiple psychosomatic orders cleared up once job stress was reduced. The body and the mind just seemed worn out.

Another reason is social pressure by family, or indeed people at work, for the person to retire. These are pull-and-push factors that persuade the perhaps dithering potential retiree finally to close the door. Clearly, being pulled is better than being pushed ... though there may be exceptions to this rule.

So why choose to stay on? Some have a sense of mission. There are tasks yet to do. They feel the task, whatever it is, remains incomplete and they want closure only when the job is finished. Others like new challenges, which they see as positive, fun and intrinsically interesting. The narcissists may even believe that they are, in some strange way, indispensable and essentially unsubstitutable.

Another group of stayers know that the job gives meaning to their lives. Their identity, status and social wellbeing are related directly to their job. Work is, central to who they are. No job, no meaning in life. And people also stay for social reasons: they like, need and appreciate their friends at work. They like that sense of community, of being valued, of being part of the group.

Those who go know that there is a weighing up to be done when retiring. Those who go may lose social status. Some hate being senior citizens, oldies, pensioners often thought of as deaf, half-witted has-beens.

Others recognize that there are often considerable and enduring adjustment difficulties: the day has less structure, and people often suffer loss of support mechanisms. And there is the loss of work contacts, some of whom, one discovers, were just fair-weather friends.

But on the positive side of the balance sheet, there are no more work responsibilities. You can sleep in every morning; and you no longer have to deal with heart-sinking staff, jealous peers, incompetent bosses or demanding customers. All retirees use the "f-word" – Freedom. Freedom to pursue passions such as, family, friends and hobbies. Free to speak your mind; to join clubs; to do something completely different. And there are new challenges: these may be travel or further education, or even retraining for voluntary work.

There *is* life beyond work, but most people have some degree of adjustment problems. Partners say they now have twice as much of their partner and half as much money. Some get a shock. Even though they were happy to retire, they did not anticipate some of the less obvious things that are lost when leaving a job.

And, yes, sadly, some get depressed. They sink into that "Not much left to live for" negativity. They see their friends popping off one by one; they seem to do less; they have less energy and less mobility. They certainly aren't a good advertisement for a fulfilling retirement.

But perhaps we retire as we worked. The energetic, enthusiastic, engaged worker becomes the active, action-oriented and adaptive retiree. The cynical, sniping, negative employee becomes the disgruntled pensioner.

It's our abilities, personality and values that drive these big decisions and how we react to events at work. But we are not passive. We make our beds and we lie in them. Some deliberately engineer, and some do not, their retirement decisions.

We shall all have to face this choice. Best ponder on it for some time...

Reference

Hendry, Leo B. (with Kloep, M.) (2006) 'Transitions to retirement: entry or exit? A Norwegian study', *Journal of Occupational and Organizational Psychology*, 79.

Understanding the internet shopper

Sales and marketing people must understand their customers. They are often engaged seriously in trying to segment those regular, irregular and non-purchasers of products and brands. They segment markets demographically and psychographically. They try to understand the motives, values and world-views of their clients. And so they should. They have to live the brand, but also get into the "mind-set" and "value system" of their customers.

So we have the pretentiously named "Science of Shopping". Observers – like those time and motion, clip-board-clutching ogres of the past – stalk around department stores trying to find out when and why people linger longer, pause and purchase.

But how to understand the internet shopper? E-commerce retailers, now of course called "e-tailers", have to understand people they never meet. Yes, they have address, post code and purchasing history, but then so do store-card shops and supermarkets. Is that enough to get under the skin of spare-bedroom, online customers who are ever-growing in number?

Internet shoppers may once have been relatively homogeneous. Affluent young males might once have made up the majority of this relatively small market at the start of the twenty-first century. But things are changing rapidly: as the word, wealth and worldliness spreads, the internet consumer may be an eight-year-old male, or just as likely, an eighty-year-old female.

The first question is, what do they buy? Are they purchasing from standard retailers or from auctions, or both? Do they tend to buy only one type of product (for example, electrical equipment), or a whole range? Do they trade on the internet – that is, buy and sell, or only one of these? And with what frequency are they purchasing? Indeed, is there a temporal pattern discernable: for example, evenings or weekends only?

So the regularly trading, auction-oriented, primarily book-purchasing customer is a very different beast from the just occasional retail-only purchaser of things such as birthday presents or airline tickets.

There are perhaps four main motives for shopping on the internet. The first is simple *convenience*. For the cash-rich, time-poor; for the house-husband and child-carer; for the 12-hours-in-the-office, stressed executive, browsing and buying online at a time to suit them is everything. It's easy, fits in with an unusual lifestyle and is very efficient.

Second, there are the bargain hunters, who take to the web mainly *to save money*. Cut out the middle-man; don't subsidize high street rates. Some people soon learn that the web is full of bargains: books, flights, clothes – the lot. The savvy, economically minded shopper who likes bargains soon signs up.

Third is *excitement*. The web is the ultimate Aladdin's Cave. A veritable treasure chest of everything in the world. All can be inspected. And then there is the thrill of the auction, which may be just as good in the spare bedroom as in a draughty, musty saleroom.

And finally, there are the *shopaphobes*: those who hate the noise and clutter of shops, but also the gaze, suggestions and just the presence of over-zealous assistants, placed there, it seems, to harass the customer as much as anything else. These internet shoppers are not necessarily retiring, non-assertive introverts scared to say boo to a goose. Rather, they may like to take their time in making their decisions.

So who avoids the internet? Those who are vigilant, suspicious, nearly paranoid and who don't trust the process. The computer phobic, who almost by definition never gets turned on, tuned in or becomes part of the action.

But the young, the curious and the fun-seeking love the idea. They like the exploratory feel of the whole enterprise. They enjoy the adventure, the quest and the possibility of price comparison. They like the idea of communicating with other users. Internet shopping can be a hobby and a stress/boredom reliever as well as a necessity.

So the field lies open for marketing researchers. The internet shopper needs segmenting. You really have to know who, when and why a growing number of people make regular and important purchasing decisions online. You need to get below their skin into that murky world of values, motives and personality traits for an understanding of what and how to market to this heterogeneous but seriously important group of shoppers.

What does it mean to be conscientious?

Nearly all the synonyms of conscientiousness are good positive words: achievement-oriented; competent; dutiful; efficient; self-controlled; responsible; rule-following.

Organizational psychologists have shown conscientiousness to be a highly significant personality trait. It predicts educational and career success, productivity, marital stability, a healthy life-style, and even longevity.

Conscientious people have the work ethic. They are honest and dependable, reliable and orderly, sensible and hard-working. They work harder and have what psychologists call "better adaptive social functioning" than their less conscientious peers. They are, for any employer, good news.

For the researcher, and the manager, there are a number of interesting and important questions associated with conscientiousness at work. Just *where* does it come from? Can and does it *change* over time? Are there any *downsides* to being excessively conscientious?

The answer to the first question remains in the area of debate and discussion. The great nature–nurture pendulum has swung convincingly to the nature end, and scientists are now looking for the gene for everything. The creativity gene, the gay gene, the criminal gene, so why not the conscientiousness gene?

But Freudians will have none of this. Conscientiousness is about the application of the conscience, which is the superego. The superego develops from early experience; particularly with parents. The conscience is a carefully honed, rather sensitive phenomenon, the result of much trauma and conflict. And it's very important. After all, the conscience*less* are what the Victorians called moral imbeciles, film directors call psychopaths, and what we now call bold executives.

Both the nature and the nurture people seem to agree that when you examine the adult of the human species, what you see is what you get. Conscientiousness is not easy to train. Ever seen an "Improve Your Work Ethic" or "Beef Up Your Conscientiousness" seminar? And those "Seven Secret" types of "how to" self-help business books never much mention the work ethic. If they do, they call it workaholism, which is more likely to be thought of as a bad thing.

So the answer to the second question above – whether conscientiousness changes over time – is "not much". Organizations often act like naïve behaviorists, with their elaborate systems of reward and punishment to encourage all aspects of conscientiousness. People can and do learn to be more responsible, more orderly, more disciplined, but it often depends greatly on their starting position. It also depends on the reward schedules. Whether the game is worth the candle?

But the most interesting question refers to the *dark side* of conscientiousness. Conscientious people are industrious, they exercise self-control, they take responsibility and they have integrity. But there are three features of conscientiousness which, if found in extremes, are certainly much less attractive. Most conscientious people are traditionalists; they are rather conservative. They are rule-upholders rather than rule-breakers. They support systems rather than try to improve them. They can therefore be anti-change, anti-innovation, with a fear of lack of order.

Related to this is the problem of perfectionism and its brother, obsessionality. The conscientious work dutifully and deliberately. They believe there is a right and wrong way of doing things, and that the rules were created for everyone to follow to ensure order and the right outcome. They seek routine, regulation and rules. And in doing so they go wildly overboard, not recognizing the difference between the means and the end, and when the product or service is good enough.

Their moralism, their integrity, their virtuousness can be of the fundamentalist and unforgiving kind. They don't tolerate the laggard, the fool or the freeloader. And this reveals another weakness. The conscientious, with that well-defined and refined work ethic, tend to be achievement-oriented strivers. After all, at the heart of the work ethic is the puritan belief that the successful and the rich are God-blessed. Success is virtuous. They work hard – very, very hard – for their just deserts. And they are intolerant of those who do not pull their weight.

Thus they can be highly competitive, individualistic, poor team players hell-bent on their (God-ordained) success.

Change-averse, mildly obsessive, competitive individualists ... the modern manifestation of the work ethic?

What's in a name?

Is it purely by chance that a chap called Rotten became interested in the consequences of unpleasant smells (Rotten and Frey, 1985)? Or that Lionel Tiger and Robin Fox collaborated in 1989 to write a book, *The Imperial Animal,* about animal behavior?

Can it really be true that one's surname influences one's choice of career or academic interests? Clearly, one's name certainly has an effect on others: hence the frequency with which media and film stars change their names to appear more desirable and attractive, while other people like the sound of exotic foreign names (this is particularly true in the world of ballet: consider the host of English girls who took Russian stage names). On the other hand, the British royal family Anglicized their name at a time when national jingoism and anti-German feeling was at its height.

Does it help clinicians to have a name that would attract and inspire confidence among their patients? For example, would a Dr Backup be particularly good with computer phobics? Dr Beebe with stutterers? Dr Colon with the anally retentive? Those who had recently suffered a shock would surely be calmed by the presence of Dr Trauma, while Dr MacLean would probably be most successful with anorexics of Scottish descent.

Would Professor Twentyman be particularly well-equipped to deal with multiple personalities; and would those patients who were in sore need of advice find comfort in the present of Dr Askew? Sociopaths would be sure to strike up an instant rapport with Drs Conway and Conwell; and is it likely that Dr Bunney and Dr Burdi would favor regressing their patients back to childhood; while Dr Bolt relies rather too heavily on ECT? Surely a Mr Dredge would specialize in psychoanalysis, while those suffering from impotence would beat a path to Dr Hardaway's door.

Those members of the medical profession who practice dentistry are surely guaranteed success with soothing names such as Mr Kalme, and Mr Titterington, but one questions the wisdom of the dentists who retained the names of Carver and Blood.

What potential lies untapped in British psychologists' and psychiatrists' lists? What academic experimental psychologist or organizational specialist is clearly unsuited to his or her job because of an inappropriate name?

When attempting a superficial and impulsive review and analysis of the many names of chartered psychologists and registered psychiatrists in Britain, it would be possible to come up with a list of practitioners who might usefully retrain in specialist areas of practice. The table allows us to speculate about possible patients with whom they may be particularly successful.

References

Rotten, J. and Frey, J. (1985) 'Air pollution, weather and violent crimes', *Journal of Personality and Social Psychology*, 49: 1207–20.

Tiger, Lionel and Fox, Robin (1989) *The Imperial Animal*. New York: Henry Holt.

Psychologist's surname	Ideal patient type
Dr Abbott	Quiet retiring types who fancy a pint of foaming real ale
Dr Abed	Patients who need a little lie-down at regular intervals
Dr Albino	Those who are obsessed with Michael Jackson and all his works
Dr Allnutt	All patients
Dr Anger	Type A patients
Dr Asch/Ashburn	Fire-setters, pyromaniacs and heavy smokers
Dr Bacon	Phobic eaters prone to fetishistic food avoidance
Dr Bakewell	General eating disorders, particularly obesity
Dr Balding/Baldwin	Elderly men
Dr Barber	Prematurely balding anxiety cases, or those wanting to be at the cutting-edge of treatment
Dr Barker	People who have taken the last train from Sanityville
Dr Barwise or Dr Beer	Recovering alcoholics
Dr Basher	Practitioners keen on physical interventions such as shock treatment, surgery and so on
Dr Batchelor	Commitment-phobics who are particularly attractive to rich patients
Dr Bellow	Hard of hearing patients
Dr Binns	Those in the last stages of personality disorders who need to be sectioned
Dr Bland	Patients without personalities
Dr Blows	Patients with respiratory problems
Dr Bullock	Those who like issues taken by the horns, and eschews those with no balls
Dr Butcher	Masochists

(Continued)

Psychologist's surname	Ideal patient type
Dr Butler	Overly polite and subservient
Dr Camp	People who are confused about their sexuality
Dr Candy	Patients with a sweet tooth and a Disney view of the world
Dr Card	Obsessive gamblers
Dr Cash	As above
Dr Charman	Patients in the grip of a merciless tannin addiction
Dr Chaste	Those suffering from satyriasis
Dr Chasty	Hysterically frigid patients
Dr Chew/Chiu/Chu/Chue	Those with jaw problems
Dr Cipolotti	Narcoleptics
Dr Cockett	Self-indulgent, heroic fantasists
Dr Comfort	Insecure, insular people who never had a teddy bear of their own
Dr Cramp/Crampin	Patients suffering from bad circulation
Dr Craze	Manic sociopaths
Dr Crowder	Claustrophobia sufferers
Dr Crystal	Those who have turned to alternative medicine
Dr Cushion	Patients fighting obesity
Dr Cutter	Patients who opt for radical surgery such as prefrontal lobotomies.
Dr Deary	Deaf geriatric patients
Dr Diaper	Patients with a long history of bowel problems
Dr Dimond	Gold-diggers
Dr Doctor	Stutterers and those who compulsively tell bad jokes
Dr Doubtfire	Hysterical cross-dressers
Dr Drinkwater	Cystitis sufferers
Dr Eayrs	Vertigo sufferers with hearing problems
Dr English	Chronically repressed patients
Dr Farewell	Those unable to terminate relationships
Dr Farmer	Those with wellie fetishes or an unnatural attraction to horses, goats, etc.
Dr Fear	Multiple phobics
Dr Fine/Fineman	Those so sick they believe they are OK
Dr Flammer	Stutterers and those unable to make decisions
Dr Fortune	Compulsive gamblers and National Lottery addicts
Dr Friendship/Friend	See Dr Comfort

(Continued)

Psychologist's surname	Ideal patient type
Dr Frost	Cold, icy patients
Dr Fuggle	Those suffering from attentional disorders
Dr Furniss	Those bewildered by the red-hot heat of modern technology
Dr Furst	Maniacally competitive people
Dr Gilfeather	Fetishists
Dr Goldfinger	Sociopaths with delusions of grandeur
Dr Gross	Adolescents
Dr Grubb	Those obsessed with cleanliness
Dr Guest	Patients with low self-esteem and few friends
Dr Gunn	Suicidal patients
Dr Haggard/Haggith	Those seeking pre-cosmetic surgery counselling
Dr Hamburger	Prader-Willi Syndrome sufferers
Dr Handyside	DIY phobics
Dr Haste	Type A patients
Dr Hatcher	Over-fertile women
Dr Heap	Those prone to fainting
Dr Hennessy	Alcoholics
Dr Hotter	People who blush easily and sweat excessively
Dr Howl/Howell	Attention seekers
Dr Huff/Hough	Over-aggressive people prone to taking offence easily
Dr Hyde	Multiple personality sufferers
Dr Inman	Delusional patients who believe they are possessed
Dr Jelly	Adolescents who refuse to grow up
Dr Jolly	Those suffering from depression
Dr Joynt	People who were at Woodstock and have never been able to forget it
Dr Kane	Sado-masochists
Dr Kindness	See Dr Comfort
Dr Knapper/Knapp	See Dr Cipolotti
Dr Kobler	Cynical patients who don't believe in doctors or medicine
Dr Kupper	Those who prefer a "nice sit down" to all that couch based introspection
Dr Laidlaw	Sado-masochism
Dr Large	See Dr Cushion
Dr Leadbetter	Those unsure of their own abilities to guide others
Dr Leech	Patients who have difficulty either forming or breaking off relationships

(Continued)

Psychologist's surname	Ideal patient type
Dr Loan	Gamblers and spendthrifts
Dr Lovelock/Lovett	Multiple divorcees
Dr Mabey	Indecisive patients
Dr Macfie	Patients who delay paying for their treatment
Dr MacLean	Obsessive cleanliness addicts from north of the border
Dr Manners	Patients who need respect
Dr Meek	Those in need of assertiveness
Dr Mercuri	Telephone addicts
Dr Mistry	Patients perplexed by the real meaning of life
Dr Money/Moola	People who feel guilty about their wealth
Dr Moss	Catatonic patients
Dr Ney	Overly negative patients
Dr Noone	Isolated, friendless, inadequate patients
Dr Nuttall	General outpatients
Dr Odd	All patients
Dr Onions/Onyon	Patients who are overly prone to weeping
Dr Ooi	Attention seeking adolescents
Dr Pace	Those suffering from sloth
Dr Paradise	Patients with unrealistic expectations of life – and of therapy outcomes
Dr Pate	People who are hypersensitive about hair loss
Dr Plumb	Patients suffering from constipation
Dr Portnoy	Self-abuse patients who frequently complain
Dr Power	Patients who like electro-convulsive therapy
Dr Price	Obsessively miserly patients
Dr Punter	Compulsive gamblers
Dr Pusey	Cat phobics
Dr Quicke	Impulsives
Dr Quirke	Most patients
Dr Rainey/Raine/Rainguard	Patients fearful of excessive weather conditions
Dr Reddi	Patients with procrastination problems
Dr Risk	Overly cautious types scared of commitment
Dr Rope/Roper	Those with suicidal tendencies
Dr Roth	People prone to outbursts of rage
Dr Royal	Patients who feel they are trapped in a gilded cage
Dr Rub	Patients phobic about aromatherapy and physical contact with the natives
Dr Saad	Very unhappy people
Dr Satten	Men who enjoy wearing ladies' underwear

(Continued)

Psychologist's surname	Ideal patient type
Dr Scarlett	Shy, easily embarrassed people with little self-esteem
Dr Schock	Easily startled, nervous patients
Dr Scotchman	See Dr Barwise
Dr Shams	Psychopaths and sociopaths
Dr Sherrif	Narcissistic, power-hungry fantasists
Dr Shine	Competitive patients with a major breakdown experience
Dr Shooter	See Dr Gunn
Dr Short	People of Napoleon-like stature with inferiority complexes
Dr Sidebottom	Anally retentive patients
Dr Sik	Hypochondriacs
Dr Sincock	Patients experiencing excessive guilt feelings
Dr Slaughter	Mass murderers
Dr Sowerbutts	Grumpy gardeners with very low EQ
Dr Speake	Selective mutes
Dr Spender	Bankrupts
Dr Spicer	Patients with olfactory hallucinations
Dr Starling	Small businessmen with a history of failure
Dr Stocks	People with an unhealthy obsession with gardening
Dr Stoner	Cannabis dependency patients
Dr Sturgeon	Spendthrifts with a taste for the high life
Dr Sugarman	Hypoglycaemia sufferers
Dr Tata	People who are unable to form lasting relationships
Dr Thinn	Anorexics and bulimics
Dr Thrasher	Sado-masochists
Dr Tibbles	Cat phobics
Dr Tinkler	Patients with weak bladders
Dr Tolliday	Workaholics
Dr Whewell	Those refusing to admit that they have a problem
Dr Whitty	Those with a sense-of-humor bypass
Prof Wigg	Balding narcissists
Dr Wildgoose	Alcoholics
Dr Wink	Habitual sexual offenders
Dr Wiseman	Exclusively inadequate members of MENSA

Writing your own development plan

"Personal development plan" (or PDP) are words that inspire fear, contempt and loathing (in that order) in many middle-aged managers. It seems to be an HR-inspired conspiracy to belittle and humiliate senior managers by requiring them to play daft and embarrassing games for no good purpose.

As a rule, opposition to personal development is concentrated most into two areas. One is in the high-tech areas of companies, where often brilliant but emotionally illiterate executives react very badly to being encouraged to be touchy-feely, psychologically-minded, empathic coaches. The other is the finance boys, equally horrified by the cost as well as the pointlessness of the whole activity. Most quite simply don't want to be developed, thank you very much – especially by "training air-heads" and "failed psychotherapists".

Some organizations are hotter on development than others. It's partly a function of national and corporate culture. Americans seem keener. Many appear to believe that development, like the pursuit of happiness, is not only an inalienable right, but a necessity. They believe not only that people *want* it (indeed, cry out for it) but also that people *should* have it. You can and should teach old dogs new tricks. It's good for them!

Of course, there are also OD (organizational development) and PD – (personal development). They are linked, but it is the latter that is being considered here. Personal development is about learning new (soft) skills, becoming more aware, being more open to change.

Some organizations really take it seriously. This is manifest in the budget and the number of people in the department once named "training", but which has possibly been through various transformations from coaching department and talent management department to development department. So there is a head of development who may even have the ear of the CEO. It is very unlikely to be the CFO or COO (chief operational manager), but some of the "developmental Johnnies" can have considerable influence. They often punch above their weight because of their (sometimes ambiguous) relationship with the CEO, which may be based on being a semi-confessor, coach or confidante.

The question, of course, is not only *what* to develop but also *how*. "I must, I must improve my bust" – not quite, but the same sentiment applies.

Development is essentially about learning. And we know a lot about this topic. How best to teach what and when. The importance of practice and reward. There are dozens of dry but worthy books on the education and psychology shelves of libraries and bookshops that should inform training managers.

For example, take distributed versus massed learning. Imagine a five-day course. From a learning perspective, should it be Monday to Friday, or five consecutive Mondays? Definitely the latter, but it is usually the former that is on offer. Why? Well, easier for the hotel and more attractive for the participants to "get to know each other properly" in the bar after the fun and games.

So how to develop people? Send them on a mini (but maxi-expensive) four-week MBA at a top business school to be well "gurued"? Give them a foreign assignment with an under-performing subsidiary in a Third-World country? Offer them a personal coach for a year? Do a job-swap for three months with a peer in a very different part of the organization? Attend a week-long development centre?

Companies have their own preferences, and what is thought to be efficacious, useful and acceptable differs between one group and another. This is often a result of the personal preferences of the HR director or CEO, who approve of certain methods but not others. Choices are frequently based on preference and cost; very rarely on any sort of data.

But we all know we like to learn in different ways. And if the goal is rather vague, why not let individuals decide? So imagine the following: people are *awarded* developmental opportunities which are seen to be positive – that is, they relate to promotion and salary.

The company offers the following: a financial budget of £5,000 and a time budget of a month. This is offered to all managers at or above a certain level. But they have to submit their own PDP. These are assessed by a committee, and if found to be acceptable, the manager has the dosh and time off to go and do his/her thing.

One option is to leave it at that: free response. The other is to demand that managers comply with a particular structure. Describe the plan; explain the process, justify the cost, and so on. The idea is that nothing is out of bounds. Thus, they may propose a yachting adventure around Cape Horn; that they do a Master of Wine Course; that they work in a Romanian orphanage; that they do four short courses.

And why not? It is not compulsory. It's a gift, albeit one that it needs to be approved. It could be fun.

The question lies in how to evaluate the proposal. Perhaps the best indices are twofold. The description of what is gained from the activity. This means the specificity of the outcomes (knowledge, insight, process, experience) and a realistic understanding of how this will occur. Next, there is the issue of value to the organization. Egotistical pleasure-seekers forget at this stage that, while the development is largely for their benefit, it is also an *investment* for the company.

Thus the committee should focus not so much on what someone proposes to do, but *how* that activity would lead to a worthy outcome that could benefit the organization. There is no reason why "writing a novel in, and about, Tuscany" for a month should be any more or less valuable than attending three workshops on creativity.

Of course, it is only the clever ones who spot that writing the plan is itself a developmental activity.